VIRGINIA WOOLF
AND LONDON

VIRGINIA WOOLF AND LONDON

THE SEXUAL POLITICS OF THE CITY

SUSAN M. SQUIER

THE UNIVERSITY OF NORTH CAROLINA PRESS

CHAPEL HILL AND LONDON

Manufactured in the United States of America

Library of Congress Cataloging in Publication Data

Squier, Susan Merrill.
Virginia Woolf and London.

Bibliography: p.
Includes index.
1. Woolf, Virginia, 1882–1941—Homes and haunts—England—London. 2. Woolf, Virginia, 1882–1941—Knowledge—England. 3. London (England)—Biography. 4. London (England) in literature. 5. Cities and towns in literature. 6. Novelists, English—20th century—Biography. I. Title.
PR6045.072Z8785 1985 823'.912 84-17376
ISBN 0-8078-1637-X

FOR GOWEN AND CAITLIN

"we are the words; we are the music;

we are the thing itself"

CONTENTS

ILLUSTRATIONS

ACKNOWLEDGMENTS

In its formulation of the struggle facing an aspiring woman writer, and its approach to the personal, cultural, and literary implications of urban scenes, this book is indebted to the work of many feminist literary critics, theorists, and Woolf scholars, in ways I have only come to appreciate at its completion. The introduction delineates ways in which earlier work has influenced my readings of Woolf's urban novels, short stories, and essays. However, some of my debt cannot be repaid, for I owe it not to any individual, but to the atmosphere of extraordinary vitality, creative interchange, controversy, and support that has characterized the field of feminist criticism—and particularly Woolf criticism—during my years of work on this book.

I am very grateful to those friends and colleagues, at Stony Brook and elsewhere, who have provided assistance, support, and valuable criticism at various stages of this project. Pat Alden was the first to read the manuscript; her insightful and encouraging comments were extremely important to me. Helen Cooper introduced me to the pleasures of collegial criticism, and our conversations together—over the years—have had an important role in shaping this book. Sallie Sears's keen eye for logic and style taught me much, and I am grateful to her. David Sheehan, David Laurence, and Adrienne Munich each contributed valuable criticism and encouragement at different stages of this project. Louise A. DeSalvo's generosity throughout the years was unflagging; she shared her work in progress with me and was always ready to comment, criticize, and encourage. Both Brenda Silver and Jane Marcus have offered models of serious scholarship along with the pleasures of genuine friendship; I have found their comments on my work invaluable, and their energy inspiring. Lucio Ruotolo, whose graduate seminar introduced me to Woolf's work, has been a steady source of encouragement, humor, and friendship, and once again I thank him.

I am grateful to Professor Quentin Bell and Mrs. Angelica Garnett, executors of the literary estate of Virginia Woolf, for permission to cite passages from the unpublished papers. In addition, I thank Dr. Lola L. Szladitz, curator of the Henry W. and Alfred A. Berg Collection of English and American Literature of the New

York Public Library, and Elizabeth Inglis, of the University of Sussex Library, for their valuable assistance. My thanks to the State University of New York for awarding me SUNY Research Foundation Faculty Research Fellowships in 1978, 1979, and 1981, and to the English Department at Stony Brook for a grant of released time for the 1982 spring semester, which enabled me to complete a draft of the manuscript. Thanks, too, to Sue Bialostosky, Gwen Duffey, and Sandra Eisdorfer for tenderly shepherding this book through the production stages.

Finally, I thank my parents, and Robin, Norman, and Virginia Squier, for their loving companionship and support over the years. I am deeply grateful to Maureen Monck for conversations which have helped clarify both the thoughts and the emotions from which this book springs. The ways in which my husband, Gowen Roper, has helped me are subtle and pervasive; his humor, encouragement, intellectual and emotional insight, and willingness to put up with the chaotic daily life at times caused by this project have been immeasurably important to me. I thank Caitlin Squier-Roper simply for being herself. Without Gowen and Caitlin, this book would have remained only an idea, not the "solid object" it has become.

ABBREVIATIONS

AHH — *A Haunted House*. Harcourt, Brace & World, 1949.

AROO — *A Room of One's Own*. New York: Harcourt, Brace & World, 1957.

B — "'Two enormous chunks': Episodes Excluded during the Final Revisions of *The Years*." Ed. Grace Radin. *Bulletin of the New York Public Library* 80 (Winter 1977): 221–51.

BA — *Between the Acts*. New York: Harcourt Brace Jovanovich, 1969.

CDB — *The Captain's Death Bed and Other Essays*. New York: Harcourt Brace Jovanovich, 1950.

CR I — *The Common Reader*. New York: Harcourt, Brace & World, 1953.

CR II — *The Second Common Reader*. New York: Harcourt, Brace & World, 1960.

DM — *The Death of the Moth and Other Essays*. New York: Harcourt Brace Jovanovich, 1970.

D I–IV — *The Diary of Virginia Woolf*. Ed. Anne Olivier Bell. New York: Harcourt Brace Jovanovich. I, 1915–19 (1977); II, 1920–24 (1978); III, 1925–30 (1980); IV, 1931–35 (1982).

F — *Flush: A Biography*. New York: Harcourt Brace Jovanovich, 1961.

JMJM — "Virginia Woolf's *The Journal of Mistress Joan Martyn*." Ed. Susan M. Squier and Louise A. DeSalvo. *Twentieth Century Literature* 25 (Fall/Winter 1979): 237–69.

L I–VI — *The Letters of Virginia Woolf*. Ed. Nigel Nicolson and Joanne Trautmann. New York: Harcourt Brace Jovanovich. I, 1888–1912 (1975); II, 1912–22 (1976); III, 1923–28 (1977); IV, 1929–31 (1978); V, 1933–35 (1979); VI, 1936–41 (1980).

LS	*The London Scene*. New York: Frank Hallman, 1975; London: Hogarth Press, 1982.
MB	*Moments of Being: Unpublished Autobiographical Writings*. Ed. Jeanne Schulkind. New York: Harcourt Brace Jovanovich, 1976.
MD	*Mrs. Dalloway*. New York: Harcourt, Brace & World, 1953.
ND	*Night and Day*. New York: Harcourt Brace Jovanovich, Inc., 1948.
O	*Orlando: A Biography*. New York: Signet, 1960.
P	*The Pargiters: The Novel-Essay Portion of THE YEARS*. Ed. Mitchell A. Leaska. New York: New York Public Library, 1977.
SM	"Street Music." *National Review* 45 (1905): 144–48.
TG	*Three Guineas*. Harcourt, Brace & World, 1966.
TY	*The Years*. New York: Harcourt, Brace & World, 1965.

Also cited:

QB	*Virginia Woolf: A Biography*. By Quentin Bell. 2 vols. New York: Harcourt Brace Jovanovich, 1972.

VIRGINIA WOOLF AND LONDON

CHAPTER ONE

INTRODUCTION

"Why do I dramatise London perpetually?" Virginia Woolf wondered in the last year of her life (*L*, VI: 434). In this book I argue that Woolf used the city in her works to explore the cultural sources and significance of her experience as a woman in a patriarchal society. Woolf's treatment of the city in her fiction and essays, where it appears as setting, image, and symbol, reveals the literary techniques she used to attain an authentic voice as a woman writer. From the personal and psychological focus of the first chapter, my analysis broadens to consider Woolf's critique of culture as a whole, for in her treatment of the city Woolf reveals not only her personal history but also her developing understanding of the political and psychological implications of gender and class distinctions.[1]

Like many women, Woolf confronted a problematic dual identification in her struggle to become a writer; she modeled herself both on her father and the male literary heritage, and on her mother and the maternal heritage, social and literary.[2] Woolf's early works reveal not only her careful discipleship to the great male writers, but also her suppressed anxiety of authorship—a fear that she would not be capable of literary creation because she was a woman.[3] In Woolf's imagination, this conflicting identification was associated with the actual geographic split in her earliest years between those months spent in London (which she saw as embodying the male tradition) and those spent in the rural, maternal atmosphere of Talland House, Cornwall. Woolf's adult response to this geographic and psychic split was to assimilate and then to revise the male literary and social heritage—*and* the city that had come to embody it. Drawing on what she called her "tea-table training," Woolf first expressed herself in a disguised fashion in her writing, despite the constraints on her voice and values posed by male literary conventions. Later Woolf revised her portrait of the city, envisioning one whose literature and culture expressed feminist values. She was thus able to negotiate a path through her early conflicting identifications to the establishment of a mature voice and subject matter of her own.

The city was crucial to this act of artistic self-creation not only because of its personal significance in Woolf's life but also—as two images from *A Room of One's Own* indicate—because it embodied both the difficulties in a woman writer's position in a patriarchal culture and the potential for their resolution in the articulation of previously unvoiced female experience. In Woolf's celebrated work of feminist criticism the life of the fictitious poet Judith Shakespeare, an aspiring writer who flees provincial life for the stimulation of the city, becomes a parable of the woman writer's experience in male-dominated culture. As Woolf explains to her imaginary listener, the novelist Mary Carmichael, the story of Judith Shakespeare's London journey has important implications for contemporary women writers. Not only does it testify to the necessity of a supportive environment if a woman is to become a writer, but it also suggests the subject with which those new writers should concern themselves. Moreover, the contrast between the London of Judith Shakespeare and the modern city of Mary Carmichael anticipates, in a compressed fashion, the developing vision of the city expressed in Woolf's oeuvre. The London she portrayed shifted from an environment hostile to women (like the city Judith Shakespeare encountered) to a later city like that experienced by Mary Carmichael, which at least held the possibility for the emergence of authentic female—even feminist—voices and values.

For Judith Shakespeare, the escape to London from the provinces ends not with fame and fortune as a playwright but with mockery, pregnancy, and suicide. Judith, like her brother, is drawn to London because she hopes to write; the city stands as the tantalizing incarnation of the cultural world she is "agog to see" (*AROO*, 49). Yet Judith's struggle to create a place for herself as a writer in London fails because her "poet's heart" is "caught and tangled in a woman's body" (*AROO*, 50). Unlike William Shakespeare, who moves easily from Latin lessons in the country to acting in London, "practising his art on the boards, exercising his wits in the streets, and even getting access to the palace of the queen," Judith Shakespeare finds no ready route to intellectual, professional, social, or political power. Instead, because she is a woman, Judith meets many barriers to the development of her "gift like her brother's, for the tune of words" (*AROO*, 49). An inadequate education, the limiting and oppressive force of her father's protective love, the heavy social restrictions placed on her both within and beyond the family—all these inner and outer obstacles to a writer's life take their heaviest toll once she has made her way, alone, to London:

> For it needs little skill in psychology to be sure that a highly gifted girl who had tried to use her gift for poetry would have been so thwarted and hindered by other people, so tortured and pulled asunder by her own contrary instincts, that she must have lost her health and sanity to a certainty. No girl could have walked to London and stood at a stage door and forced herself into the presence of actor-managers without doing herself a violence and suffering an anguish which may have been irrational . . . but were none the less inevitable. . . . To have lived a free life in London in the sixteenth century would have meant for a woman who was a poet and a playwright a nervous stress and dilemma which might well have killed her. . . . That woman, then, who was born with a gift of poetry in the sixteenth century, was an unhappy woman, a woman at strife against herself. All the conditions of her life, all her own instincts, were hostile to the state of mind which is needed to set free whatever is in the brain. [*AROO*, 51–52]

Woolf's tale of Judith Shakespeare vividly represents the impact of the urban environment, which can either nurture or annul a woman writer's creativity. Forced to endure ridicule, exclusion, and finally sexual exploitation, Judith Shakespeare ironically ends her days as part of the London scene that scorned her, buried "at some cross-roads where the omnibuses now stop outside the Elephant and Castle" (*AROO*, 50). The city's inhospitable treatment of Judith Shakespeare is significant, Woolf points out, because it reflects society at large. A woman had to be conscious of countless constraints imposed because of her gender, and to adopt the public role of writer was to be unchaste. Woolf develops her most celebrated argument from the tale of Judith Shakespeare: that a writer must be serenely unconscious of sex in order to create with genius, and that possession of money and a room of one's own are essential for such a state of sexual unconsciousness.[4] But while Woolf's point is well known, what has been overlooked is the extent to which it is grounded in the urban environment, as the place in which Judith Shakespeare painfully encounters the cultural obstacles to her personal aspirations.

The city is equally important to the experience of the modern woman writer, as Woolf presents it in *A Room of One's Own*. If London swallows up both Judith Shakespeare and her writer's voice in the sixteenth century, in the twentieth it testifies to woman's hitherto unexpressed and immensely powerful presence—or so Woolf explains to Judith's descendant, the novelist Mary Carmichael. The task of the contemporary woman writer, Woolf asserts, is to put that female presence into words:

> All these infinitely obscure lives remain to be recorded, I said, addressing Mary Carmichael as if she were present; and went on in thought through the streets of London feeling in imagination the pressure of dumbness, the accumulation of unrecorded life, whether from the women at the street corners with their arms akimbo, and the rings embedded in their fat swollen fingers, talking with a gesticulation like the swing of Shakespeare's words; or from the violet-sellers and match-sellers and old crones stationed under doorways; or from drifting girls whose faces, like waves in sun and cloud, signal the coming of men and women and the flickering lights of shop windows. All that you will have to explore, I said to Mary Carmichael, holding your torch firm in your hand. [*AROO*, 93]

The women whose unspoken, unrecorded presence swells the London streets are the proper subject of the woman writer, Woolf asserts to Mary Carmichael.[5] And, in turning her attention to those women, the contemporary writer is transforming her art as surely as Woolf intended to when, in "Mr. Bennett and Mrs. Brown," she urged writers, "Let us not take it for granted that life exists more fully in what is commonly thought big than in what is commonly thought small" (*CR* I, 155). The city streets and shops, and the women who walk and work in them, are as rich a subject for the imagination as all the conventional masculine themes and settings of literary history:

> [In] imagination I had gone into a shop; it was laid with black and white paving; it was hung, astonishingly beautifully, with coloured ribbons. Mary Carmichael might well have a look at that in passing, I thought, for it is a sight that would lend itself

> to a pen as fittingly as any snowy peak or rocky gorge in the Andes. And there is the girl behind the counter too—I would as soon have her true history as the hundred and fiftieth life of Napoleon or seventieth study of Keats and his use of Miltonic inversion which old Professor Z and his like are now inditing. [*AROO*, 94]

Contemporary London and the experiences of the city's women are ideal subjects for the modern woman writer because the reality they embody has been passed over by literary tradition.[6] Woolf's attention to them in *A Room of One's Own* typifies the revisionist impulse characteristic of her mature writing. From her early view of the city as male territory often hostile to women, Woolf deepened her perspective to include an appreciation of the city's power to embody women's experience. While Woolf's portrait of the city shifted during her writing career, what did not change was the city's central position in her art, as a context in which to explore the personal, cultural, and literary lives of women.

In Woolf's development as a writer, the city served as a means of exploring and integrating various areas of experience. London had a specific set of personal meanings related to Woolf's own memories, from the Kensington Gardens walks of her childhood to the urban rambles of her adulthood.[7] She wrote of London's personal importance to her throughout her life, in essays, letters, and her diary. From her longing for the city when forcibly exiled as an adolescent, to her adult despair at the ravaged face of London after the German bombings, Woolf's writings reflect the city's deep significance to her political analysis, the progress of her art, her hope for the future. Yet Woolf's treatment of the city was more than mimesis: the city she wrote about, particularly in her essays and fiction, was shaped both by early experience and by adult intention. Consciously and unconsciously, Woolf drew on her childhood encounters with the city in order to organize both her later experiences and her writings.[8] Late in her life she used her memories of the contrast between two London neighborhoods, experienced before she had published her first novel, to express the nature of "Old Bloomsbury," that milieu which has drawn so much of its fame from her accomplishments as a writer:

> At Molly's command I have had to write a memoir of Old Bloomsbury—of Bloomsbury from 1904 to 1914. Naturally I see Bloomsbury only from my own angle—not from yours. For this I must ask you to make allowances. From my angle then, one approaches Bloomsbury through Hyde Park Gate—that little irregular cul-de-sac which lies next to Queen's Gate and opposite to Kensington Gardens . . . though Hyde Park Gate seems now so distant from Bloomsbury, its shadow falls across it. 46 Gordon Square could never have meant what it did had not 22 Hyde Park Gate preceded it. [*MB*, 159–60]

Having been asked to write an intellectual and social history of "Old Bloomsbury" for the Memoir Club, Woolf instead responds, characteristically, with something closer to an evocation of the cityscape. She presents her literal "angle" on Bloomsbury—the physical contrast between the cramped space of 22 Hyde Park Gate and 46 Gordon Square—as a way of understanding the sources of the "Old Bloomsbury" sensibility, and she parodies the physical angle of vision one must adopt in order to see Bloomsbury (even in the imagination) from Kensington.

Woolf's technique of presenting her memories concretely, in a spatial rather than a conceptual form, made it possible for her to accommodate both aspects of her strategy as a writer: assimilation and revision.[9] Taking "angle" not as a mental perspective on a subject but as an actual physical relationship between objects or places in space, Woolf testified to the importance of what she called "scene making" to her writing. As she described this technique in "A Sketch of the Past," it was her "natural way of marking the past," "a means of summing up and making innumerable details visible in one concrete picture" (*MB*, 122).

> Always a scene has arranged itself: representative; enduring . . . why do they survive undamaged year after year unless they are made of something comparatively permanent? Is this liability to scenes the origin of my writing impulse? . . . . Obviously I have developed the faculty, because, in all the writing I have done, I have almost always had to make a scene, either when I am writing about a person; I must find a representative scene in their lives; or when I am writing about a book, I must find their poem, novel. . . . [*MB*, 122]

The preservative impulse behind "scene making" is evident in this passage. However, Woolf's description also hints at a less docile motive: "In all the writing I have done, I have almost always ***had to make a scene***" (emphasis mine). Disruption of her inherited literary and social worlds was an inevitable part of Woolf's struggle to make a place for herself in the literary tradition. The very act of expressing her own vision was disruptive to a world in which women's experiences were stifled; she had to make a scene by the very act of writing in her authentic voice. Scenes were useful to Woolf, then, not only as ways of preserving a past she hated to lose, but also because they embodied the disruptive act of assuming her authorial voice. In fact, "scene making" exemplifies Woolf's dual literary strategies, the acts of assimilation and of revision that were central to her writing career. Small wonder, then, that she speculated, "Is this liability to scenes the origin of my writing impulse?" (*MB*, 122).

Urban scenes offered particularly fertile possibilities to Woolf's creative imagination because, in addition to their personal meaning, they held cultural significance; she could see embodied in them the social and cultural principles shaping her personal situation. To explore this cultural dimension of city scenes, I consider their symbolic meaning in Woolf's works, where they reveal the relationship between the personal and the cultural, reflecting a truth both about the writer who created them and about the culture in which she lived. City scenes can be "read" in two directions: *in* to the personal and psychic life of their creator, which they express symbolically and by which they are to some degree shaped, and *out* to the culture they symbolize and reflect, and by which they are also influenced.[10] For example, Leonore Davidoff has delineated the urban scene's role in linking the personal and cultural dimensions of experience and has demonstrated that, for middle-class children in Victorian England, attitudes toward class and sexuality were "reflected in a spatial view of their world—a view which started with their own bodies, extended to the houses where they lived and eventually to their village, town, or city."[11] The anus was associated with the back areas of the house, where servants dwelt; servants were consequently associated both with the "unclean" areas of the body and with the nether regions of the city, where refuse was handled and industrial production went on. By implication, one could deduce a child's attitude toward class, sexuality, and gender from her or his vision of the city. Having been a late Victorian middle-class child, Woolf herself reflected the residue of this associative chain in her manuscript draft of "The Docks of London." There the industrial areas of the city and its rubbish heaps are associated with female servants and with the working classes in general, although Woolf's essay adds an implicit critique of the culture maintaining that association. Woolf's street scenes both reveal the larger culture within which she wrote and offer her critique of that culture: so in *Mrs. Dalloway* the characters' thoughts, like the city through which they walk, illustrate the split between public and private, male and female, characterizing patriarchal postwar London, while in *Flush* and *The Years* Woolf's serious feminist critique of that culture is expressed both in the city scenes and in the characters' urban experiences.[12]

Not only do I understand the city as having both personal and cultural significance to Virginia Woolf, but I also find in Woolf's treatment of it a reflection of her own position in a complex textual network. As a literary subject, the city has featured prominently in a long line of texts. Woolf's treatment of it in her writing was shaped not only by her experience, by the prevailing culture and her quarrel with it, but also by her response to and experience of other literary treatments of the city.[13] Her diaries abound with moments of confrontation with earlier literary portraits of London. When reading Defoe's *Moll Flanders*, for example, she noted in her diary:

> These ten minutes are stolen from Moll Flanders, which I failed to finish yesterday in accordance with my time sheet, yielding to a desire to stop reading & go up to London. But I saw London, in particular the view of white city churches & palaces from Hungerford Bridge through the eyes of Defoe. I saw the old women selling matches through his eyes; & the draggled girl skirting round the pavement of St. James' Square seemed to me out of Roxana or Moll Flanders. Yes, a great writer surely to be thus imposing himself upon me after 200 years. [*D*, I: 263]

In 1920 Woolf noted in her diary, "Nowadays I'm often overcome by London; even think of the dead who have walked in the city" (*D*, II: 47). From the literary geniuses buried in Westminster Abbey whom she celebrates in an early London essay, to the memory of Elizabeth Barrett's escape from Wimpole Street which she dramatizes in *Flush*, the dead of London—its great writers—are a constant presence in Woolf's works, a source of influence, dialogue, debate. Because Woolf so frequently considered other literary portraits of the city as she was composing her own, her treatment of the urban environment reveals her strategies for responding to a textual tradition in which she wished to make a place for herself. Writing about London, Woolf was not only paying tribute to the cities of writers preceding her—Defoe, Fielding, Blake, Barrett Browning, and others—but revising them as well, to reflect her own urban experiences.

Addressing the archetypal contemporary woman writer Mary Carmichael, Woolf urged her in *A Room of One's Own* to record the "infinitely obscure lives" embodied so evocatively in the streets of London (*AROO*, 93). Woolf's diaries and letters testify that she took her own advice, using strolls through the city streets to stimulate her creative imagination, to untangle a difficult passage in a work in progress, and to find fresh material for essays and fiction alike. From the map of Green Park and Bond Street which she drew by hand shortly before writing *Mrs. Dalloway*, to her letters replete with London gossip and sketches of street scenes, to her diary entries exploring the moods overtaking her as she walked through the streets, Woolf's personal writings reflect her interest in the city as both tangible and symbolic entity.[14] Perhaps a diary entry best incarnates the city's centrality to Woolf's intellect and imagination. Echoing the task of Mary Carmichael, she there evokes both the struggle and the solution that she found in the city streets: "I keep thinking of different ways to manage my scenes; conceiving endless possibilities; seeing life, as I walk about the streets, an immense opaque block of material to be conveyed by me into its equivalent of language" (*D*, I: 214).

"Why do I dramatise London perpetually?" Woolf wondered. This book argues that the city was of such lasting concern to Virginia Woolf not just because she lived there virtually all of her life ("all these years of being Cockney!" she marveled in her last year) or merely because, as a modern writer, she was drawn to the quintessential modern setting, but because, as a woman writer, she found in the city the confluence of her personal, cultural, and aesthetic concerns (*L*, VI: 460).[15] Linking personal history to culture and yoking both to the literary tradition, the city provided a rich vehicle for Woolf's creative imagination and her political analysis. The goal of this book is to attain a fuller appreciation of each through an exploration of the city in which they were nurtured.

CHAPTER TWO

TALLAND HOUSE AND HYDE PARK GATE

In a diary entry written on the anniversary of her mother's death, Virginia Woolf pledged to herself, "One of these days I will write about London, & how it takes up the private life & carries it on, without any effort" (*D*, II: 301). Woolf's intense interest in the city was very much a reaction to the tragedy of her mother's death, which left her struggling alone to define herself as a woman and a writer in what she called the "circus" of patriarchal London. To understand her treatment of the city in her adult writings, where it vividly evokes women's private and public concerns, we must return first to the early years of Virginia Woolf's life.[1]

The comfortable rhythm of summers in Cornwall and winters in London shaped Virginia Stephen's first thirteen years. From March 1878, when Leslie Stephen married Julia Duckworth, the Stephen family owned a house in London, at 22 Hyde Park Gate, Kensington. From the time of Virginia Stephen's birth, they also owned Talland House, St. Ives, Cornwall, where they spent every summer from 1882 to 1894. The year thus divided, each half had its significant geography, its duties and pleasures, its special mood. Winter in London was the Broad Walk and Kensington Gardens, sailing luggers in the pond and reading *Tit-Bits*. If the days contained large spells of boredom or purely unconscious activity (what Woolf would later call "non-being"), they were also punctuated by moments of painful or pleasurable intensity: the dumb horror she felt when faced suddenly by the mewing, slit-eyed idiot boy (to whom, in pity and terror, she gave her entire bag of Russian toffee); the sharp-edged perceptions that turned balloons and shells into objects of extreme distinctness. Summer at St. Ives was the bay, the beach, walks along the cliffs; fishing for tidbits from adult dinners sent up to the nursery window in a wicker basket tied to a string; fishing for mackerel or gurnards from a sailboat. Most of all, it was the pure delight bred by the evanescent beauty of the Cornish coast (*MB*, 64–137).

Woolf's vivid, scenic memories of childhood in London and Cornwall were recorded retrospectively in her memoir essays, particularly "A Sketch of the Past," "22 Hyde Park Gate," and "Old Bloomsbury." However, many of those memories also figure in early diaries spanning the years 1897 to 1909.[2] I have chosen to begin my consideration of Woolf's treatment of the city not with those early diaries but with the late adult memoirs, in whose narratives of childhood experience I find more than merely biographical significance. In their structure and content these scenes from *Moments of Being*, like all literary scenes, are overdetermined: both the unintentional product of an unconscious psychological process and the intentional product of a conscious literary process. They are privileged by their position in Woolf's memoirs. Because she chose them to express her unique personal narrative as she framed it toward the end of her life, they reveal the strategies she chose for composing and presenting her self, in life and in art. Retrospective reconstructions of her psychological reality rather than faithful recountings of actual childhood experiences, they show us an identity in the process of being formed in relation to culture and society. They reveal both her own psychic structure (as it was shaped by her earliest human relationships) and her social and literary responses to her position as a woman and an aspiring writer in male-dominated modern London.

A survey of the scenes with which I began reveals that London clearly suffered from any comparison with Cornwall. Whatever conflict resulted from the contrasting geography, activity, and mood of each period was resolved by the one constant in Virginia Woolf's first thirteen years: her mother. She reconciled all differences. "She was the whole thing; Talland House was full of her; Hyde Park Gate was full of her" (*MB*, 83). In earliest childhood, although she associated the country most strongly with her mother, Woolf felt both city and country suffused by the soothing presence of Julia Stephen. When her mother died, however, the harmony that Woolf felt with her surroundings ended. Within six months of the funeral, Talland House was sold; those ecstatic Cornwall summers were over forever. Over, too, was the atmosphere of unity and serenity that Julia Stephen had created by the mere fact of her presence.

Not only did the harmony between Talland House and London end in the primacy of London upon Julia Stephen's death, but the values associated with each world also came into overt conflict. The rifts implicit in Stephen family life became manifest without Julia Stephen's healing influence, much as, in *To the Lighthouse*, discord erupts in the Ramsay household once Mrs. Ramsay is no longer a part of it. And since identity is formed in relationship, both with people and with places, with the death of her mother Virginia also lost a harmony within the self. Left in an urban environment where her own place, as a female, was marginal at best, she was forced to struggle with an obdurate inner conflict between her identification with her mother (and with women and outsiders) and her later identification with her father (and with men and insiders). Careful study of four important memories from Virginia Woolf's childhood, three before and one after her mother's death, reveals Woolf's changing sense of self and social place in a changed presentation of the environment. An analysis of these memories reveals the intrapsychic and social shift that Woolf experienced with her mother's death: from fusion to separateness and finally to marginality, a shift echoed in Woolf's movement from country to an indeterminate locale and finally to the city.

Woolf identified a recollection of the St. Ives nursery as her "first memory . . . the most important of all my memories. If life has a base that it stands upon, if it is a bowl that one fills and fills and fills—then my bowl without a doubt stands upon this memory" (*MB*, 64). Emphatically rural, this memory presents a moment of harmony with the environment: "It is of lying half asleep, half awake, in bed in the nursery at St. Ives. It is of hearing the waves breaking, one, two, one, two, and sending a splash of water over the beach; and then breaking, one, two, one, two, behind a yellow blind. It is of hearing the blind draw its little acorn across the floor . . . and hearing this splash and seeing this light, and feeling, it is almost impossible that I should be here; of feeling the purest ecstasy I can conceive" (*MB*, 64–65). Cradled in semi-sleep in the country nursery, she heard the soothing repetition of waves upon the shore like the soothing rhythm of breathing a child would hear as she nestles, after feeding, at her mother's breast. As René Spitz has described the newborn, he or she "cannot distinguish one 'thing' from another; he cannot distinguish an (external) thing from his own body, and he does not experience the surround as separate from himself. Therefore, he also perceives the need-gratifying, food-providing breast, if at all, as part of himself. Furthermore, the newborn *in* himself is not differentiated and organized either. . . ."[3]

The feeling of maternal presence in Woolf's memory, even though her actual mother was absent, arises from the vivid detail with which she presents the various aspects of her surroundings—the blind, with its little acorn; the light; the rhythmic splash of waves upon the beach. In light of Spitz's understanding, this intense and unmediated vision suggests that the child is still in harmony with her surroundings, still thinks of the world as part of herself. As an aspect of that pleasurable and gratifying world, the mother is also perceived as part of the child; her presence suffuses the room, the blind, the acorn, and, most explicitly, the beach upon which the waves beat. The scene thereby embodies the relaxed satiation and dim sensory awareness of a newly fed infant, and her pure ecstasy (the purest she can conceive) arises from the paradoxical conviction that "it is almost impossible that I should be here." That statement, initially disturbing with its overtone of nonbeing, expresses the feeling of being so merged with the mother, as though she is in fantasy cradled in her mother's arms, that the self is only minimally distinct from the pleasure associated with that position. The wonder of the new summer's day at Talland House thus echoes an earlier wonder—the symbiotic experience of a self completely dependent upon the mother's care.

In this first memory Virginia Woolf expresses the ecstasy arising from union with the mother in earliest infancy, associating it explicitly with the country and with Talland House. As psychoanalysts know, the ability to use experiences creatively depends upon the earlier sense of Being itself as pleasurable.[4] So it is accurate enough for Virginia Woolf to assert that this memory is the most important of all her memories, and that it forms the base for the accumulation of life experiences to follow. The adult woman's accomplishments are grounded in this primitive moment of preverbal pleasure in merely existing. This moment, in turn, is grounded in two entities: the mother and Talland House.

Yet for the adult woman to be able to engage in cultural creativity, she must have moved as a child from the necessary first position of fusion with the mother to a later, pleasurable position of relative separation, and the exploration of "transitional space" through play. This movement is embodied in Woolf's next childhood memory—which, surprisingly, she also identified as her "first memory." Choosing to begin with it when, at the age of fifty, she wrote her memoir essay entitled "A Sketch of the Past," Woolf created a scene of extraordinary clarity. "This was of red and purple flowers on a black ground—my mother's dress; and she was sitting either in a train or in an omnibus, and I was on her lap. I therefore saw the flowers she was wearing very close; and can still see purple and red and blue, I think, against the black; they must have been anemones, I suppose. Perhaps we were going to St. Ives; more probably, for from the light it must have been evening, we were coming back to London" (*MB*, 64). Although this memory presents itself as being "about" one image, "red and purple flowers on a black ground," in reality it presents a human relationship and the emotions it engenders. More than the contrasts between color and absence of color, pattern and solid space, we are moved by the contrast of the small child and the mother, whose secure lap provides the setting for this memory.

The structure of this memory provides the key to its meaning, as well as suggesting why Woolf labeled this, too, as her "first memory." The two levels of response, visual and emotional, are linked by the structure implicit in each of them: the figure/ground relationship, best exemplified perhaps by that familiar type of perceptual puzzle in which a white vase on a grey background shifts suddenly to become a pair of silhouetted profiles facing each other. Whether we apprehend it visually or emotionally, according to the psychoanalyst Roy Schafer the figure/ground relationship presents us with two social positions: "figure" suggests "definition, boundaries, articulation, structure, prominence, and impact—it is that which is seen as such; it is what is looked at; it shows itself by standing out; it is remembered." Ground, or milieu, in contrast, is "amorphous, unbounded, unarticulated, unstructured—it is seen only through what it does for or to the figure; it is necessary for the sake of something else; it is modest, recessive, anonymous, set back or behind."[5] In its embodiment, visually and emotionally, of a figure/ground relationship, this "first memory" captures the complexity of a social situation: the first moment of independent consciousness.

Securely placed on her mother's lap, the small child feels herself a figure, a separate individual with needs, hopes, and desires, against the ground of her mother's sheltering presence. This "first memory" may have primacy for Woolf because it commemorates a new experience for her. Mother and daughter are in a train or an omnibus together, yet what is unusual is not the travel, but the sustained attention to her child which travel seems to have made possible for Julia Stephen. She was, as Woolf remembered her, generally inaccessible: "Can I remember ever being alone with her for more than a few minutes? Someone was always interrupting." There were incessant demands on her time "with seven children, some of them needing grown-up attention, and four still in the nursery; and an eighth, Laura, an idiot, yet living with us; and a husband fifteen years her elder, difficult, exacting, dependent on her; I see now that a woman who had to keep all this in being and under control must have been a general presence rather than a particular person to a child of seven or eight" (*MB*, 83). General though her mother's presence may have been, it provides the only definite background to the anemone corsage memory. In fact, it may be because Julia Stephen is so emphatically the important background that the more specific setting is in doubt. What is significant is that the mother provides a background for the young girl against which she can, possibly for the first time, experience herself as a separate, autonomous, distinct individual.

Although in its careful evocation of the mother's sheltering presence this alternate "first" memory seems initially to celebrate a moment of closeness between mother and daughter, in its structure it also intimates their impending separation. As the child sits on her mother's lap, she sees her mother anew as a background against which she emerges as a figure, just as the anemones become distinct in their varied colors when set against the mother's black dress. The moment thus embodies both the secure mother-child unity and the child's growing separate selfhood. This separation of identities, which is a normal and positive aspect of growing up, foreshadows another inevitable but painful separation: the mother's death. The somber mood of the passage also evokes an association, in the image of the black dress and in the corsage of anemones, that recalls the later time when the hall of 22 Hyde Park Gate "reeked with flowers" and Virginia Stephen, feeling bleakly that "everything had come to an end," watched from an upstairs window as the attending doctor walked away up the street (*MB*, 92, 84). In its spatial relations this last image recalls the scenes in *A Room of One's Own* when the narrator stops at the upstairs window to stare at the city street below as she muses about the relationship between women and fiction. Here, as there, the rhythm of the scene suggests that a relationship exists between the events in the street below and the emotions of the perceiver in the window above, a relationship Woolf would explore in her fiction and essays. As I suggest in this chapter, the death of Julia Stephen had a pivotal impact upon an issue central to *A Room of One's Own*: female authorship. This alternate "first memory" presents a moment of poised ambivalence in content and tone; the separation it celebrates prefigures a sorrowful later separation enforced by death. Its setting is tellingly ambiguous. Are they going to St. Ives? Or are they returning to London, as the evening light bathing the remembered scene suggests? Whatever their destination, the significance of each (London's associations with her mother's death; St. Ives's with childhood union with her mother) turns ambiguity of setting into ambivalence, just as in its mixture of lively color and ominous black the memory itself betrays ambivalence about the separation of daughter from mother as both healthy and tragic, both willed and involuntary.

This second memory introduces a young Virginia Stephen who already associates separation from her mother with issues of figure and ground, and with ambivalence about the physical environment. However, the reliance on figure/ground, city/country contrasts appears to be a literary strategy devised to express the impact of the memory the scene presents: separation from the mother, particularly the mother's death. In acknowledging that "it is more convenient artistically to suppose that we were going to St. Ives," Woolf reveals the influence of aesthetic decisions in the presentation of the raw materials of memory. Similarly, her irrational claim for the primacy of both "first" memories indicates the persistent influence of unconscious forces on the nature and shape of what is remembered. Finally, the interplay of the two memories shows a change in the nature of the young girl's sense of herself and of her physical and social setting. In the country memory the mother has no discrete place. Her presence is everywhere; the setting is distinctly perceived, but the self is diffuse. In contrast, in the memory of the anemone corsage the nascent moment of independent consciousness is accompanied by a highly distinct sense of the maternal presence and an indeterminate, even problematic setting. In contrast to the self-absorbed flavor of the first memory, the second memory expresses a social experience, as an identity is formed through the encounter with another person. To move from the nursery memory to the memory of the mother's lap and her corsage is to trace a self in the process of separation and individuation.

Yet even this moment of developing identity is grounded in, and determined by, the reassuring presence of the mother. Julia Stephen gave a shape to experience, as her daughter described it in a third childhood memory from *Moments of Being*, that was awesome, even spiritual. "Certainly there she was, in the very centre of that great Cathedral space which was childhood; there she was from the very first" (*MB*, 81). If childhood is a great cathedral, the object of worship in this memory seems to be Julia Stephen herself. Like the God worshiped in a cathedral, she is paradoxically central yet invisible, part of the atmosphere or environment rather than a distinct presence. "Of course she was central. I suspect the word 'central' gets closest to the general feeling I had of living so completely in her atmosphere that one never got far enough away from her to see her as a person" (*MB*, 83). Angel in the house, she mingles the functions of madonna and hostess. Although she is the object of her daughter's reverent concentration, she never acts as a figure in the scene herself. Instead, she provides the ground against which life stands out and with respect to which it acquires focus and meaning.

Perhaps nothing can more vividly convey the devastating effect of the loss of that central figure upon her daughter than to consider a fourth childhood memory from *Moments of Being*, a memory from the days at Hyde Park Gate after Julia Stephen's death.

> I felt as a tramp or a gipsy must feel who stands at the flap of a tent and sees the circus going on inside. Victorian society was in full swing; George [Duckworth] was the acrobat who jumped through hoops, and Vanessa and I beheld the spectacle. We had good seats at the show, but we were not allowed to take part in it. We applauded, we obeyed—that was all. . . . I felt, at twenty, that George no less than Herbert Fisher was obeying the laws of patriarchal society. [*MB*, 132]

It may surprise us to hear Virginia Woolf describe her childhood self as a "tramp or a gipsy," for the facts of her upbringing as she narrates them in "A Sketch of the Past" seem so clearly to contradict that image of an impoverished drifter. "Who was I then?" she asks, and responds, "Adeline Virginia Stephen . . . descended from a great many people, some famous, others obscure; born into a large connection, born not of rich parents, but of well-to-do parents, born into a very communicative, literate . . . late nineteenth century world" (*MB*, 65). Yet, if we consider her comparison of herself to a tramp or a gipsy as a characterization of her relationships with the people closest to her in the years following her mother's death, the image takes on meaning. Woolf's relationship to the people and places around her changed significantly with the loss of her mother, and inevitably her own sense of self shifted as well. Woolf wrote of herself as plagued during those years by the "outsider's feeling," and she was an outsider in several senses. Just as before she had been evicted by her mother's death from the "Cathedral space" of childhood, now not only her mood but more especially her gender made her unwelcome in the "circus" of patriarchal society, which was organized around the belief, so tenaciously held by Leslie Stephen, that "women must be pure and men strong" (*MB*, 130). So it was that Virginia Stephen had fifty pounds a year to George Duckworth's thousand pounds. She was limited to the social sphere while so many of her male relations were testing themselves in public life, to emerge "at the age of sixty or so, a Headmaster, an Admiral, a Cabinet Minister, a Judge" (*MB*, 132).

The contrast in the very images of "circus" and "Cathedral" embody Woolf's changed social role. "Cathedral" presents an image of female centrality whose predominant mode is worship; "circus" reveals male centrality (as she imagines it) and has as its predominant mode display and competition: the "schoolmasters' reports . . . scholarships, triposes and fellowships" that Leslie Stephen laid such enormous stress upon (*MB*, 132). While she is a spectator in both scenes, the young girl in the first scene worships a woman whose generalized presence leaves her (the worshiping one) as the only figure in the scene. Furthermore, she adores a woman whose place she may one day fill. Because of her gender, she has the capacity (socially and biologically) to become that central mothering one, although that capacity is a mixed blessing. In contrast, as a spectator to George Duckworth's performance in the "circus" of patriarchal society, she is and must remain marginal. Because of her gender she is banished—first to the sidelines, and then from the tent altogether. Her empathy with tramps and gipsies reveals that, even in her position at the tent flap, she feels transitory, impoverished, powerless.

The different spatial locations and configurations of these memories suggest the effect of the central figures upon the worlds they organize or dominate. The Cathedral scene echoes the spatial indeterminacy of Woolf's two earlier memories, although its mood of fusion is more characteristic of the Talland House memory. Like the scene of the mother's lap, setting scarcely matters, so fixed is the perceiving intelligence on the twin facts of her mother's unifying background presence and the figure of her own distinct self as worshiper. In contrast, the circus scene is definitely urban, not only because of its Hyde Park Gate location but also because of its metaphoric connotations. Circuses were permanently attached to the great cities of the world in the nineteenth century, and, as Neil Harris has pointed out, to many spectators circuses mirrored those great industrial cities in their complexity, variety, and modernity.[6] In its centralized, stylized, ritualized texture Woolf's circus image also recalls the regimentation of city life in late Victorian and early modern England.

Woolf's relationship to the circus as tramp or gipsy in turn embodies her alienation from that urban society in which she was growing to maturity. The contrast between the stability of the circus and the rootlessness of the spectator may be less accessible to a modern reader, who will tend to think of circuses as traveling entertainments. In fact, circuses were stable parts of city life in the nineteenth century, whereas the tramp or the gipsy was forced, by social codes and poor laws, to keep moving. Woolf's metaphor reveals that as a young girl she felt in an unstable, powerless relation to her social milieu, which she scorned for its fascination with gaudy feats meaningless to her. No longer able to experience herself as even potentially included in her environment, Woolf chose an urban image that expressed her new sense of society as alien, dramatized, and shallow, and her sense of self as sidelined.

This shift in social position from insider to outsider, figure to ground, powerful agent to powerless spectator came about when Woolf's mother died. Rather than continuing to experience herself as an independent figure, she found herself expected to act as ground and spectator for the men in her family. Of course, some such shift was inevitable for a woman in her society. Even had Julia Stephen lived, it is likely that her daughter would eventually have suffered a similar loss of place and power. Yet the loss might have been less drastic, a gradual socialization into "womanhood" rather than the abrupt exile from personhood that Woolf's memory reveals. Instead, Virginia Woolf was presented in her adolescence with a difficult dilemma: how to negotiate an active, workable identity as a woman and a writer in a world that was fundamentally alien to her and where her position was one of powerless irrelevance. The death of her mother marked far more than the loss of one individual for Virginia Woolf. In initiating the shift from a country setting to a city one, from a Cathedral-based model for experience to a circus-based one, and—most important—from a sense of self as significant figure to a sense of self as insignificant ground, it initiated the complete restructuring of self and environment, both actual and psychic, external and internal. She expressed the meaning of this shift most poignantly in her image of London society as a patriarchal circus.

Woolf understood that identity is formed in a network of relationships, by what she described as the influence of "invisible presences," "the consciousness of other groups impinging upon ourselves; public opinion; what other people say and think." "Those magnets," she argued in "A Sketch of the Past," "attract us this way to be like that, or repel us the other and make us different from that" (*MB*, 80). In extrapolating Woolf's developing sense of self and world from the content and structure of four early memories, I have been drawing on the object-relations formulation of identity formation, which holds that "becoming a person is the same thing as becoming a person in relationship and in social context."[7] By capturing a moment of relationship (even if only with fantasied aspects of the maternal presence, as in the nursery memory), Woolf's early memories offer important glimpses of the early social processes that shaped her identity: maternal identification, gender differentiation.[8]

In addition, however, to the early formation of primitive internal object relations that account for the structure of the developing personality, human character is also formed by other, later influences. Chief among these is education, formal or informal. The tea table at 22 Hyde Park Gate provided an informal education in diversity for the young Virginia Stephen. Not only did she encounter the "great men" of the Victorian and Edwardian eras—Symonds, Watts, Meredith, Lowell, James—who were family friends, but she listened too while

> George [Duckworth] and Gerald [Duckworth] and Jack [Hills] talked of the Post Office, the publishing office, and the Law Courts. And I, sitting by the table, was quite unable to make any connection. There were so many different worlds: but they were distant from me. I could not make them cohere; nor feel myself in touch with them. And I spent many hours of my youth restlessly comparing them. No doubt the distraction and the differences were of use; as a means of education. . . . [*MB*, 137]

Distractions and differences were the rule, too, for the more formalized sorts of education given the Stephen women in the years at Hyde Park Gate following their mother's death, manifest in a geographical and psychic polarization between "Downstairs [where] there was pure convention" and "upstairs," where there was "pure intellect" (*MB*, 135). Even the days themselves were split in two for Vanessa and Virginia: "It was when the lights went up in the evening that society came into force. During daylight one could wear overalls; work. There was the Academy for Nessa; my Liddell and Scott and the Greek choruses for me. But in the evening society had it all its own way. . . . Dress and hairdoing became far more important than pictures and Greek" (*MB*, 129–30). The pleasant rigors of art school and Greek lessons (conventionally male intellectual endeavors) were permitted during the daylight hours of freedom, along with "overalls" (practical clothing with masculine overtones). When the gas was lit, however, the social world prevailed, enforcing the more subtle rigors of "feminine" behavior. Those evening lessons in "feminine" deportment could be quite unpleasant: Woolf's memoirs record many public and private struggles with George Duckworth, as he tried first to coax the sisters into "proper" behavior, evoking the example of their late mother, and was finally content merely to impose such behavior upon them.

While Virginia and Vanessa plainly reveled in their daytime freedom for intellectual and artistic inquiry, they responded in a more mixed fashion to their nighttime training in feminine deportment, fluctuating between submissive assimilation to the expected role and subversive revolt against it. Because each response was to figure in Woolf's literary strategies as well as her social ones, I shall delineate their nature and significance more fully. Assimilation resulted in part from the persuasive power of "invisible presences," those people, ideas, or institutions that, Woolf felt, formed the identity by impinging upon it. Another way of describing such a psychic response to surrounding phenomena is identification: "in this process the subject modifies his motives and behavior patterns, and the self representations corresponding to them, in such a way as to experience being like, the same as, and merged with one or more representations of [an] object."[9] Identifications are established roughly sequentially in early life, in much the same order as Woolf constructs her list of "invisible presences" that shaped her character and identity. While the first and most vivid of those "invisible presences" was her mother, Woolf lists other later influences in relation to which she constructed her self: the Cambridge Apostles, that secret society to which her father, brother, and many of her male friends belonged; the Galsworthy-Bennett-Wells school of fiction; the struggle for female suffrage; the Great War (*MB*, 80–81). Woolf's list implies that her identity was formed in response or reaction to people, organizations, and events both congenial and inimical, conventionally feminine and conventionally masculine, aligned with the mother and aligned with the father. It also traces a progression from intensely personal relations (with the mother) through more socially and culturally oriented ones (with the Apostles, and the father and brother they represent, and the Galsworthy-Bennett-Wells school of fiction) and finally to relationships with social and historical events.

Object-relations psychoanalytic theory would concur with such a model for the development of identifications, holding that Woolf would have moved from primary identification with the mother into a later defensive identification with aspects of the mother, father, and siblings in order to prevent her frustration or control by those significant figures, and finally to an oppositional identification with the father and, beyond him, with aspects of the social world, once a secure and gendered sense of self had been established.[10] Furthermore, object-relations psychoanalytic theory's understanding of the development of female personality now holds that women emerge from the oedipal crisis with a more complex psychic structure than men, one that echoes the conflicting identifications with which Woolf struggled. Maintaining ties to the mother while consolidating a new, sexualized attachment to the father, the oedipal and post-oedipal daughter, this theory holds, is doomed to suffer divided loyalties. Though still tied by her intense primary identification to the mother, she is now also drawn by social and sexual needs to the father, with whose system of values she is likely to identify. The primitive intrapsychic division enforced by the oedipal crisis in the "daughters of educated men" can be seen as the foundation upon which later socially enforced conflicts will be built: the maintenance of a distinction between "male" intellectual and "female" social/emotional education in the Stephen daily routine, and the resulting conflict between affectionate affiliation with the mother (and the mother's memory) and intellectual affiliation with the father, whose role as writer his daughter emulated.[11]

That Woolf experienced such deeply rooted and socially reinforced conflicting identifications even in her adult years can be seen if we return to her fourth memory and consider her description of the spectacle of George Duckworth negotiating the circus routines of patriarchal society: "He was in the swim; going through hoops; doing the required act. I could feel his adherence; he accepted the convention; he believed. A belief which is commonly accepted, as his was by all his friends, has an atmosphere of authority; it impresses even the outsider. It seems right, natural, taken for granted" (*MB*, 132). The curiously conventional language in this passage reveals that Woolf has been drawn to accept Duckworth's equally conventional values against her will. In its use of generalization, as in its balance, the passage recalls the "man's sentence" current "at the beginning of the nineteenth century," as Woolf inventively illustrated it in *A Room of One's Own*: "The grandeur of their works was an argument with them, not to stop short, but to proceed. They could have no higher excitement or satisfaction than in the exercise of their art and endless generations of truth and beauty. Success prompts to exertion; and habit facilitates success" (*AROO*, 79). While the consequence of such an involuntary, momentary identification with the commonly accepted belief seems minor—the current of conviction that Woolf feels while listening to "God Save the King" she criticizes almost immediately—in reality the effect on her language and perception of self as a writer was more lasting. The conflict even surfaces in her memoirs, in the admission that it "is by such invisible presences that the 'subject of this memoir' is tugged this way and that every day of his life; it is they that keep him in position" (*MB*, 80). While linguistic convention accepts the generic use of the masculine pronoun, still the passage suggests an unchallenged, involuntary identification with masculine authorship in its elision of the fact that the "subject of this memoir" is a woman. Tugged by invisible presences, by the influence of a role that is conventionally masculine—the memoir writer—the self becomes a "he," and Woolf is pushed into a position of marginality and invisibility. No wonder she feels the futility of "life-writing": she is like "a fish in a stream; deflected; held in place; but [unable to] describe the stream" (*MB*, 80). Woolf here captures her struggle with conflicting identifications, her paralyzed position between the masculine expectations of her literary milieu and the female identity to which she must, as a writer, remain faithful. Without the freedom to acknowledge her womanhood, she cannot escape the medium of male identification which surrounds her in her culture. Nor can she anatomize it, since that would require an unattainable degree of distance from her experience of coercion into male models. Consequently, she is deflected from her task as a memoirist, from the task of describing her experiences as a (woman) writer and her perceptions of the stream of life surrounding her. If the discovery that she identifies momentarily with George Duckworth, or that she can be moved by a patriotic song, shakes her superficial sense of self, this identification with the memoirist as masculine writer challenges her deepest identity as a woman and as a writer.

However, the very feminine education enforced at 22 Hyde Park Gate also offered Woolf a way out of the incompatibility of "woman" and "writer." "Tea-table training" was her shorthand for the Victorian art of indirect speech that she learned to cultivate during the early years of the twentieth century. As she remembered it, this convention was imposed by the same society that set the rules of George Duckworth's conduct in its "circus" ring. "Nobody ever broke the convention. If you listened, as I did, it was like watching a game. One had to know the rules" (*MB*, 129). Clearly, there were drawbacks to this particular game: it meant perpetuating the Victorian values of "restraint, sympathy, unselfishness—all civilised qualities" (*MB*, 129).

Yet this submissive social persona had a distinct advantage for a young girl struggling to create a position for herself in male society while still retaining her own perspective on experience. As Woolf described "this surface manner," it permitted "one to say a great many things which would be inaudible if one marched straight up and spoke out" (*MB*, 129). If their training in "proper" feminine behavior constrained Virginia and Vanessa from criticizing the circus of cultivated life that they watched from the sidelines, that very training also offered them an escape from their mute spectatorship. That "Victorian game of manners" made it possible for them to express covertly their many passionate, unsympathetic, even uncivilized feelings about the world of crimson velvet, mounds of plush, and black folding doors picked out in raspberry red that was 22 Hyde Park Gate. As the *lapsus linguae* in Woolf's definition of "tea-table training" reveals, it was at first the most promising form of self-expression, since any direct and forceful criticism of society was doomed to be "inaudible." Like the scene-making habit that enabled Woolf to recapture past experiences vividly and nondiscursively, this way of speaking—because she learned to subvert it to her own uses—made it possible for Woolf to express her own vision without sacrificing her position at the family tea table, just as in *Night and Day* it would enable Katharine Hilbery to express her sense of isolation through a remark about a cousin in Manchester. "When I re-read my old *Common Reader* articles," Woolf wrote in "A Sketch of the Past," "I detect it there. I lay the blame for their suavity, their politeness, their sidelong approach, to my tea-table training. I see myself handing plates of buns to shy young men and asking them, not directly and simply about their poems and their novels, but whether they like cream as well as sugar" (*MB*, 129). While this manner in one sense perpetuated the conflicting identifications that were to present stylistic and thematic difficulties in her writing, it can also be said to have made writing possible for her.

Yet as she matured as a woman and a writer, Woolf also developed another response to the limitations of her social position, a response grounded in her earliest childhood experiences as well as in the Hyde Park Gate days after her mother's death. In "A Sketch of the Past" Woolf asserted that "the shock-receiving capacity is what makes me a writer," and she identified three episodes of sudden, violent shock that taught her the technique central to her creativity (*MB*, 72). The sociologist Alfred Schutz has argued that our sense of what is "real" is determined by the way we frame the world within which we experience events and people; furthermore, we "experience a special kind of 'shock' when suddenly thrust from one 'world' . . . to another." To Schutz, these shock experiences are the product of ontological relativism: "There are as many different shock experiences as there are different finite provinces of meaning upon which I may bestow the accent of reality."[12] Virginia Woolf's use of shock experience is a familiar aspect of her novels, whether it is as major a shock as the effect of the news of Septimus Smith's death upon Clarissa Dalloway or as minor a shock as Ralph Denham's sudden realization, while looking at London from his Highgate window, that he loves Katharine Hilbery. In either case, the shock (which may be internally or externally caused) partakes of several of the qualities Schutz described: it occurs when one framework for reality is jostled by the introduction of another, and it challenges the priority of any particular conception of reality. It also has a sociopolitical dimension, for it schools the subject in openness to unfamiliar experiences, alien ways of being, strange people. Woolf drew upon the ability to adapt to new situations acquired in these three early shock experiences when, in her adolescence, she found herself an outsider in a masculine world after the death of her mother. With her sister Vanessa she saw "life as a struggle to get some kind of standing place" in society apart from the role of angel in the house, a role that they watched destroy first their mother and then their half-sister, Stella Duckworth Hills (*MB*, 124).

The two sisters became adept at reframing society in order to define themselves as insiders in a woman-focused world. As Woolf remembered it, they maintained a "very close conspiracy. In that world of many men, coming and going, we formed our private nucleus . . . we made together a small world inside the big world. We had an alliance that was so knit together that everything . . . was seen from the same angle; and took its shape from our own vantage point" (*MB*, 123–24). Reframing, the act of redefining a social situation, held out to the adolescent Virginia the possibility of recapturing the harmony with her environment that she had enjoyed before her mother's death without abandoning her sense of separate identity. The act of reframing evokes once more the memory of the young girl on her mother's lap, for implicit in that scene is the potential for a reversal of figure and ground. The mother acts as both ground and figure for the young girl who is (actually and potentially) both figure and worshipful, affectionate ground to her mother. Reframing is implicit in figure/ground relationships: the essential fascination of such puzzles is that they are reversible. While Virginia joined Vanessa in refashioning their perspective on the world in adolescence, the basis for that skill was laid much earlier, in her three childhood moments of violent shock. Those childhood shock experiences were all instances in which Woolf reframed her concept of the world, both to make connections between issues previously kept separate in her mind and to broaden her conception of the nature of reality. Woolf spoke of them as the source of her writing impulse, and examination reveals that they made possible the crucial shift in political and aesthetic allegiances that led to a room of her own in the house of fiction as well as in a house in Bloomsbury.

Three "exceptional moments" reveal Woolf's ways of responding to a shocking experience and dealing with issues crucial to her as a woman writer: power and powerlessness, alienation, and community (*MB*, 71). Furthermore, these moments from before the death of Julia Stephen suggest the response her daughter could later make, because of this early preparation, to the new role in which that death cast her: as spectator and background to the men at 22 Hyde Park Gate. While all of the episodes occur at Talland House, they demonstrate an openness to alien experience that would be central to Woolf's transformed view of the city in adult life and to the political and aesthetic vision grounded in that urban environment. "The first: I was fighting with Thoby on the lawn. We were pommelling each other with our fists. Just as I raised my fist to hit him, I felt: why hurt another person? I dropped my hand instantly, and stood there, and let him beat me. I remember the feeling. It was a feeling of hopeless sadness. It was as if I became aware of something terrible; and of my own powerlessness" (*MB*, 71). This first remembered moment of violent shock produces a complex insight, for the young girl's feeling of hopeless sadness has an ambiguous origin. Had she become aware for the first time of her drive for power and its potentially oppressive effects? Did she suddenly feel the forbidding force that Thoby could wield? Both raw, new emotions may have overwhelmed her in this moment of shock; yet in identifying them we have still not completely traced the origin of her terror and depression. This youthful moment dramatizes Woolf's adult understanding of the vicious circle of oppression and complicity that characterizes male-female relations in patriarchal society, and that (as we will see in chapters to come) arises from woman's enforced position as "magnifying mirror" to men (*AROO*, 100). The essential elements of what Woolf would call "subconscious Hitlerism," in her brilliant late essay entitled "Thoughts on Peace in an Air Raid," are present in this early childhood experience: a boy and a girl are fighting; when the girl prepares to defend herself, her will to fight paradoxically disappears, and in its place she finds passivity and willing victimization. It is impossible for her willingly to deny man his role as dominator, victor; out of her love is bred her acquiescence. The loved brother who would later inspire Woolf's eloquent antiwar novel, *Jacob's Room*, is here an oppressor with the ideal accomplice: his sister, his victim.[13]

Woolf's first experience breeds passivity and sadness because of its shocking revelation that a connection exists between power and powerlessness, will and the loss of will, woman's loving attention to man's actions and her own inability to act. The young girl is tortured by alienation both from her brother and from her own sources of strength. In the next moment of shock, alienation confronts her in its most universal and acute form, as the unsettling discovery of a family friend's suicide plunges her into an abyss of immobility and impotence.

> We were waiting at dinner one night, when somehow I overheard my father or my mother say that Mr. Valpy had killed himself. The next thing I remember is being in the garden at night and walking on the path by the apple tree. It seemed to me that the apple tree was connected with the horror of Mr. Valpy's suicide. I could not pass it. I stood there looking at the grey-green creases of the bark—it was a moonlit night—in a trance of horror. I seemed to be dragged down, hopelessly, into some pit of absolute despair from which I could not escape. My body seemed paralyzed. [*MB*, 71]

Like the discovery of powerlessness, the discovery of alienation from human society—as she is dragged down into "some pit of absolute despair"—paralyzes the young girl. She is unable to defend herself, incapable of skirting the ominous apple tree whose bark is hellish rather than edenic to her transfixed gaze. As before, the sudden shock introduces her to a new world, and her response is a spiritual and sensory numbness. Furthermore, if isolation wounds her, connection is also paradoxically painful. Virginia's closeness to Thoby prevents her from legitimate self-defense; the apple tree's mysterious association with Mr. Valpy's suicide turns it from a benign shape in the family garden to a sinister, moonlit sentinel blocking her escape from that "pit of absolute despair."

A similar trancelike, eidetic stasis characterizes Woolf's initial response to the third moment of violent shock that she analyzes in "A Sketch of the Past." The significance of this third moment for Woolf's aesthetic theory is far reaching because it shows a dramatic difference in her ultimate response to shock experience. Both the fight with Thoby and the discovery of Mr. Valpy's suicide were externally caused shock experiences that produced "a peculiar horror and physical collapse." In retrospect, Woolf felt that her relationship to the new world glimpsed in each episode was the same: it seemed "dominant," while she seemed "passive" (*MB*, 72). In contrast, the third "exceptional moment" contains an internally motivated shock that produces a satisfying calmness in her, and its structure embodies the life-giving force of connection. Although in its elements the third moment echoes the other two (the time is still early childhood; the place is her family's summer home at St. Ives; the setting is the formerly ominous garden by the front door), its outcome diverges dramatically. "I was looking at the flower bed by the front door; 'That is the whole,' I said. I was looking at a plant with a spread of leaves; and it seemed suddenly plain that the flower itself was a part of the earth; that a ring enclosed what was the flower; and that was the real flower; part earth; part flower" (*MB*, 71). While the third "exceptional moment" differs from the previous two in that its "shock" is in the nature of a sudden perception rather than a sudden (and assaultive) action or fact, there is a further reason why Woolf found this third moment "likely to be useful to me later" (*MB*, 71). As she explains in "A Sketch of the Past," it marks her development of a new and more positive response to shock experience. Rather than numbly cowering under the "assault" of a new vision of the world, Woolf accepts it, even embraces it. Faced with the shock of the new, she has learned to use reason to "provide an explanation" that can blunt "the sledge-hammer force of the blow" (*MB*, 72). Although this use of reason can be called defensive, both Woolf's childhood memories and her adult essays reveal that she uses reason not to avoid the new but to admit it, welcome it, and assimilate it. With the wisdom that may accompany experience, Woolf learns in this progression of three childhood moments of shock to oppose the conscious, willed power of the creative mind to the powerless passivity that can be engendered by sudden shocks. In the third moment, rather than recoiling numbly or shielding herself from the startling realization of a flower's organic unity with earth and air, she makes a Keatsian move toward it. With a "greeting of the intellect," she introduces the experience that shocked her to a world made richer and more complex by its inclusion.

Both the moments of shock and the affirmative response to them persisted into Woolf's adulthood, then to form an integral part of her writer's vision: "[Though] I still have the peculiarity that I receive these sudden shocks," she wrote in her last years, "they are now always welcome; after the first surprise, I always feel instantly that they are particularly valuable" (*MB*, 72). The ability to heal splits between worlds, people, or parts of the self that Woolf learned in this series of three violent shocks was of crucial importance to her in adolescence and early adulthood. Bereft of her mother's unifying presence, she was faced with a personal life fissured into public and private, male and female, active and passive realms. This dichotomous worldview resulted both from the conflicting identifications forged in earliest infancy and from the dual educations given the Stephen women.

Profoundly affected by her mother's death and the radically new perspective it enforced on herself and her world, Woolf found in her "shock-receiving capacity" a response both self-protective and reparative that enabled her to salvage an autonomous, creative self from the ruins of her childhood. "It is only by putting it into words," she explained in "A Sketch of the Past," "that I make it [a shock experience] whole; this wholeness means that it has lost its power to hurt me; it gives me, perhaps because by doing so I take away the pain, a great delight to put the severed parts together" (*MB*, 72). But Woolf was not merely stitching together riven halves of experience; she was using her intellect to imagine a new world, one larger and more responsive to alien experience.

This internal psychic action corresponded to an external development as well. On 22 February 1904 Sir Leslie Stephen died, ending a lengthy period of decline. Virginia had served as his devoted and most tender nurse, yet her careful ministrations concealed intense ambivalence about the sacrifices his life demanded, sacrifices that made a speedy death appealing. Woolf wrote in her diary in 1928, on her father's birthday, "He would have been 96, 96, yes, today; & could have been 96, like other people one has known; but mercifully was not. His life would have entirely ended mine. What would have happened? No writing, no books;—inconceivable" (*D*, III: 208). If the loss of Julia Stephen ushered in an era of marginality and conflict for Virginia, the loss of her father led to a period of intellectual and social discovery, for with his death the Stephen children decided to move from Kensington to Bloomsbury. "Vanessa—looking at a map of London and seeing how far apart they were—had decided that we should leave Kensington and start life afresh in Bloomsbury" (*MB*, 162). Not merely a change of house but a rebirth, this shift in spatial surroundings was electrifying: light, air, roaring traffic, strange prowling people and an "extraordinary increase of space" all made 46 Gordon Square a significant new environment. Once again, with the changed setting came a corresponding change in social relations and individual aspirations. "We were full of experiments and reforms . . . we were going to paint; to write. . . . Everything was going to be new; everything was going to be different. Everything was on trial" (*MB*, 163).

In her early memories Virginia Woolf reveals her changed relationship to others and the changed psychic structure that came into being upon her mother's death. Faced with a new view of the world as hostile, urban, and male-dominated, and of the self as powerless and marginal, Woolf forged two responses to the dilemma before her: how to make a place for herself in society as a woman and as a writer. First she learned to fit in, using a decorous tone to couch her more critical visions. Then she learned to reframe her world. This strategy, exemplified by her developing response to shock in the three "exceptional moments" of her childhood, enabled her to envision an autonomous, creative life as a woman writer in the male-dominated modern city. Rather than cowering in the Hyde Park Gate drawing room, Virginia and her sister made themselves at home in Bloomsbury. The perspective she gained there—on the city and on herself—remains the most important accomplishment of Virginia Woolf's early adulthood.

CHAPTER THREE

ACHIEVING AN AUTHENTIC VOICE

Woolf wrote about the city from the years of her apprenticeship as a writer (1897–1904), through her literary eminence in the mid-1930s, until her death in 1941. While all of her writings reveal to some degree her interest in such feminist issues as the social position of women, the experience of the woman writer, and the distribution of material possessions between the sexes, those works that treat the urban environment are particularly significant to the feminist critic. Because they juxtapose Woolf's feminist concerns with an environment traditionally hostile to women, the urban novels and essays reveal Woolf's struggle to achieve an authentic voice and vision within a masculine cultural domain. In her London essays, freed from fiction's demands for plot and characterization, Woolf's political beliefs encounter her lifelong reluctance to preach; as a result, her essays explore issues indirectly, using a portrait of the city to initiate either a social critique or the exploration of feminist values. Careful study of her London essays written between 1903 and 1932 reveals not only the development of "tea-table training," that indirect method of expression, but also her continuing battle between identification with the male literary and social tradition into which she was born and identification with the more subversive tradition of women and outsiders.

From 1897 to 1909 Virginia Stephen kept a number of diaries and exercise books in which she experimented with different kinds of writing.[1] While all of these merit careful study for the developing writer they reveal, the Hyde Park Gate Diary of 1903 makes the most creative and extensive use of the urban environment to explore feminist themes. A sampling of its contents reveals that London was one of the author's most frequent subjects. Its geography, society, and mood are captured in "A Dance in Queen's Gate," "Thoughts upon Social Success," "A Garden Dance," "An Expedition to Hampton Court," "An Artistic Party" (an essay upon an Academy soiree), "The Country in London," "Earls Court" (on the Earls Court Exhibition), "London," and "The Serpentine" (on the suicide of a young woman). Of course, one of Woolf's reasons for writing so copiously about the city was that she lived there; thinking of the diary as analogous to an artist's sketchbook, she took the city around her as material on which to practice her exercises. Yet these seven diaries of Woolf's apprenticeship, and particularly the Hyde Park Gate Diary of 1903, reveal her struggle to find a place as a woman writer in the predominantly male-defined literary and social tradition embodied for her by London. They show Woolf struggling with issues central to her experience as an aspiring writer: the significance of social demands in a woman's life; the struggle to find solitude; the legitimacy of a woman's vision of experience. Trying out her pen, Woolf is also trying out her voice, alternating between the ironic or tentative tone of women and outsiders and the serene or objective tone of male writers, as she would later (and so wittily) exemplify in *A Room of One's Own*.

In *Moments of Being* Woolf recalled the years between her mother's death in 1895 and her father's death in 1904 as ones of anxiety and gloom. Her memoirs reveal that London then seemed a place hostile to her aspirations, permitting her little freedom, solitude, or sense of belonging as an apprentice writer. The Hyde Park Gate Diary of 1903 testifies in detail to the fidelity of this general impression. Its tone is epitomized by one of the last entries, a writing exercise on "The Country in London" which presents the city as hostile to learning—at least for a woman: "The London atmosphere is too hot—too fretful. I read—then I lay down the book and say—what right have I, a woman, to read all these things that men have done? They would laugh if they saw me." What right have I, a woman? This question is crucial to the 1903 diary, in which Woolf uses writing exercises on urban topics to explore such issues as the legitimacy of women as writers and readers, the female fear of trespassing upon the male preserve of literary culture, and woman's struggle to mediate between social and intellectual demands upon her time. Moreover, the diary excitingly anticipates a number of episodes and themes in Woolf's later fiction and essays.

The first entry in the Hyde Park Gate Diary is "A Dance in Queen's Gate." This writing exercise anticipates the "1907" chapter of *The Years*, in which Sara Pargiter, kept awake by dance music playing in an adjoining garden, reads Sophocles' *Antigone* and imagines a romantic encounter between a young man and woman at the dance. The exercise begins as music awakens the speaker (who seems to be Woolf herself—she possesses similar childhood memories and a similar London address), reminding her of her childhood, when she would crawl for comfort to her sister's bed. Although initially recalling the "blind terror" of her childhood, "when awake enough to think at all about it," the "critical mind" of the adult woman converts terror into understanding, informing her that the terrifying music is "token of a ball—not in our street—but in Queen's Gate—the tall row of houses that makes a background to the mews." The exercise continues by contrasting the weary professionalism of the musicians to the primeval energy of the music they play. In an image anticipating the ballroom scene of *The Voyage Out*, but without its optimistic exuberance, Woolf evokes the sinister power the music exerts over the dancing couples:

> they dance as pale phantoms because so long as the music sounds they *must* dance—no help for them. . . . They are sucked in by the music. And how weary they look—pale men—fainting women. Crumpled silks & rumpled flowers. They are no longer masters of the dance—it has taken possession of them—And all joy & life has left it—& it is diabolical—a twisting livid serpent, writhing in cold sweat & agony, & crushing the frail dancers in its contortions.

The compulsion to dance recalls aspects of Woolf's description of a similar time in her own life, in *Moments of Being*: the mysterious fascination of society, the inexorable social code relegating women to the drawing room and men to the public world of professional life, the mingled humiliation and pleasure such dancing parties evoked. Woolf found her writer's vision a useful support during such social occasions. As in the writing exercise, it helps her to ascertain the meaning of that initially frightening dance music. As she explained in *Moments of Being*:

> I remember of these parties humiliation—I could not dance; frustration—I could not get young men to talk; and also, for

happily that good friend has never deserted me—the scene as a spectacle to be described later. And some moments of elation: some moments of lyrical ecstasy. But the pressure of society in 1900 almost forbade any natural feeling. Perhaps I was too young. Perhaps I was wrongly adjusted. At any rate I never met a man or a woman with whom I struck up any real relationship. All the same there was the excitement of clothes, of lights, of society, in short; and the queerness, the strangeness of being alone, on my own, for a moment, with some complete stranger . . . when I was once more in my own room I would see it small and untidy: I would ride the waves of the party still: I would lie in bed, tossing up and down on the things I had said, heard and done. And next morning I would still be thinking, as I read my Sophocles, of the party. [*MB*, 134]

Woolf's memories of adolescent partygoing inform not only "A Sketch of the Past," but also her writing exercise more than thirty years earlier. "A Sketch of the Past" makes explicit what "A Dance in Queen's Gate" only implies: dances were not merely entertainments for the Stephen women, but "wrangles . . . efforts . . . humiliations," painful social encounters enforced by the will of George Duckworth (*MB*, 135). In "A Dance in Queen's Gate" the music becomes a diabolical serpent enforcing that will on men and women alike; it crushes the frail dancers as Duckworth crushed his sisters' individual desires, subjecting them to the "competent machine" of a society that "was convinced that girls must be changed into married women . . . had no doubts, no mercy; no understanding of any other wish; of any other gift" (*MB*, 135). In "A Sketch of the Past," Woolf thinks of last night's party as she reads Sophocles—perhaps because his portrait of Creon, in *Antigone*, recalls the tyrannical stepbrother George Duckworth. Woolf's antipathy to such patriarchal coercion stayed with her throughout her life. In a late work, *Three Guineas*, she recalled "The voice of Creon, the dictator": "'Whomsoever the city may appoint, that man must be obeyed, in little things and great, in just things and unjust. . . . We must support the cause of order, and in no wise suffer a woman to worst us. . . . They must be women, and not range at large'" (*TG*, 141). Similarly, in *The Years* Sara reads *Antigone* while her sister is attending a party—to be "changed into" a married woman. As Eugenie Pargiter later explains to her daughter, "'You don't go to parties, my dear Maggie, to talk to your own cousins. You go to parties to—' Here the dance music crashed out" (*TY*, 142). In "A Dance in Queen's Gate," the sinister dance music embodies a central theme of Woolf's mature work: the social pressures on women that prevent them from exploring their other wishes, other gifts.

Woolf uses writing in the exercise as a defense against social pressures, just as she used it in her own life. It enables her first to identify the origin of the frightening music (a dance in Queen's Gate), and then to convert the local and troubling power the dance music brings to mind (George Duckworth's command that his sisters accompany him to such dances, ultimately in order to find husbands) into a more generalized, mystical (with its serpentine force coercing the phantomlike dancers), and consequently less personally threatening force. The writing exercise uses the description of a characteristic urban event—overhearing music or noise of some kind—to initiate an exploration of feminist themes that have recurring importance in Woolf's works.

A second writing exercise in the Hyde Park Gate Diary, "Thoughts upon Social Success," might be described as the answer to "A Dance in Queen's Gate," this time from the perspective of one who enjoys such social rituals. The exercise contrasts a hypothetical young lady who is a social success, and who counts her evenings as more important than her mornings, with the Stephen women, who have clearly not cultivated their social gifts and who (as we know from *Moments of Being*) count their mornings as precious respite from the evening hours of social obligations. While the essay shares a technique with Woolf's mature London essay, "Oxford Street Tide," using a "moralist" to comment on the question at hand, that character's function here is diametrically opposed to his later role. This "moralist" seems to speak for Woolf herself, suggesting that a preoccupation with society is "very artificial." Yet in its conclusion the essay overrules the moralist: "The truth is, to be successful socially one wants the courage of a hero." While this second exercise seems to express the victory of conventional values over an authentic (and more typically Woolfian) distaste for society's artificiality, it, too, uses a meditation upon a characteristic urban phenomenon—the society woman—to introduce subjects of deep personal concern to the writer: the contrasting demands of social and intellectual life upon a woman's time; the courage required for venturing into society; the morality of dedicating one's life to social pursuits.

A brief study of other London entries in the Hyde Park Gate Diary reveals further instances of Woolf's use of the city to initiate an exploration of feminist concerns, as well as other passages anticipating Woolf's mature works. In "A Garden Dance" she describes the intense pressure of social intercourse at a dance just three blocks from Kensington Gardens. People seem to her like "flies struggling in a dish of sticky liquid," an image that recurs in "The New Dress." In "An Expedition to Hampton Court" she celebrates the unexplored London suburbs but bemoans the crowds surrounding her at that familiar landmark, invoking the love of solitude that would figure in *A Room of One's Own*. "An Artistic Party" anticipates *Three Guineas* in its contrast between male and female clothing. Gazing at the people attending a London Academy soiree, examining them as if they were works of art, the speaker considers how women, "as though to atone for their want of definite orders, dress up in the oddest ways." The image prefigures her vision of women decorated for motherhood with "a tuft of horsehair on the left shoulder" (*TG*, 21). Finally, in the haunting exercise "The Serpentine," Woolf records the wording of a suicide note left by a young woman who has drowned herself in that London pond: "No father, no mother, no work." The essay eerily anticipates much of Woolf's own future: motherless already, she was soon to become fatherless. (Leslie Stephen died in February of the following year.) And while, to her lasting satisfaction, she had her work as a writer, when writing finally became impossible, suicide was to be her end as well. "The Serpentine" suggests the life-or-death nature of Woolf's commitment to her writing, which led her to overrule the anxieties, figuring so largely in the years between 1894 and 1904, concerning her competence and legitimacy as a woman writer in patriarchal London.

While the city seemed a hostile environment through 1903, it came to take on a very different meaning following the death of Leslie Stephen in February 1904. Woolf's second severe mental breakdown in May 1904 resulted in a long period of enforced exile from London, on the advice of the family physician, Dr. George Savage (QB, 90). Woolf stayed first at Violet Dickinson's house in Welwyn, then in Nottinghamshire, and with her Aunt

Caroline Emelia Stephen in Cambridge, and finally with Madge and Will Vaughan at Giggleswick, Yorkshire. Letters of the time reflect her intense frustration at being kept from her beloved London, which she more and more associates with the pleasures of intellectual and physical labor—also forbidden her by Dr. Savage as potentially dangerous to her mental health. Portions of two letters written during this period to her first intellectual mentor, Violet Dickinson, testify to Woolf's yearning to return to the city, as well as to her association of London with intellectual and physical work:

> People say how lucky I am, and how glad I ought to be to be out of London. They dont realise that London means my own home, and books, and pictures, and music, from all of which I have been parted since February now,—and I have never spent such a wretched 8 months in my life. [*L*, I: 147]

> That silly old Nessa has been absorbing Savages theories as usual. I cant conceive how anybody can be fool enough to believe in a doctor. I know he will soon climb down and tell me what is the fact. That I am quicker and better in London than anywhere else—just as he had to give in about walking alone, and being isolated. My life is a constant fight against Doctors follies, it seems to me. [*L*, I: 159]

Discharged by Dr. Savage as cured in January 1905, within one month Woolf had incorporated her new view of London into an article published in the *National Review*. A January diary entry hints at the rebellious message carried by this seemingly slight piece: "Wrote all the morning at a paper which may, with luck do for Leo [Maxse]. It is about music!—naturally depends much more upon the imagination than upon facts. Rather amuses me to write, since I have been ordered not to write for my brains [*sic*] health." "Street Music," the first of Woolf's published essays dealing with an urban theme or setting, reflects her recent experience of being forbidden intellectual work, physical exertion, solitude, and urban life. The essay focuses on street musicians, those peripatetic urban outsiders. In a tone mingling condescension and irony, it paints a fanciful portrait of the street musician as pagan god or prophet come back to earth to bring to humanity the potent, otherworldly art of music. The essay's conclusion, while far from being Woolf's best social criticism (like the fiercely logical *Three Guineas*), mingles with the elements of whimsy a vision of the socially transforming potential of music that anticipates Woolf's mature work:

> If . . . instead of libraries, philanthropists would bestow free music upon the poor, so that at each street corner the melodies of Beethoven and Brahms and Mozart could be heard, it is probable that all crime and quarrelling would soon be unknown, and the work of the hand and the thoughts of the mind would flow melodiously in obedience to the laws of music. It would then be a crime to account street musicians or any one who interprets the voice of the god as other than a holy man, and our lives would pass from dawn to sunset to the sound of music. [SM, 148]

The fantasy of free music for the poor, of Beethoven, Brahms, and Mozart at each corner, prefigures Mrs. Hilbery's impulsive desire, in *Night and Day*, to "stand at that crossing all day long and say: 'People, read Shakespeare!'" (*ND*, 306). Moreover, it anticipates Woolf's mature philosophy, formulated in "A Sketch of the Past," of the interrelationship between art and human experience: "It is a constant idea of mine . . . that the whole world is a work of art; that we are parts of the work of art. *Hamlet* or a Beethoven quartet is the truth about this vast mass that we call the world. But there is no Shakespeare, there is no Beethoven; certainly and emphatically there is no God; we are the words; we are the music; we are the thing itself" (*MB*, 72).

In a diary entry of November 1923 Woolf expanded on this notion that humanity constitutes a work of art, linking the insight, as in "Street Music," to the urban environment. The entry also exemplifies the important distinction, in all of these passages, between the art kept sequestered in libraries, museums, or concert halls and the art that exists in the streets. Woolf revises the concept of art by emphasizing not its formal, intentional creation but its serendipitous occurrence, whether in street music or in the random pattern of the city itself: "It was so lovely in the Waterloo Road that it struck me that we were writing Shakespeare; by which I mean that when live people . . . produce an effect of beauty, & you dont have it offered as a work of art, but it seems a natural gift of theirs, then—what was I meaning?—somehow it affected me as I am affected by reading Shakespeare. No: its life; going on in these very beautiful surroundings" (*D*, II: 273).

Those urban outsiders, street musicians, 1884 (from Pictures Collection, New York Public Library).

Seeing aspects of the work of art in ordinary life, Woolf proposes not to elevate art, but to exalt the ordinary. So, in "Street Music," she strikes the note which was to resound through her mature works: recognition of the countless potential artists among us who, for want of the right encouragement, environment, or gift of expression, go unnoticed:

> Whatever the accomplishment, we must always treat with tenderness the efforts of those who strive honestly to express the music that is in them; for the gift of conception is certainly superior to the gift of expression, and it is not unreasonable to suppose that the men and women who scrape for the harmonies that never come while the traffic goes thundering by have as great a possession, though fated never to impart it, as the masters whose facile eloquence enchants thousands to listen. [SM, 145][2]

The voice of "Street Music" is that of a young writer. Not only is she understandably gentle to aspiring talents, but she is also more conventional and tentative than the mature Woolf of *Moments of Being*. Still, in her first published London essay Woolf anticipates qualities in her later work: the emphasis upon artistic engagement with ordinary life, and the use of an urban theme to initiate exploration of issues important to her as an apprentice writer. Most significant among these issues were the possibility of hostile criticism, the effect upon an artist of an extensive education, and payment for artistic production. Most remarkably, perhaps, this essay presents an eloquent if unspoken analog to the woman writer in the portrait of the street musician. Like the woman writer, the street musician is not generally a socially welcome creature: "'Street musicians are counted a nuisance' by the candid dwellers in most London squares, and they have taken the trouble to emblazon this terse bit of musical criticism upon a board which bears other regulations for the peace and propriety of the square" (SM, 144). Like the woman writer who perseveres, the street musician has learned not to pay "the least attention to criticism": "the artist of the streets is properly scornful of the judgement of the British public" (SM, 144). Like women writers (and women in general), the street musician is poorly paid—or not paid at all—for his or her labors. And just as the woman writer has seemed, to male writers from Johnson to Lawrence, a scandalous aberrance from the customary feminine role, so the street musician plies a trade which seems "vagrant and unorthodox" to the well-ordered mind of the legitimate householder. In fact, street musicians join "artists of all kinds" in being seen by the British public as "unmanly," because they "give expression to the thoughts and emotions . . . which it should be the endeavour of the good citizen to repress" (SM, 145). Emotional and expressive, unconventional, unpaid or poorly paid, liable to hostile criticism and social ostracism—in affirming the street musician as "holy man," "Street Music" uses an urban theme to present a powerful though unspoken defense of the role Woolf had chosen for herself: woman writer.

In "Street Haunting" (1927) Woolf again used an urban topic to approach a number of themes explored in "Street Music": a comparison of respectable householders to disreputable vagrants; the liberating character of the city environment; social strictures against spiritual vision or emotional expression. An entry in Woolf's diary for 1925 suggests some further themes underlying the simple plot of "Street Haunting": the importance of writing in Woolf's life; the pleasure of making imaginative connections between disparate experiences; the significance of the city in making such connections possible:

> Happiness is to have a little string onto which things will attach themselves. For example, going to my dressmaker in Judd Street, or rather thinking of a dress I could get her to make, & imagining it made—that is the string, which as if it dipped loosely into a wave of treasure brings up pearls sticking to it. Poor Murphy is in the glumps [*sic*], . . . She has no string dipping into the green wave: things don't connect for her; & add up into those entrancing bundles which are happiness. And my days are likely to be strung with them. I like this London life in early summer—the street sauntering & square haunting, & then if my books (I never speak of L.'s pamphlet) were to be a success; if we could begin building at Monks . . . if—if—if— [*D*, III: 11]

Although the diary specifies London strolls in early summer while the essay dictates that "The hour should be the evening and the season winter," there are a number of ways in which "Street Haunting" dramatizes themes with which Woolf was concerned in this diary entry of two years earlier. The literary theme with which the diary entry ends ("if my books . . . were to be a success") is part of the essay's initial pretext: the need to buy a pencil, which gives one the excuse for "walking half across London between tea and dinner" (*DM*, 20). (This journey is, in turn, analogous to the diary entry's fantasy of a trip to Woolf's dressmaker in Judd Street.) "Street Haunting" has the episodic structure that Woolf celebrated in the diary entry, for it is punctuated by brief tales of pathos, drama, and joy which together constitute the joys of "street haunting." Just as in the diary entry she attributed her happiness to the "little string onto which things will attach themselves," so in "Street Haunting" she finds the "greatest pleasure of town life in winter" through "rambling the streets of London," accumulating different urban experiences. Finally, just as Woolf distinguishes between "poor Murphy," who lacks the imagination to make things connect and so is "in the glumps," and her own ability to connect disparate experiences and so find happiness, so the essay celebrates the cohesive power of the author's imagination.

"Street Haunting" describes a walk through London during the period between tea and dinner, ostensibly to buy a pencil. The initial effect of this escape from the protective surroundings of the private home is the rupture of habitual patterns of experience and a heightened sense of visual acuity: "when the door shuts on us . . . [the] shell-like covering which our souls have excreted to house themselves, to make for themselves a shape distinct from others, is broken, and there is left of all these wrinkles and roughnesses a central oyster of perceptiveness, an enormous eye" (*DM*, 21–22). While this "eye" is able to appreciate beauty, even in the incongruous setting of a London street or square, it is unable to move beyond such surface appreciation: "The eye is not a miner, not a diver, not a seeker after buried treasure. It floats us smoothly down a stream; resting, pausing, the brain sleeps perhaps as it looks" (*DM*, 22). So, desiring stimulation, the street haunter moves from simple observation to a more curious, critical encounter with several seemingly unrelated episodes of city life, whose real common denominator is their challenge to complacency and self-satisfaction: a dwarf trying on shoes; the sudden encounter with a hungry, poverty-stricken man and woman; the fantasies spawned by the goods displayed in Oxford Street; the innumerable tales contained on the shelves of a secondhand bookshop; an overheard conversation; the sight of two lovers on a Thames bridge; a quarrel in a stationer's shop in the Strand.

While the ostensible subject of "Street Haunting" is an evening walk through London, its real subject is the acrobatics of a writer's consciousness as well as the spectacle of contemporary city life that the walk reveals. Written in 1927, after Woolf had achieved a large measure of literary success (she had published four novels and several volumes of short stories), "Street Haunting" displays a more marked identification with insiders than did "Street Music." The earlier essay, although decorously conventional in voice and viewpoint, affirmed in its conclusion the outsider's vision of the street musicians: "It would then be a crime to account street musicians or any one who interprets the voice of the god as other than a holy man, and our lives would pass from dawn to sunset to the sound of music" (SM, 148). In contrast, the voice and viewpoint of "Street Haunting" oscillate between insider and outsider. Description has free rein in this imaginary tour of London, but social criticism is markedly restrained. While the street haunter embraces the "vast republican army of anonymous trampers" and empathizes with the dwarf to such an extent that her normal-sized attendants swell to "giantessess," still her viewpoint is that of the outsider only as long as it will not force her to examine her own privilege (*DM*, 20, 24). When empathy for the dwarf seems to have transformed the entire city into a world of "the humped, the twisted, the deformed," the narrator's voice becomes far more distanced and her point of view alienated from those she observes. Rather than exploring what it must be like to live as one of "the maimed company of the halt and the blind" who have "such queer names, and pursue so many curious trades," however, the narrator retreats into a rationalization: "It seems as if the lady in the sealskin jacket must find life tolerable, passing the time of day with the accordion pleater, or the man who covers buttons; life which is so fantastic can not be altogether tragic. They do not grudge us, we are musing, our prosperity" (*DM*, 26).

Even when the street haunter encounters a miserable man and woman, like alter images (in age, religion, and even garb) of the successful Leonard and Virginia Woolf, the resulting challenge to complacency is short lived: "Suddenly, turning the corner, we come upon a bearded Jew, wild, hunger-bitten, glaring out of his misery; or pass the humped body of an old woman flung abandoned on the step of a public building with a cloak over her like the hasty covering thrown over a dead horse or donkey" (*DM*, 26). Although "the nerves of the spine seem to stand erect; a sudden flare is brandished in our eyes," the question prompted by that sight of human suffering—Does my privilege cause or maintain their misery?—is "never answered" (*DM*, 26). Any social criticism the question might have instigated is abandoned, the brief vicarious experience of hopeless hunger and poverty is forgotten, and the street haunter retreats to the security of her own home. The stroll through London leaves her neither morally, spiritually, nor politically changed, but merely entertained. The essay concludes not with an affirmation of the outsider (as in "Street Music"), but with a reaffirmation of the privileged insider: "Still as we approach our own doorstep again, it is comforting to feel the old possessions, the old prejudices, fold us round; and the self, which has been blown about at so many street corners . . . sheltered and enclosed" (*DM*, 35–36). Although tempted and entertained by the experience of urban outsiders, still in "Street Haunting" Woolf ultimately casts her lot with insiders such as the "respectable householder."

While in "Street Music" the description of the street musicians suggested a buried, possibly unconscious analogy with the situation of women writers, in "Street Haunting" the linguistic resonance of the title (also probably unconscious) testifies to the essay's flaw: "street haunter" calls to mind "streetwalker." The former is a woman who is economically self-sufficient, possesses a secure social situation, and enjoys a large measure of control over her experience; the latter is a woman economically dependent on the men who are her customers, socially stigmatized, and possessing significantly less control over her experience. Still, the echo indicates Woolf's inability to resolve the struggle between the identification with men and insiders, and the identification with women and outsiders. While it is doubtful that Woolf consciously intended the auditory allusion to "streetwalker," it points to the political conflict at the essay's heart. A woman walking through twilight London is always at risk of being seen as a streetwalker, and treated as such, by the men she encounters. This gender-based risk of being taken as an urban outsider, unwelcome in polite society, might move the street haunter to examine the nature of her own social situation and to realize her kinship with those people whom she observes during her twilight walk. Yet the street haunter makes no such connections between her own experience and that of the characters she meets in the streets. While she does enter briefly into their experiences, she never sees their situation as relevant to her own as a woman in patriarchal society. In "Street Haunting," the experience of other lives is merely diverting, not enlightening: "[One] could tell oneself the story of the dwarf, of the blind men, of the party in the Mayfair mansion, of the quarrel in the stationer's shop. Into each of these lives one could penetrate a little way, far enough to give oneself the illusion that one is not tethered to a single mind, but can put on briefly for a few minutes the bodies and minds of others. One could become a washerwoman, a publican, a street singer" (*DM*, 35). Yet when the illusion of being someone else fades, "one" is left far from being a washerwoman or a street singer. Not only the comfortable possessions and prejudices of the private home, but also the choice of pronouns places the speaker squarely in a comfortable class. "One"—with its upper-class linguistic orthodoxy—undercuts the speaker's identification with the "vast army of anonymous trampers," suggesting that, although she enjoys the experience of classlessness and multiple identity attained in the city streets, she may also fear it.[3] In her use of the pronoun "one," as in her occasional lapses into conventional, even sentimental language ("the champagne brightness of the air"), Woolf undercuts the affirmation elsewhere in "Street Haunting" of the "streaked, variegated" nature of the true self whom we can know only if we "give the rein to its wishes and let it take its way unimpeded" (*DM*, 28–29). Yet Woolf is neither snobbish nor sly in this conflict between two sorts of diction; her language here betrays ambivalence about sex and class issues because of her problematic position as a street haunter who is a woman in a patriarchal society.[4] Outsider or insider; member of the community of the "halt and the lame," or one defined by the "old possessions, old prejudices" of the private home; ground or figure; mirroring or mirrored: throughout her life Woolf struggled with such "contrary instincts" and divided loyalties. As she explained in *A Room of One's Own*, her experience is characteristic of that of women writers in general, who have been plagued by such conflicts since the time of Shakespeare's hypothetical sister (*AROO*, 51). To condemn Woolf because she reproduces in her language the voice of the dominant culture is to condemn her for a tautology. She speaks in the language of the culture which has oppressed her because, as a contemporary woman writer, she has no other language. In literature as in history, as Woolf explains in *A Room of One's Own*, woman's voice and being have been silenced, suppressed (*AROO*, 44).[5]

"Street Haunting" may at times seem frustrating and inauthentic to readers who wish Woolf would explore the relationship between class oppression and sexism, between the poverty-stricken individuals encountered during the London stroll and the street haunter herself. Still, the essay is significant because it makes use of an urban situation to initiate a consideration of the origins of social stratification and the impact of gender, class, and material possessions upon one's sense of self. Becoming part of "that vast republican army of anonymous trampers," the street haunter vicariously experiences the lives of a dwarf, of beggars, of a Mayfair partygoer in pearls and silk, of an old man and old woman selling pencils. In demonstrating how the street haunter relaxes into habitual patterns of thought once she returns to the private home, the essay shows the relationship between material possessions and political prejudice. Possessions, by shoring up one's customary sense of self, make it possible to avoid questioning familiar assumptions about others as well.

The movement from exploration to isolation takes place gradually for the street haunter. When she moves out of the private home at the beginning of the essay, she is temporarily liberated from custom, free to discover her true self. The essayist wonders, is it possible that the true self is "neither this nor that, neither here nor there, but something so varied and wandering that it is only when we give the rein to its wishes and let it take its way unimpeded that we are indeed ourselves?" (*DM*, 28–29). Yet society, and the rules it perpetuates, works against such a free and various identity, and against the critical social perspectives it might adopt:

> Circumstances compel unity; for convenience' sake a man must be a whole. The good citizen when he opens his door in the evening must be banker, golfer, husband, father; not a nomad wandering the desert, a mystic staring at the sky, a debauchee in the slums of San Francisco, a soldier heading a revolution, a pariah howling with scepticism and solitude. When he opens his door, he must run his fingers through his hair and put his umbrella in the stand like the rest. [*DM*, 29]

As the umbrella slips into the umbrella stand, so the challenging variety of selves experienced in the city streets slips away; the individual takes *his* "proper" place in society, "for convenience' sake." Woolf's essay portrays the cultural repression of those "instincts and desires" originally possessed even by the most staid of bankers, while in the conclusion enacting that repression as well. Nomad, mystic, debauchee, soldier, pariah—all those alternate selves which are discarded when the good citizen opens his door have two common qualities that would be inconvenient for society. Each lacks a stable social niche reinforced by accumulated possessions; moreover, each represents a marginal—even a critical—perspective on that society to which it does not belong: the nomad as a result of his mobility; the mystic by virtue of a different spiritual focus; the debauchee and pariah by their disregard for social conventions and moral laws; the soldier as one who endures uncivilized discomfort and suffering in order to protect a civilization he has left behind.

A further aspect of this threshold drama explains why "Street Haunting" finally retreats from the multiple selves it explores and temporarily affirms: the "good citizen" is clearly male. Woolf typically associates the qualities of critical skepticism and social marginality with women; one of the alternate selves that the street haunter acknowledges is simultaneously "walking to the Strand to buy a pencil" and "on a balcony, wearing pearls in June"

(*DM*, 28). Yet both the critical perspective and the explicitly female self (in pearls) embodying it are abandoned with the thud of the solid front door.[6] Whatever identity exists in the streets, masculine identity predominates once the private home is entered. Domestic space, conventionally seen as feminine, here falls under male control and reflects male values, perhaps because the possessions and privileges with which the private home shapes its identity are so overwhelmingly held by men. The objects in the private home "perpetually express the oddity of our own temperaments and enforce the memories of our own experience," and since men have traditionally had more latitude for both temperament and experience, those objects tend to reflect male experiences. The bowl on the mantelpiece recalls a quarrel between an Italian innkeeper and his wife and the "melancholy Englishman, who rose among the coffee cups and the little iron tables and revealed the secrets of his soul"; the brown stain on the carpet recalls Mr. Cummings's anger at Lloyd George ("'The man's a devil!' said Mr. Cummings, putting the kettle down with which he was about to fill the teapot so that it burnt a brown ring on the carpet") (*DM*, 21). The narrative voice further emphasizes the fact that possessions perpetuate class and sex prejudices and restrict freedom when it makes such a dramatic shift upon the street haunter's return to the private home. From being plural, first-person, and implicitly female ("How . . . are we also on a balcony, wearing pearls in June?") the voice becomes singular, third person and implicitly male ("When he opens his door") (*DM*, 27–29). With possessions comes prejudice, which in turn gives the pleasure of self-absorption. The privileged need not suffer painful empathy for the impoverished; instead, they may surrender fellow feeling for the relief of complacent distance—a retreat into easy prejudices created by possession, whether of a mantelpiece bowl, a stained carpet, or an umbrella. Once safe in the private home, the self is monolithic, male, and moneyed.

While "Street Haunting" reflects a more male-identified perspective than does "Street Music," it also has a more acute social vision, revealed both in its documentation of the varied lives encountered and in its honest admission that the pleasure afforded by imaginative participation in those lives is merely temporary. Little more than four years later Woolf would return to the unspoken question raised by the street haunter's experience: What is the relationship between women and the working classes?

While throughout her life Woolf relied on the urban environment to raise issues of identity, social position, and access to material possessions, her most extended and straightforward use of urban portraiture as a vehicle for social commentary was in *Six Articles on London Life*. This series of essays on London, which appeared from December 1931 to December 1932 in *Good Housekeeping*, surveyed the highs and lows of the city: "The Docks of London," "Oxford Street Tide," "Great Men's Houses," "Abbeys and Cathedrals," "'This is the House of Commons,'" and "Portrait of a Londoner."[7] Although the "London Scene" essays celebrate a conventionally modernist setting—the city—their approach is not typically modernist. Rather than documenting the city as "environment of personal consciousness, flickering impressions, Baudelaire's city of crowds, Dostoyevsky's encounters from the underground, Corbière's (and Eliot's) *melange adultère de tout*,"[8] Woolf's "London Scene" essays, informed by her feminism, encounter the city as both the center of patriarchy and the testing ground of feminist values. They reveal Woolf's struggles between identification with insiders (men, the upper classes) and outsiders (women, the working classes), and they exemplify the strategies she forged to accommodate her personal vision while remaining compatible with her vehicle, *Good Housekeeping*. Moreover, at their best the "London Scene" essays subvert the often complacent genre of the urban travelog to portray gender and class relations.

Woolf used a variety of strategies to cope with her conflicting identifications and to accommodate or subvert the requirements of the *Good Housekeeping* milieu. In "The Docks of London," with two major deletions, she omitted social criticism, established her identification with the consuming middle class, and avoided friction with the magazine's tone. In "Oxford Street Tide" Woolf used the contrast between an appreciative observer of city life and a sour "moralist" to suggest her divergence from the conventionally anti-urban sentiments of Victorian and modernist thinkers, expressing her love for the commercial quarter of the city, with its throngs of outsiders and workers. In "Great Men's Houses" she subverted the demands of the standard journalistic house tour, making it instead an ironic challenge to the values implicit in Thomas Carlyle's *On Heroes, Hero-Worship, and the Heroic in History* and transforming it into an exposé of woman's exploitation, whatever her class (as she considered the chore of keeping house for Thomas Carlyle), by those heroic "great men." In "Abbeys and Cathedrals" and "'This is the House of Commons'" Woolf explored the great London churches and the House of Commons. Her point of view wavered between insider and outsider, perhaps due to her persistent allegiance to the concept of a literary elite even when she remained ideologically opposed to the existence of social hierarchies. In the final essay, "Portrait of a Londoner," Woolf nostalgically evoked a characteristic Victorian Londoner, Mrs. Crowe, only to bid farewell both to her and to the rational, ordered city she chronicled. In so doing Woolf established her own point of view, distinguished from those of her Victorian forefathers and her modernist brethren, by affirming the freedom and vitality of the outsider over the security of the insider.

"The Docks of London"

In manuscript, "The Docks of London" provides one of Woolf's most sustained visions of the industrial or commercial city. The draft is worth quoting at length, because in revision Woolf made two drastic deletions which completely changed its character. Juxtaposing the romance of the sea with the anti-romantic details of laboring London, the essay considers, in the first deleted passage,

> the process, which is daily discharged in the port of London, of receiving this immense merchandise, of taking it on shore, of opening it, sorting it, sampling it, weighing it, selling it, distributing it, & passing it on, in its crude state, to be cooked, baked, tanned, worked, seasoned, rolled,—made in short into the million different luxuries & necessities upon which not only London but all England will feed; will wear—will use in its cars in its houses, in its streets—this vast patient skillful & [unremitting] labour is full of sweat & agony & squalor & horror. Looking out to sea is one thing, at the splendid ship, crowding her white sails, leaning across the bosom of the argent West, but turn East; look at the blight & squalor that surrounds us; as we turn, to go towards the voracious city which those white sails feed. Nothing can be much more dismal. Factories & offices line the shore; stand crowded in the mud. Behind are the meanest streets in London. The line of

> warehouses is black, dingy, decrepit looking. Here & there are vast factories; whether new or old does not matter—The same dingy grey black coats them all. They crowd without order or intention. If a window is broken broken it remains. They have neither size nor strength. They seem run up & purely utilitarian & to fall. When one of them has been blackened by fire it seems scarcely more derelict & ruinous than the other. Behind them in ridges of grey rise the mean streets—which house the dock laborers.[9]

Suffering and horror; squalor and sweat. The blame for this painful melange of facts and feelings lies with the utilitarian producers and unthinking consumers of England. Woolf details the complicated process of commercial production, whose price is pain and whose habitat is this dismal quarter of the city. She forces upon our attention the dramatic difference between the romantic dreams of the Thames view to the West, where "splendid ships" sail the seas, and the squalor of the city's East End. The contrast is historical as well as geographic: on land once graced by grass and trees, churches and country inns, now squats the "voracious city" with its factories and warehouses, the detritus of careless, greedy, haphazard industrial production. In this passage Woolf creates a memorable image for a painful fact: the price, in human suffering, paid by the working classes to produce the necessities and luxuries that middle- and upper-class England consumes.

Yet the published version of this scene presents only architectural disorder; its only pain is the visual discomfort of the sensitive, detached aesthete who perceives it. Facts, before so firmly presented—the price of industry and commerce, the human cost of refining raw materials—have melted into atmosphere. Whether consciously or unconsciously, independently or following editorial suggestion, Woolf toned the facts down as she revised "The Docks of London." By the final version she had deleted the social criticism, and the narrator's sympathy for the workers had given way to a more comfortable, less guilt-inducing alienation from them—a sense of them as tainted and sinister and of their area of the city as mysterious, dingy, freakish, a "dwarf city of workmen's houses" (*LS*, 8).

One way of explaining this shift would be to say that anticipation of the audience's probable negative response shaped Woolf's revisions. Yet her own discomfort with the "facts" of dockside London, of which she complained in a letter to Ethel Smyth in March 1931, seems also to have bearing on the deletions: "I'm being bored to death by my London articles—pure brilliant description—six of them—and not a thought for fear of clouding the brilliancy; and I have had to go all over the Thames, port of London, in a launch, with the Persian Ambassador—but that I liked—I dont like facts, though" (*L*, IV: 301). While Woolf clearly resented being confined to the facts of her "pure brilliant description" and restrained from any thought "for fear of clouding the brilliancy," she may also have felt torn between her sense of privilege—riding in a launch with the Persian ambassador, herself the daughter of Sir Leslie Stephen—and her empathy with the working people she saw on her tour of the London docks. We know that her experience as a woman had, as early as her adolescence, kindled in her what she called the "outsider's feeling," and it is not unlikely that her river tour rekindled that painful, if now vicarious, sense of exclusion and powerlessness (*MB*, 132). It may have been in response to this surge of uncomfortable empathy that the locus of allegiance changed, in her revisions of "The Docks of London," from identification along gender lines, as a powerless woman, to identification along class lines, as one of the privileged London elite. However, gender is at times only implicitly present in the portrait of working-class London, and class privilege belongs to the narrator, as to Woolf herself, by virtue only of her ancillary position as one of the "daughters of educated men."

In the second extensive deletion, gender relations overtly join class relations. When Woolf compares the space of servants to that of the "master," the result is a vision of London divided between messy, exploitative male masters and overburdened female housekeepers. When the passage begins, we survey an area in which it seems

> as if fortifications were being raised. But in fact these dykes are built of old fires & vegetables. London is sending out the contents of her dustbins. Barges come down heaped with tin cans. The Londoner leaves behind him every day a fire [tin] & fish, bones, ashes, vegetables. And here they are, being dumped by men out to these ancient fifty year old rubbish heaps, by the river; which grow & grow; & sometimes catch fire—smoul-

> der; & sometimes remain damp & sodden, so that weeds flourish & rats accumulate. And here is an ambiguous vessel, neither ship nor machine, but something between the two, which is dredging the river bottom. The silt will be carried out seventy miles & dropped into the sea. All is activity & [housemaids] Everywhere things are being sorted, ordered, kept in being. Here is London's scullery, its washing up place, its kitchen offices. And then, just as we are given up to thinking of London as the master, where men, whose habit of throwing away tins, cabbage, skittles keeps the whole population here busy clearing [cleaning] up after her, down comes a great steamer bound for India. . . .[10]

Woolf's traditional identification of the city as female, "she," is tellingly undercut by her potent description of it as the "master." In a domestic metaphor that splits London dramatically along the lines of gender and class, the great city becomes a garbage-spewing upper-class man and the populace becomes working-class housemaids. This dichotomy anticipates *The Years*, which, as Jane Marcus has pointed out, "shows us men making money, making war, making love, making books, and making a colossal mess—and women cleaning it up after them. Only a woman like Virginia Woolf could conceive of the metaphor of the artist as charwoman to the world."[11] And only Virginia Woolf could conjure up the "ambiguous vehicle, neither ship nor machine," who bears such an evocative analogical relationship to its creator, with her divided sense of self and social place. Which was she, Woolf may have wondered: A glorious white ship bound for imperial India? Or a dredge, a drudge, a prosaic female machine?

The published version of this fascinating passage, once again, is safe, brief, and rather flat:

> Barges heaped with old buckets, razor blades, fish tails, newspapers and ashes—whatever we leave on our plates and throw into our dust bins—are discharging their cargoes upon the most desolate land in the world. The long mounds have been fuming and smoking and harbouring innumerable rats and growing a rank coarse grass and giving off a gritty, acrid air for fifty years. The dumps get higher and higher, and thicker and thicker, their sides more precipitous with tin cans, their pinnacles more angular with ashes year by year. [*LS*, 9–10]

Woolf's shift in identification is unmistakable: now the ash heaps are built by invisible workers from "whatever *we* leave on *our* plates and throw into *our* dustbins" (emphasis mine). She has joined her audience in the consumer mentality of the middle class, rather than sharing the workers' drudgery.[12]

From "voracious city" and garbage-spewing "master," London has changed to "noble city," just as the narrator has shifted allegiance from the workers to the consumers. The deletion of these two passages of implicit social criticism lends an air of resignation to the essay's conclusion. Instead of the ironic voice that we might have heard if the social criticism had remained to create a context for it, we hear only self-congratulation:

> It is we—our tastes, our fashions, our needs—that make the cranes dip and swing, that call the ships from the sea. Our body is their master. We demand shoes, furs, bags, stoves, oil, rice puddings, candles; and they are brought us. Trade watches us anxiously to see what new desires are beginning to grow in us, what new dislikes. One feels an important, a complex, a necessary animal as one stands on the quayside watching the cranes hoist this barrel, that crate, that other bale from the holds of the ships that have come to anchor. [*LS*, 14]

The workers have become invisible. "One" only feels of such importance, prominence, and power if "one" is a member of the consuming class—standing at quayside watching, rather than operating a crane or hoisting barrels. From the subversive vision of the essay's earlier draft, Woolf has moved to complacency: "one" is no longer the housemaid who cleans up after him, but the "master" himself.

"Oxford Street Tide"

Like so many of Woolf's essays, "The Docks of London" ends at full tide. A wool auction is over; now the "cart horses are struggling and striving to distribute the wool over England" (*LS*, 15). "Oxford Street Tide," next in the series, describes that wool when it has been transformed into finished products, "thin vests and soft stockings," for the Oxford Street stores. Although it, too, reflects conflicting identifications, in this essay Woolf more steadily maintains her control over voice and point of view by using the double perspective, a device familiar from *A Room of One's Own* as well as from an early writing exercise, "Thoughts upon Social Success." In "Oxford Street Tide" the primary perspective is that of an appreciative narrator, impressed with the variety of Oxford Street's finished goods and with the attitudes toward life that they exemplify. Played off against that perspective is the view of a "moralist," brought in only as a parody of the Victorian values he mouths. While the appreciative observer celebrates the street for its manifestation of the stimulating shock and change characteristic of the urban spirit, the moralist points the "finger of scorn" at Oxford Street, proclaiming his distaste for its "blatant and raucous" commercialism, its profusion of bargains and sales. This division of perspectives emphasizes the distinction between Victorian and modern valuations of the city, just as the image of Oxford Street as a "tide" both recalls the Victorians' characteristic figures for the city as "a stream, a tide" and contains the modern image of urban life as a river of sensation and activity.[13]

The appreciative observer celebrates "Oxford Street" as a synesthetic delight: "The mind becomes a glutinous slab that takes impressions and Oxford Street rolls off upon it a perpetual ribbon of changing sights, sounds and movement" (*LS*, 17). His vision of the city not only challenges the moralist's Victorian antipathy to urban commercialism but also queries the assumption of such modern writers as T. S. Eliot and D. H. Lawrence, as well as the sociologist Georg Simmel, that urban stimulation produces alienation and anomie.[14] Instead, he reports that the city-dweller thrives on sensation in an almost visceral way: "News changes quicker [in Oxford Street] than in any other part of London. The press of people passing seems to lick the ink off the placards and to consume more of them and to demand fresh supplies of later editions faster than elsewhere" (*LS*, 17). The commercial Oxford Street "palaces" are equally changing, and they please us, therefore, in new ways: "The charm of modern London is that it is not built to last; it is built to pass. Its glassiness, its transparency, its surging waves of coloured plaster give a different pleasure and achieve a different end from that which was desired and attempted by the old builders and their patrons, the nobility of England" (*LS*, 19–20). While nobility wanted the illusion of permanence, the new democratic crowds swelled by shoppers and working-class street vendors prefer an architecture reflecting their own spirit of creative innovation: "We knock down and rebuild as we expect to be knocked down and rebuilt. It is an impulse that makes for creation and fertility. Discovery is stimulated and invention on the alert" (*LS*, 20). The new egalitarian political vision accompanying such a stress on change is expressed in both "Street Haunting" and, later, *Three Guineas*: possessions, whether they are of the private home or of the college, not only define one's identity but threaten to constrain it as well—as in the case of the alternate female selves in "Street Haunting." Better, therefore, to have only those possessions which, being cheap and easily discarded, can be changed at will, and even lost without regret. Oxford Street offers just such ephemeral possessions to its customers.

For Woolf's appreciative observer, London offers more than just a pleasant experience. Oxford Street induces empathy with the varied voices of the street crowd, enabling identification with the less fortunate, even with the criminal, which expands one's political perspective:

> I grant, says the middle-class woman, that I linger and look and barter and cheapen and turn over basket after basket of remnants hour by hour. My eyes glisten unseemlily I know, and I grab and pounce with disgusting greed. But my husband is a small clerk in a bank; I have only fifteen pounds a year to dress on; so here I come, to linger and loiter and look, if I can, as well dressed as my neighbors. I am a thief, says a woman of that persuasion, and a lady of easy virtue into the bargain. But it takes a good deal of pluck to snatch a bag from a counter when a customer is not looking; and it may contain only spectacles and old bus tickets after all. [*LS*, 21]

This moment of empathy with the travails of a thief seems to have originated in Woolf's own experience of being robbed on 23 December 1930. In the diary entry recording the event, as in "Oxford Street Tide," curiosity and empathy prevail over anger as Woolf's imagination goes to work, leading her to expand her social horizons by imagining the thief's home and her relations with her husband:

> I will make this hasty note about being robbed. I put my bag under my coat at Marshall & Snelgrove's. I turned; & felt, be-

> fore I looked "It is gone." So it was. Then began questions & futile messages. Then the detective came. He stopped a respectable elderly woman apparently shopping. They exchanged remarks about 'the usual one—no she's not here today. Its a young woman in brown fur.' Meanwhile I was ravaged, of course, with my own futile wishes—how I had thought, as I put down my bag, this is foolish. I was admitted to the underwor[l]d. I imagined the brown young woman peeping, pouncing. And it was gone my 6 pounds—my two brooches—all because of that moment. They throw the bags away, said the detective. These dreadful women come here—but not so much as to some of the Oxford St. shops. Fluster, regret, humiliation, curiosity, something frustrated, foolish, something jarred, by this underwor[l]d—a foggy evening—going home, penniless—thinking of my green bag—imagining the woman rifling it—her home—her husband. . . [*D*, III: 339–40]

Coincident with the loss of her possessions ("my 6 pounds—my two brooches") Woolf experiences a moment of imaginative union with the "brown young woman" who stole from her; the experience is a model for the insight into property's impact on human relations that she developed in "Street Haunting" and expands in "Oxford Street Tide." Moreover, the passage in "Oxford Street Tide" emphasizes the city's role in shaking individuals loose from habit to transform their sympathies: "if the moralist chooses to take his afternoon walk along this particular thoroughfare, he must tune his strain so that it receives into it some queer, incongruous voices" (*LS*, 20–21).

The introduction of the moralist, whose stodgy political, aesthetic, and social values Woolf mocks, permits a consideration and a dismissal of the Victorian anti-urbanism he embodies. "[Even] a moralist," Woolf ironically asserts, "who is, one must suppose, since he can spend the afternoon dreaming, a man with a balance in the bank—even a moralist must allow that this gaudy, bustling, vulgar street reminds us that life is a struggle; that all building is perishable; that all display is vanity" (*LS*, 21–22). Yet the consolations of philosophy are purchased by a fat bank balance; no such portentous summations are accessible—happily, Woolf implies—to the lively but impecunious crowds of Oxford Street. No moralist or philosopher, the observer mocks such contemplative tendencies as alien to the spontaneous commercialism of the city. "[Until] some adroit shopkeeper has caught on to the idea and opened cells for solitary thinkers hung with green plush and provided with automatic glowworms and a sprinkling of genuine death's-head moths to induce thought and reflection, it is vain to try to come to a conclusion in Oxford Street" (*LS*, 22). The essay ends with the moralist's parody of Victorian judiciousness, mocking the impulse to retreat into contemplation as an escape from the salutary immediacy of urban experience.

"Great Men's Houses"

The next essay in the series, "Great Men's Houses," fights the popular myth of a great man's house as a "cell for solitary thinkers." It purports to offer a tour of the homes of Thomas Carlyle and John Keats, yet Woolf's real goal in this essay is subversive: to fight the image of the "great man" created by Carlyle himself, who asserted that "it is the spiritual always that determines the material,"[15] by focusing on the *material conditions* of the great man's life. Woolf intends to show a "Man of Letters" who is not the "Hero" or "most important modern person," as Carlyle saw him to be, but merely a prosaic domestic master.[16] To Carlyle's definition of history as "at bottom the History of the Great Men who have worked here," Woolf opposes this small chapter in the history of women, both great and ordinary, behind the great man.[17] Lighting on the one telling fact about the Carlyles' establishment—its lack of running water—she movingly describes the enormous effort that went into the daily operation of that great man's home—an effort put forth by women.

While Carlyle sat "in the attic under a skylight . . . as he wrestled with his history," down in the lower quarters of the house his wife and maid worked to keep the bathwater hot and the dirt at bay. "All through the mid-Victorian age the house was necessarily a battlefield where daily, summer and winter, mistress and maid fought against dirt and cold for cleanliness and warmth" (*LS*, 24). This vertical division in the Carlyles' home recalls the division of London into male parlor and female scullery, as deleted from the published version of "The Docks of London." Politically, the vision is radical in its subversion of patriarchal authority: mistress and maid are united in one battle, the fight to clean up the very mess produced by Thomas Carlyle. While Carlyle asserted, in *On*

Heroes, Hero-Worship, and the Heroic in History, that "The Hero as Man of Letters . . . is one of the main forms of Heroism for all future ages," Woolf's essay reveals the reality of *woman's* labor and the extent of woman's heroism.[18] The ostensible portrait of a great man's house becomes a portrait of the tortures his requirements inflicted upon maid and wife alike. Even the portrait of the great man has been subverted into a striking portrait of his wife, the long-suffering Jane Welsh Carlyle:

> By pumping and by scrubbing, days of victory, evenings of peace and splendour were won, of course. Mrs. Carlyle sat, as we see from the picture, in a fine silk dress, in a chair pulled up to a blazing fire and had everything seemly and solid about her; but at what cost had she won it! Her cheeks are hollow; bitterness and suffering mingle in the half-tender, half-tortured expression of the eyes. Such is the effect of a pump in the basement and a yellow tin bath up three flights of stairs. [*LS*, 25]

Jane Carlyle's hollow cheeks ask how splendid or peaceful any evenings could be that failed to free her of next day's chore: filling that tin bath up three flights of stairs. Woolf's sympathy for the mistress is unmistakable, as is her concern for the working-class maid beside whom she toiled.

The spatial imagery of the Carlyles' house explicitly connects sexual and class oppression, mistress and maid. Emphasizing the amount of time women spend in physical labor each day, it suggests that the forms of labor, rather than her familial or class ties, really define woman's place in society. Because both Jane Welsh Carlyle and the maid are responsible for the hot water, clean rooms, and regular meals that Thomas Carlyle requires to write his history, both women are associated with the same space in the home. While the great man fills the top floors, the women cluster in the lower regions: kitchen, washroom, scullery, basement. This spatial analysis has both a sociological and a psychosocial dimension: just as women's domestic tasks keep them in the lower reaches of the home, so they limit them to the lower reaches of society. And though the Victorian home, like the mind it could be seen to mirror, was strenuously and repeatedly purified, its metaphoric spatial relations revealed the repressed reality. Leonore Davidoff has demonstrated that, in the Victorian era, for middle-class children "social divisions and their erotic overtones were also reflected in a spatial view of their world—a view which started with their own bodies, extended to the houses where they lived, and eventually to their . . . city."[19]

In "Great Men's Houses" Woolf guides the reader to consider the value of a great man's love, which finds itself impotent against "bugs and tin baths and pumps in the basement" (*LS*, 26). Unfortunately, she was not yet ready to sustain the implications of that vision: a complete reevaluation of the meanings of both greatness and heroism. Instead, she retreated to a comfortable fatalism familiar from the conclusion of "The Docks of London": "But then, we reflect, as we cross the worn threshhold, Carlyle with hot water laid on would not have been Carlyle; and Mrs. Carlyle without bugs to kill would have been a different woman from the one we know" (*LS*, 26). The echo of that difference remains to haunt the reader.

"Abbeys and Cathedrals" and "'This is the House of Commons'"

After the exuberance and expressive imagery of "Oxford Street Tide" and "Great Men's Houses," the next two essays seem subdued, wavering between the perspectives of insider and outsider. Woolf's topic is now the hub of patriarchal London which she saw from Parliament Hill, and she walks us softly round church and state as if trying to disturb neither the illustrious inhabitants of the splendid buildings (living or dead) nor her *Good Housekeeping* readers. The theme, which runs throughout the "London Scene" series, is the contrast between two Londons, the surface city of respectable convention and what Woolf called "the underworld" (*D*, III: 339–40). In "The Docks of London" this contrast figures in an exploration of the little-known (to middle-class *Good Housekeeping* readers) methods of unloading, distributing, and processing that turn a cargo of raw material into a fixed amount of finished merchandise, as well as in the vision of subterranean class struggle arising from that endeavor. "Oxford Street Tide" contrasts the moralist's easy, superficial criticism of the trivial vulgarity of modern London to the appreciative narrator's more complex understanding of an "underworld" that finds its meaning, and even its survival, in the flimsy social network of London's commercial sector. Though to different degrees and at different stages of composition, both essays embody Woolf's response, in a debate waged in 1925, to Logan Pearsall Smith concerning the morality and aesthetic effect of writing for the fashion papers. Against his assertion that those magazines were a trivial, superficial, and inappropriate environment for serious thought, Woolf argued that the fashion magazines were less damaging to aesthetic or social freedom than were the so-called "deeper" journals of official high culture such as the *Times Literary Supplement*. Pearsall Smith decried "modern writers who . . . [have not] deemed it beneath the dignity of letters to insert, between articles on Cosmetics, and advertisements of Exclusive Underwear, little snippets and butterfly-dishes of Art and Culture."[20] However, responding to his fears that Bloomsbury intellectuals would be corrupted by "writing articles at high rates for fashion papers," Woolf scoffed, "Ladies' clothes and aristocrats playing golf don't affect my style; and they would do his [Pearsall Smith's] a world of good" (*L*, III: 154). Woolf's assertion that what was to Pearsall Smith superficial was to her deep, and what was to him exemplary and worthwhile was to her lifeless and unoriginal, reflects a radical reframing of experience that anticipates the truly independent social criticism of *Three Guineas*, where Woolf would assess the impact of professional life upon humanity and find it purely negative, producing not enlightened workers but merely "a cripple in a cave" (*TG*, 72).

The distinction between surface and underworld, convention and originality obtains in "Abbeys and Cathedrals." St. Paul's embodies the former in its tidy pomposity, while Westminster Abbey's sometimes bawdy vigor embodies the latter. Yet the very difficulty we have with the idea of Westminster Abbey as representative of the "underworld" reveals the flaw in this essay: while Woolf scorns social snobbery and elitism, she still holds to the idea of a literary aristocracy. The respect she shows for "poets and statesmen" and for the kings and queens who were their patrons gives little hint of the more iconoclastic stance she would adopt only six years later, in *Three Guineas*, toward all those who elevate themselves above the great crowd of common readers.

Still, a quiet irony here may have escaped the editors of *Good Housekeeping*, if the captions and illustrations may be taken as representing the editors' expectations of their "distinguished author."[21] The caption to the title page of "Abbeys and Cathedrals" is "The splendour and serenity of St. Paul's"—a phrase that omits the ironic undertone not merely of the passage as it reads in its

The splendour and serenity of St. Paul's (from General Lew Wallace, ed., Scenes From Every Land *[Springfield, Ohio: Mast, Crowell & Kirkpatrick, 1893], p. 22).*

entirety, but of the whole essay.[22] The complete passage suggests not merely the glory of St. Paul's but its inhuman, static aridity as well: "Something of the splendour of St. Paul's lies simply in its vast size, in its colourless serenity" (*LS*, 31). To this grand tidiness Woolf opposes the untidy vigor of Westminster Abbey; once again, the caption suggests that the expectations of editors and author diverged. "Westminster Abbey, full of potent royalty," accompanies a photograph of the Abbey's interior.[23] While the caption suggests that Woolf is celebrating hereditary political power, in its entirety the phrase reveals that she is assessing the *inferiority* of kings, dukes, and princes next to the "more potent royalty" of English literature, the "dead poets" who lie "still musing, still pondering, still questioning the meaning of existence" (*LS*, 34).

The House of Commons also disappoints the narrator's expectations in ways that seem to elude the *Good Housekeeping* editors. While the caption dwells on the power and scope of the institution—"Here the destinies of the world are altered. . . . It is by these men we are governed. We obey their orders every day of the year. . . . But we have to remind ourselves—'This is the House of Commons'"—in the body of the essay the narrator clearly finds the opposite quality remarkable.[24] Far from glorifying the members of the House of Commons, she celebrates their prosaic nature. Just as the crucial detail about a man's house is not the writing desk and chair upon which he left his imprint but the inadequate facilities for hot water which left their mark upon his wife and maid, now the wonderful thing about the members of the House of Commons is not their dignity but their *commonness*: "But how, one asks, remembering Parliament Square, are any of these competent, well-groomed gentlemen going to turn into statues? . . . the transition into marble is unthinkable. Mobile, irreverent, commonplace, snub-nosed, red-jowled, squires, lawyers, men of business—their prime quality, their enormous virtue lies surely in the fact that no more normal, average, decent-looking set of human beings could be found in the four kingdoms" (*LS*, 40). Although Woolf jokes about the effect Mr. Baldwin would make, mounting a plinth and wrapping himself "decorously in a towel of black marble," the deeply serious point of this essay would form a central theme in *The Years*. In an ideal society we would make no statues of great men; there would be no boundaries between "great men" and ordinary people, any more than there would be between men and women. Trade, fame, religion, politics—all have the dangerous potential to isolate one group from another, insiders from outsiders, the great from the obscure, men from women. Whether insiders possess fame, money, or power, their isolation in turn creates prejudice, as Woolf revealed in "Street Haunting."

In contrast to that world of rigid distinctions between those possessing greater and lesser power, at the end of "'This is the House of Commons'" Woolf imagines a different kind of political organization: a world beyond art, which abandons the egotism of statues for the communal endeavor of architecture:

> If the days of the small separate statue are over, why should not the age of architecture dawn? That question asks itself as we leave the House of Commons. Westminster Hall raises its immense dignity as we pass out. Little men and women are moving soundlessly about the floor. They appear minute, perhaps pitiable; but also venerable and beautiful under the curve of the vast dome, under the perspective of the huge columns. One would rather like to be a small nameless animal in a vast cathedral. Let us rebuild the world then as a splendid hall; let

Westminster Abbey, full of potent royalty (from General Lew Wallace, ed., Scenes From Every Land *[Springfield, Ohio: Mast, Crowell & Kirkpatrick, 1893], p. 26).*

> us give up making statues and inscribing them with impossible virtues.
>
> Let us see whether democracy which makes halls cannot surpass the aristocracy which carved statues. [*LS*, 43]

Calling for a world no longer dedicated to the celebration of great men but able instead to celebrate all individuals, female and male, great and ordinary, Woolf imagines that world in the familiar shape of her earliest experiences with her mother, when she felt herself to be a "small, nameless animal in a vast cathedral" (*LS*, 43). The image is far from fortuitous, because at issue here is an alternate social system that would permit people enough space to feel "venerable and beautiful" while dedicating no alcove to one man alone. Woolf's early memories, and her scene-making imagination, reveal an implicit liberation from gender categories in this world without statues. Stony figures whose names and "impossible virtues" are inscribed on pedestals for the admiration of faceless viewers give way to the splendidly anonymous cathedral space, analog to the sheltering environment first furnished by the mother, in which children first experience their separate selfhood. This age of architecture is no doubt female in its inspiration, but in its embodiment in Woolf's fantasy it promises to transcend the normal gender-inscribed roles. The positions of figure (or agent) and ground (or spectator) are not only reversed but also freed from any connection to gender, and thus may be enacted by both men and women. Even space itself partakes of both male and female aspects, combining in "the curve of the vast dome" and the "perspective of the huge columns" both male and female "architecture" to suggest a world transcending gender polarities.

Woolf attains this vision only briefly. Unfortunately, she temporizes at the essay's end, holding out to her readers the rather dubious possibility of a social compromise between such an egalitarian world and one that still erects statues of great men: "So let us hope that democracy will come, but only a hundred years hence, when we are beneath the grass; or that by some stupendous stroke of genius both will be combined, the vast hall and the small, the particular, the individual human being" (*LS*, 44). The ambivalent closure attests to Woolf's own uncertainty about her position in society, as in her earlier surveys of the waterfront, commercial, literary, and religious districts of London. She continues to waver between empathy for common people and temptation to grasp at prominence and privilege.

"Portrait of a Londoner"

"Portrait of a Londoner," the last essay, combines roles that were riven in "Great Men's Houses," to create Mrs. Crowe, the housekeeper/historian, who mediates London life through her own idiosyncratic perspective. Alone among all the "London Scene" essays, "Portrait of a Londoner" was not reprinted in the limited edition of 1975, entitled *The London Scene*, edited by Frank Hallman. While Mrs. Crowe's nature as a broad parody of Cockney London may account for the essay's exclusion, a careful reading of the essay reveals some astringent social criticism beneath Woolf's gentle regional satire.

A "collector of relationships," Mrs. Crowe objectifies the people around her: "She looked out of place among other people's chairs & tables; she must have her own chintzes and her own cabinet and her own Mr. Graham under it to be completely herself." Yet, once secure in her familiar surroundings, Mrs. Crowe turns to the text of the city around her, which she interprets in her conversation: "Mrs. Crowe by no means dwelt on the past—she by no means exalted it above the present. Indeed it was always the last page, the present moment that mattered most. The delightful thing about London was that it was always giving one something new to look at, something fresh to talk about." Sharing her creator's technique for safeguarding her place in society while still assuming the central role of speaker, she pitches her tale to her audience, avoiding obvious cleverness or profundity lest it alienate someone, particularly some *man*. Instead, she entertains by retailing what resembles village gossip, though the "village was London, and the gossip was about London life."

There is a real power in Mrs. Crowe's homely conversation, however. Her gossip creates a world and shapes it to her needs: "Mrs. Crowe's great gift consisted in making the vast metropolis seem as small as a village with one church, one manor house, & twenty-five cottages." Though without formal institutional sanction, the urban history which she creates at her tea table plays a crucial role in city life. It makes the unmanageable and chaotic suddenly comprehensible, intimate:

> Thus, to know London not merely as a gorgeous spectacle, a mart, a court, a hive of industry, but as a place where people meet and talk, laugh, marry, and die, paint, write and act, rule and legislate, it was necessary to know Mrs. Crowe. It was in her drawing room that the innumerable fragments of the vast metropolis seemed to come together into one lively, comprehensible, amusing and agreeable whole. Travellers absent for years, battered and sun-dried men just landed from India or Africa, from remote travels and adventures among savages and tigers, would come straight to the little house in the quiet street to be taken back into the heart of civilisation at one stride.[25]

Mrs. Crowe not only brings London's rich texture into focus, humanizes it, and gives it a past; she also distorts it. Reducing the vast metropolis to a feudal village in her gossip, she civilizes and moralizes it as well. So, to the colonial administrators who turn first to Mrs. Crowe's drawing room upon returning from their savage jungles, the city seems not challenging and diverse but "comprehensible, amusing and agreeable." Urban interpreter for imperialists, Mrs. Crowe embodies the intrinsic conservatism that

Woolf at times revealed, and with which she struggled, in her "London Scene" essays.

Such a homogeneous, ordered, and rational perspective cannot long prevail in the modern city. Perhaps it is for this reason that Mrs. Crowe dies at the end of "Portrait of a Londoner": "Even London itself could not keep Mrs. Crowe alive forever. It is a fact that one day Mrs. Crowe was not sitting in the arm chair by the fire as the clock struck five; Maria did not open the door; Mr. Graham had detached himself from the cabinet. Mrs. Crowe is dead and London—no, to some people London will never be the same city again." With Mrs. Crowe's demise, London seems irreparably changed—"to some people." The qualifying phrase suggests that, when her unifying, stabilizing perspective is gone, the city splinters into a thousand different vistas. With the new relativism in perspective comes a change in social organization as well. Rather than the single, established hierarchy of imperial Victorian London, we have a new and perhaps more egalitarian modern city. Now Marias are free to find jobs other than as maidservants; now Mr. Grahams, who have held up the drawing-room cabinet all these years thanks to leisure provided by inherited wealth, must remove themselves from the furniture and venture out to make a living.

Mrs. Crowe's death is a fitting end to the "London Scene" essays because her preoccupation mirrors that of her creator. In these essays of 1931 and 1932 Woolf struggled to subsume under one voice her conflicting perspectives on life in London. As a result, the brilliantly amusing travelog appropriate to *Good Housekeeping* frequently drowned out both realistic portrait and social criticism. However, the death of Mrs. Crowe at the end of the series symbolizes Woolf's decision to stop attempting to reconcile her conflicting identifications. No longer would she disguise her perspective as a woman and an outsider under the smooth, unchallenging voice of the insider. In the works to come, particularly in *Three Guineas* and *The Years*, Woolf's portrait of the city would reflect more and more her own experience as a woman in a patriarchal society.

CHAPTER FOUR

TRADITION AND REVISION

THE CLASSIC CITY NOVEL AND WOOLF'S *NIGHT AND DAY*

Completion of her first novel in 1913 had left Woolf agitated and delusional. When rest, balanced meals, and doses of "Robin's Hypophosphate" failed to cure her, she was sent, on doctor's orders, to the Twickenham convalescent home. There she endured the rest cure developed by Dr. Silas Weir Mitchell: quiet country life, bed rest, and countless glasses of milk. Yet, in March 1915, her progress toward recovery ended; a relapse raised the possibility that Virginia and Leonard Woolf's temporary residence in Richmond, where they had been living in lodgings since October, should become permanent. "Certainly [Richmond] is the first of the suburbs by a long way, because it is not an offshoot of London, any more than Oxford or Marlborough is," Woolf considered in her diary (*D*, I: 31). Yet her attempt to reconcile herself to suburban life, half-hearted as it was, did not disguise London's continuing fascination for her; she was still searching for rooms there on every visit to the city. In particular, she was drawn to Holborn and Bloomsbury, enjoying their "tumult & riot & busyness" (*D*, I: 9).

London's activity alone did not explain her reluctance to leave it for a home in the suburbs. Woolf seems to have associated the city with the ability to do serious intellectual work, finding in its "Crowded streets . . . the only places . . . that ever make me what-in-the-case of another-one-might-call think" (*D*, I: 9). London was "serious life" to her, unlike Richmond, where she had "always come . . . for an outing" (*D*, I: 29–30). The last entry in her diary before the relapse of March 1915 records a day spent in the city and captures London's importance to her as a writer. "Then I had tea, & rambled down to Charing Cross in the dark, making up phrases & incidents to write about. Which is, I expect, the way one gets killed" (*D*, I: 35). While the actual risk Woolf seems to have taken is disturbing, perhaps even more disquieting is her offhand dismissal of it as "the way one gets killed." London is clearly a source of creative inspiration for her, but at this time it also appears to have been a dangerous environment—physically and psychologically. Prudence, it seemed, dictated the move to the more sedate Richmond, which occurred only one day before publication of *The Voyage Out*, just as Woolf began her second—and successful—convalescence.

Although this second cure was successful, a mood of caution lingered. When Woolf began to plan her second novel a year later, a similar desire to avoid stimulation seems to have shaped that venture. As she confessed long afterward to Ethel Smyth:

> After being ill and suffering every form and variety of nightmare and extravagant intensity of perception . . . after all this, when I came to, I was so tremblingly afraid of my own insanity that I wrote Night and Day mainly to prove to my own satisfaction that I could keep entirely off that dangerous ground. I wrote it, lying in bed, allowed to write for only one half hour a day. And I made myself copy from plaster casts, partly to tranquillise, partly to learn anatomy. Bad as the book is, it composed my mind, and I think taught me certain elements of composition which I should not have had the patience to learn had I been in full flush of health always. [*L*, IV: 231]

To understand what Virginia Woolf learned in *Night and Day*, her second novel, we must consider the emotional and aesthetic reasons for what E. M. Forster called her curious condescension to classicism.[1] It is generally agreed that the center of the novel was Woolf's beloved sister, Vanessa Bell. In a letter to her Latin teacher, Janet Case, she hinted, "Try thinking of Katharine [the protagonist] as Vanessa, not me; and suppose her concealing a passion for painting and forced to go into Society by George [Duckworth]" (*L*, II: 400). Yet her explanation of the novel's origin, in the letter to Ethel Smyth, suggests that Woolf identified strongly with Vanessa's dilemma: she appropriates the art student metaphor to acknowledge the novel's stilted, derivative nature, explaining that it derives from her use of real people and events as "plaster casts" from which to copy.

Those real events and people that formed the basis for *Night and Day* were, first of all, the educational divisions of daily life for Vanessa and Virginia Stephen in their years at 22 Hyde Park Gate, Kensington. The novel's title recalls them, inverting the culturally established expectations that "night" will be a time of creative fantasy and "day" a time of practical labor; the Stephen women were free to engage in creativity during the day, while at night they found themselves duty bound. Torn between her duties as hostess around the tea table and her hidden passion for mathematics, Katharine Hilbery in *Night and Day* recalls Vanessa Stephen, torn between the social duties prescribed by George Duckworth and her own passion for painting.[2] And if the novel originates in that struggle to find the time and place to do serious work, it speaks of a similar struggle on the part of many Victorian and modern women: to resist the "duty" to serve as "angel in the house" in order, instead, to do the work one has chosen.

In turning her attention to woman's struggle to work, Virginia Woolf seems to have chosen a topic highly unlikely to provide the "tranquillising influence" for which (as she told Ethel Smyth) she hoped in her second novel. Yet in asserting that she made herself copy from "plaster casts," Woolf was not just speaking of the biographical origins of the novel's theme and characters, but defining its form as well. An early scene in which Katharine Hilbery chooses her parents' postprandial reading reveals Woolf's formal solution to the problem of how to express herself without alienating others or treading on "dangerous ground." Katharine first tries to interest her parents in modern fiction, but her attempt is futile; her father mocks the authors as if they were promising children, while her mother dismisses the "light, gold-wreathed" volume of a contemporary author as "too clever and cheap and nasty for words" (*ND*, 104). They urge her, instead, to read them something "real." She chooses at last a "portly volume in sleek, yellow calf," a novel by Henry Fielding (*ND*, 104). Selection of her parents' reading poses risks for Katharine. Choosing the modern novel, she runs the risk of being mocked or condemned as tasteless; choosing the safer, classical alternative, she runs another risk—of losing her audience. And in fact she does lose it, not to clashing tastes but to sleep. The Fielding novel has "directly a sedative effect upon both her parents" (*ND*, 104).

This early scene in *Night and Day* can be read as a metatextual gloss upon Woolf's dilemma in writing her second novel. Both the classical and contemporary models available to her had certain risks. With the former, she chanced charges of being derivative; with the latter, she risked alienating her audience or (worse still) being laughed at. Furthermore, there was the overarching risk of losing her sanity, which was perhaps her greatest concern at this time. The reading scene suggests that Woolf joined her heroine in opting for the sedative restraint, the tranquilizing effect, of the classical model; moreover, it suggests specifically what that model might have been. I suggest that Fielding offers an important precursor for *Night and Day*. As Irving Howe has pointed out, Henry Fielding originated the classic city novel, with its "dominant literary pattern of discovery and withdrawal in regard to the city."[3] Cautious, concerned with her own mental stability yet convinced that London's crowded streets were "the only places . . . that ever make me what-in-the-case of another-one-might-call think," Woolf had herself recently undergone a process of discovery and withdrawal in regard to the city. She had moved, upon her father's death, from the confines of Kensington to the spacious squares of Bloomsbury, only to retreat after her marriage to the calm of suburban Richmond. She turned to the classic city novel to explore an issue intimately related to her own response to the city in 1915: a woman's struggle to do her own work.

Several elements characterize the classic city novel. It is a drama of emotional education whose shape is a spiral journey from country to city and back. Implicitly, it embraces what Raymond Williams has called "the ideology of improvement," since the journey through the city must result, with more or less coincidence as the tradition becomes established, in a good match. Finally, its protagonist learns of life in the city only to live it in the country. For the youth propelled there by necessity or fortune, the city has little appeal in itself; rather, it is only a way-station where he may remain until attaining emotional and economic majority, when he may retire gracefully to a comfortable country seat.[4]

Night and Day resembles the classic city novel in a number of ways, perhaps most obviously in the shape of Katharine Hilbery's story. Like the Fielding novel that she reads to her parents in Chapter 7, it concerns a marriage choice laced with comic elements. Each principal is identified by geographical coordinates, leading E. M. Forster to observe that the characters "are screwed into Chelsea and Highgate as the case may be, and move from their bases to meet in the rooms and streets of a topographical metropolis."[5] "Katharine Hilbery [of] Chelsea (Cheyne-walk, that is, not the King's Road or the side streets), mellow, august, exquisite" must choose between "Ralph Denham [of] Highgate, strong, raw, ugly" but a hard worker, and William Rodney, the country gentleman who comes "of the oldest family in Devonshire" and places supreme importance not on work but on social conventions and family traditions.[6] Despite her Chelsea setting, Katharine's heritage is rural; her family's country seat is Stogden House, home of the passive, prolific Aunt Charlotte. Even the Cheyne-walk drawing room in which we first meet Katharine has something of the rural retreat about it, at least in the perception of a visitor, Ralph Denham. "With the omnibuses and cabs still running in his head, and his body still tingling with his quick walk along the street and in and out of traffic and foot passengers, this drawing-room seemed very remote and still; and the faces of the elderly people . . . had a bloom on them owing to the fact that the air in the drawing-room was thickened by blue grains of mist" (*ND*, 10).

Katharine's original distaste for the city also bespeaks her rural origins. The view from her Chelsea window reflects an experience of blocked avenues, frustrating enclosures, and immobility, for Katharine sees in the city merely a mirror of her life at Cheyne-walk, where she is oppressed by the incessant demands of family and friends: "The incessant and tumultuous hum of the distant traffic seemed . . . to represent the thick texture of her life, [which] was so hemmed in with the progress of other lives that the sound of its own advance was inaudible" (*ND*, 106). Katharine's familial heritage of passivity has made the city horrible to her, because its every connection implies an obligation. "Even now, alone, at night, looking out into the shapeless mass of London, she was forced to remember that there was one point and here another with which she had some connection. William Rodney, at this very moment, was seated in a minute speck of light somewhere to the east of her, and his mind was occupied, not with his book, but with her" (*ND*, 106). In short, to Katharine the city is merely the territory for a marriage plot. Its shapeless mass will reveal to her, on closer examination, not a future but a future husband, who (at least at the book's opening) seems to be William Rodney.

Under the influence of Ralph Denham, however, Katharine is drawn out of her secluded, "remote" drawing room into the streets, parks, omnibuses, and offices of London, where she comes to question her submission to social and familial obligations. Like the "Young Man from the Provinces" who is the protagonist of the classic city novel, Katharine encounters "pleasures, adventures, and lessons to last a lifetime"; also like him, she chooses her lifetime companion, the man who has educated her emotions so that she can now "read poetry . . . and feel poetry, and look poetry" (*ND*, 488). Finally, her adventures in the city over, she plans to return with her husband-to-be to the country, where (we assume) she will study mathematics while he writes his "history of the English village from Saxon days to the present time" (*ND*, 226).

While Katharine's story recalls the classic city novel in its spiral to and away from the city and in its stress on emotional education, it is somewhat looser in its enactment of the good match. In one sense, of course, Ralph Denham is the ideal husband for Katharine since he intuitively grasps her perspective on life. Yet, to the more practical mind, his prospects cannot seem ideal: "Hasn't a penny . . . and a family more or less dependent on him" (*ND*, 462), according to Katharine's Aunt Celia Milvain. The economic side of that spiral journey is represented by the mercurial Cassandra Otway's momentous trip from the country to her cousin's city home; after some comic contretemps, her London visit concludes in the classic good match with William Rodney and his exceedingly old Devonshire family. Rodney's appreciation of country society makes him the perfect candidate to marry the daughter and rescue the sinking Otway line, while Cassandra's conventional, malleable nature makes her a perfect protagonist for the realistic narrative of economic improvement that is also a part of the classic city novel. Once married, Cassandra and William will flee the city for their country estate and their journey will be complete.

Night and Day takes an attitude toward country life that is also characteristic of the classic city novel. Nostalgia for a rural, unmechanized past pervades the novel, clashing with an urban world of telephones, motorcars, the suffrage movement and the elided presence of the Great War. These anachronisms tempted Katherine Mansfield to label the novel "Miss Austen up-to-date," and she raged against it as "a lie in the soul."[7] As J. H. Raleigh has pointed out, however, in "the novel in particular the nostalgic mood is built into the medium, nowhere more so than with the urbanists themselves . . . where the *ubi sunt* theme is in many ways the dominant one."[8] Cassandra and Katharine feel nostalgia for the rural past partly because their mothers are its primary purveyors: Mrs. Hilbery's mental time ranges from Shakespeare's day to the "fair summer of 1853" but is rarely more current, while Lady Otway's way of life revolves around the charming ritual of a carriage ride to Lincoln, in a day of motorcars and railroad trains (*ND*, 218, 217). Even the forward-looking Ralph Denham seems to be succumbing to the *ubi sunt* emotion as he falls in love with Katharine, for he determines to quit the bar and retire to the country, where he will write a book celebrating that passing rural world. And although the definition of a good match varies, from Cassandra's pragmatic socioeconomic criteria to Katharine's more intangible guides in her search for a soulmate, once the matches are made the principals plan a retreat to the country. The city may be the setting for their adventures and their searches for mates, but it is never a goal in itself. At the end of the novel Katharine suggests to Ralph that they take the country cottage he has been dreaming of. "And leave all this?" he protests. To Katharine, however, "all this" is already hers whether they settle in city or country, for the phrase evokes merely a satisfying domestic prospect mingling mathematics and marriage. "She thought, looking at the sky above Chancery Lane, how the roof was the same everywhere; how she was now secure of all that this lofty blue and its steadfast lights meant to her; reality, was it, figures, love, truth?" (*ND*, 502). The high sky of the city sinks, in this passage, to the snug roof of the connubial home, much as Katharine's expectations are confined to the happy marriage with which her story ends.

I have been suggesting how, in some important ways, *Night and Day* resembles the classic city novel. It is important to note, however, that Woolf's novel diverges from the morality customary in its model in such a way as to accommodate her political and aesthetic vision, and consequently to make the novel more than the uniformly traditional and derivative work that some critics have thought it to be.[9] The classic city novel associates the town with worldliness and vice, the country with innocence and virtue. This contrast, Raymond Williams has argued, "depends, often, on . . . the suppression of work in the countryside, and of the property relations through which this work is organised."[10] Yet work, specifically Vanessa Stephen's passion for painting, provided the inspiration for *Night and Day*. It is therefore not surprising that the novel reverses the customary town/country morality of the classic city novel, instead associating the city with honest work and virtue, and the country with worldly leisure and, if not vice, at least petty dishonesty. In Stogden House, for example, Katharine learns that "to marry someone with whom you are not in love is an inevitable step" (*ND*, 216). This reversal of values appears in several ways in *Night and Day*, but it can perhaps be seen most clearly in the criteria by which the reader is invited to judge Katharine Hilbery's two suitors.

Forster wrote that *Night and Day* takes place in a "topographical metropolis"; in this metropolis, topography reveals psychology. I have already described how Katharine's view of the city reflects the immobility and oppression that are her lot when the novel opens; even more important is that, *in their reactions to the city*, her suitors also reveal their characters, in particular their fitness as potential husbands. In four scenes whose formal symmetry clearly owes something to the classic city novel, Woolf develops a study in contrasts based on a morality that reverses that of its traditional model. We see William Rodney and Ralph Denham each in four moments that are critical indicators of the amount of agency and autonomy each man would "allow" Katharine: upon first encountering Katharine (in the text); walking with her through the city streets; observing her walking through the streets on her own; and in their own rooms. At issue in each scene is Katharine's ability to act, to occupy the position of figure in a relationship with the man in question, and his willingness or ability to provide her with a background. A survey of these scenes reveals that the two men have characters almost diametrically opposed in terms of their attitudes toward the city, toward work, and—most important—toward Katharine herself.

Ralph Denham, fresh from the brisk, bustling city streets, feels ill at ease in the secluded drawing room at Cheyne-walk where he first meets Katharine Hilbery. In particular, his tour of the "relic room" moves him to protest that he should hate to be "cut off" from a course of action, as Katharine admits she has been by her illustrious family. "Almost savagely," Denham challenges the motives for Katharine's self-abnegating devotion to her ancestors and her willingness to provide a "rich background for her mother's more striking qualities," thus forgoing hopes of accomplishing anything striking herself (*ND*, 19, 45). If Denham besieges Katharine with questions in their first meeting, William Rodney lectures her (among others) upon his predecessors' achievements in the use of metaphor. And, during a literary conversation with Ralph Denham, Rodney goes on to cut Katharine off "from all communication with the outer world" by a succinct bit of body language, "adjusting his elbow and knee in an incredibly angular combination" (*ND*, 57).

As this pair of scenes reveals, Rodney joins the Hilbery family in restricting Katharine's liberty; she is "cut off" by Rodney's knee and elbow just as she is "cut out" of literary activity by her famous family. While Denham urges Katharine to act by describing to her the pleasure of "making discoveries," Rodney reduces her to a passive spectator, keeping her from conversation by creating a barrier first with the podium, then with his body language. The spatial or topographical distinction between the two men echoes the argument of one of Woolf's most interesting and whimsical essays; "Why?" asserts that the urban environment encourages an open, questioning attitude that reveals as absurd the practice of delivering a lecture, whether on the "origin of the French Revolution" or the "evolution of the Elizabethan sonnet" (*DM*, 230, 233). Not surprisingly, Rodney, the inveterate lecturer, is almost always seen indoors in *Night and Day*, while the perpetually inquisitive Ralph Denham is the "champion walker in the novel," seen almost always in the streets.[11]

A further pair of scenes reveals that Rodney and Denham differ, too, in the amount of autonomous thought and action they "allow" Katharine as they walk with her through the city. After his lecture Rodney and Katharine stroll together along the Embankment; he continues to lecture her, now on the topic of marriage as the only proper means of feminine fulfillment. Rodney's deference to conventional occupations is matched by his consternation when he realizes that the unconventional Katharine actually intends to make her way home through London alone. Though she protests, he asserts his masculine dominance neatly by beckoning a taxi (with a "despotic gesture") and placing her inside (*ND*, 68). Rodney's controlling stance is different indeed from Denham's malleable companionship: having met Katharine quite by chance in Rodney's rooms, Denham follows her back outside and allows her to set the pace. Then, when at his suggestion they board an omnibus, rather than invoking tradition and custom in a lecture on her proper route to female self-fulfillment, Denham talks haltingly about his own hopes and plans for the future. Finally, when Katharine decides to leave him, he uses no masculine power tactics to prevent her departure. Though he at first introduces the question of her own future plans in an attempt to hold her interest, when that gambit fails his last view of her affirms her autonomy: he sees her "standing on the pavement edge, an alert, commanding figure" (*ND*, 96). In tone and context, that final glimpse of Katharine is dramatically different from William Rodney's; Rodney looks after the taxi into which he has unceremoniously shoved Katharine "suspiciously, half suspecting that she would stop it and dismount," and then he sums her up to Denham by saying, "But she's a woman, and there's an end of it" (*ND*, 69, 71). Philosophically and physically, Rodney tries to circumscribe Katharine's freedom, while Denham affirms it.

Since William Rodney begrudges Katharine any independent action or identity while they are together, it is understandable that he should be horrified when once he passes her on the street and she is too absorbed in her own thoughts to acknowledge him. "Once throw conventions aside," he sputters, "once do the things that people don't do. . . ." His inarticulate objections express "William's code," according to which, for a woman, "it was considerably more damning to be seen out of doors than surprised within" (*ND*, 454). Ralph Denham's contrasting affirmation of Katharine's autonomy also extends to his unexpected glimpse of her, self-absorbed and unaware of his presence, in the street. As she walks past him, lost in thought, "immediately the whole scene in the Strand wore that curious look of order and purpose which is imparted to the most heterogeneous things when music sounds; and so pleasant was this impression that he was very glad that he had not stopped her" (*ND*, 130).

The contrasts between Rodney and Denham extend to their origins. Rodney's country gentry background provides him with a conversational agenda for country women; he sticks to it in the city as well, with the unhappy result that he invariably seems to underestimate Katharine's goals and abilities. "You talk to them about their children, if they have any, or their accomplishments—painting, gardening, poetry—they're so delightfully sympathetic. Seriously, you know I think a woman's opinion of one's poetry is always worth having. Don't ask them for their reasons. Just ask them for their feelings. Katharine, for example—" (*ND*, 205).

Rodney clearly holds little promise of being a husband supportive of Katharine's right to act autonomously; he expects her to join in the female chorus of his praises. And just as he expects paper-doll women, so his London is a cardboard mock-up of a city, "a town cut out of gray-blue cardboard, and pasted flat against the sky, which was of a deeper blue" (*ND*, 72). Rodney presents himself as passionately involved with Katharine and as an inveterate Londoner, when in fact he is merely involved with the pleasant figure of himself—as lover, as urban sophisticate—revealed against the backdrop of an admiring woman and a stage-prop city.

In contrast, Ralph Denham sees both woman and city as exhilaratingly free from his own influence. Allowing each the status of central figure, Denham adopts the role of admiring spectator or background. Perhaps this ability to value or admire the city arises from the nature of the comparison he is able to make, for Denham, alone among all the characters in *Night and Day*, lives in the suburbs. In this, of course, he resembles his creator, who struggled with the same emotional and intellectual balancing act as her character, attempting to preserve some independence from suburban values. Woolf's diary records distaste for the smug competitions in respectability, the hypocrisy, and the hideous taste that she found surrounding her in Richmond. Denham's origins also echo those of Leonard Woolf, whose family still lived in Putney after he married Virginia Stephen.

Yet if Denham's origins are pinched and suburban, his orientation is deliberately, even defiantly urban. His habit of gazing out from his attic window—"The great advantage of Highgate is the view over London," he brags when Katharine visits him—leads him ultimately to link his admiration for the city with his feelings for her in a revelation of compact significance. "'But I'm in love with you!' he exclaimed, with something like dismay . . . looking over the city as she had looked. Everything had become miraculously different and completely distinct" (*ND*, 380, 386). Denham is dismayed in this scene because he has suddenly found a word for the tumultuous and hitherto unnamable feelings that Katharine has aroused in him; that the word is the right one is made clear by the instantaneous clarity it grants to the scene before him, as to his understanding of the relationship. The language of his insight, furthermore, echoes the earlier scene in which Denham passed Katharine in the street and she, self-absorbed, failed to recognize him. Denham's response to both woman and city is affirmative, respectful, responsive, admiring: he accepts their innate autonomy, rather than attempting to force them to mirror him. In fact, part of his dismay seems to be due to the realization that it is a personal emotion—his love for Katharine—that accounts for his response to her, rather than some quality in the woman herself, detached from his experience.

A system of values the inverse of that characteristic of the classic city novel figures in the contrast between Katharine's suitors. Denham is fit to be Katharine's husband precisely because he is a hard-working city dweller who is not afraid of a woman who also works hard and loves the city. Although styling himself an urbane ladies' man, William Rodney, in contrast, is revealed as capable of only the most conventional and egotistical response to Katharine. Clearly, the two men would have very different responses to the passion for work that drives her and that was the donnée of *Night and Day*. Denham would likely support any attempts to study mathematics as a way of "making discoveries," while Rodney's impatience with her playing any but the role of admiring spectator, along with a philosophy that upholds marriage as a woman's fulfillment, make him likely to support Katharine's work only if and while it redounds to his credit, and to resent anything that would draw her attention away from its "proper" focus on him. If Rodney seems destined to be Katharine's husband when the novel opens, he occupies that position only as long as she remains reconciled to the constricted prospects for her future reflected in the city that she sees from her Chelsea window.

In fact, the novel's plot turns upon the word *prospect*. The city reveals all three types of prospects to the characters in *Night and Day*: spatial, mental, and existential. The nature of a character's visual prospect either reflects his or her mental prospect, or indicates the existential prospect. Once Katharine abandons her self-abnegating posture as dutiful daughter, she abandons William Rodney as well. Accepting him, she had accepted his prospect: the adherence to social roles and traditions, the roots in country society, the merely superficial understanding both of London and of herself. When her love shifts to Ralph Denham, she then accepts a new prospect: affirmation of work, innovation, intellectual and social independence. This explains why the country gentleman William Rodney, whose work is only a misty backdrop to his carefully cultivated role as *litterateur* (as he describes himself to Denham, without a job "I should be ten times as happy with my whole day to spend as I liked"), and the dilettante Cassandra Otway are presented with less seriousness and respect than the hard-working solicitor Ralph Denham, who repeatedly defends the merits of work over leisure, and Katharine Hilbery, who at least aspires to do serious work in mathematics (*ND*, 74, 20). Finally, the turns of the plot invert the customary morality of country and city. Both Katharine and her friend Mary Datchet are tempted, when in the country, to make fundamentally dishonest decisions about their futures—Katharine, to remain engaged to William Rodney; Mary, to become engaged to Ralph Denham. Both recover their ability to act with emotional honesty upon their return to the city.

Yet if *Night and Day* is indebted to its precursor, the classic city novel, a return to the scene from Chapter 7, which I have taken as a metatextual commentary on Woolf's strategies of approach to the emotionally charged issue of women's struggle to work, suggests that the novel may also reflect an interest in contemporary fictional models. Katharine's attention is first drawn to the "light, gold-wreathed" volume by a living author, although she ultimately discards it when her father mocks its author and her mother dismisses the book in distaste. This scene suggests that Virginia Woolf, too, may have yearned to experiment with contemporary fictional forms, to consider not just the struggle of Hyde Park Gate but also the joyful creativity of the Bloomsbury years that followed.[12] If Vanessa Bell was central to that first period, she was also instrumental in making the second possible, for it was Vanessa who, "looking at a map of London and seeing how far apart they were—had decided that [the Stephen children] should leave Kensington and start life afresh in Bloomsbury" (*MB*, 162). Fears—of shocking her contemporaries, of being dismissed by the strong literary "fathers" she longed to please, of getting onto mentally "dangerous ground"—may have kept Virginia Woolf from making extended use of contemporary literary models in *Night and Day*, but in its urban iconography, as in its system of values, the novel reveals evidence of an impulse toward contemporary fiction.

Images of the city as a maze are particularly characteristic of the modern perspective, according to Irving Howe: "If the pattern of nineteenth century fiction forms a spiral to and away from the city, it is in sharpest contrast to later novels in which the city becomes a maze."[13] The bewilderment, disorientation, and lack of direction induced by a maze typifies not only Cassandra's experience of London but even her sense of life itself. In fact, it is in part to escape these feelings that she turns to William Rodney, whose solid center promises to stabilize Cassandra's wayward, impulsive nature. Mazes and the experience of the city as a maze punctuate their courtship. Other London excursions originally bring the couple together, but a visit to the Hampton Court maze cements their union; during that absence from Chelsea, Aunt Celia Milvain informs Cassandra's uncle, Mr. Hilbery, of their improper romance. When he, enraged, banishes Cassandra from Cheyne-walk, the mazelike qualities of London save the lovers. Cassandra loses her way to the station, misses her train to the country, and, after "wandering about London all day," is finally forced to return to the Hilbery home (*ND*, 494). There William claims her as his own, to protect her, with his well-meaning paternalism, from any future experiments in self-direction.

London is also a maze to Mary Datchet, yet, unlike Cassandra, she finds it "wonderful" because she knows exactly where she belongs—"at the very center of it all"—and, unlike Katharine, she finds her centrality not an oppressive reminder of her obligations to others but an affirmation of her self-sufficiency and personal worth (*ND*, 49). Mary's centrality seems enviable to Katharine precisely because it bespeaks a control over and distance from routine familial turmoil. In an image that mythologizes Mary's work in the Suffrage Office, Katharine sees her and her co-workers as "enchanted people in a bewitched tower, with the spiders' webs looping across the corners of the room," and imagines them "flinging their frail spiders' webs over the torrent of life which rushed down the streets outside" (*ND*, 93, 94). This use of web imagery is another characteristic modernist element in *Night and Day*, linking the novel to important precursors by Samuel Butler and Charles Baudelaire. As Allen McLaurin has demonstrated, by "using the image of the cobweb, which was to be one of Virginia Woolf's favorite images," Samuel Butler illustrated "the strange nature of shock."[14] For Baudelaire, too, as Walter Benjamin has observed, "shock experience [lay] at the very center of his artistic work," and he used the web image to convey the curious nature of that sensation. In his dedication to the urban prose poems *Spleen de Paris*, Baudelaire demanded: "Who among us has not dreamt, in his ambitious days, of the miracle of a poetic prose? . . . This ideal, which can turn into an *idée fixe*, will grip especially those who are at home in the giant cities and the web of their numberless interconnecting relationships."[15] Educated by Ralph Denham to "read poetry . . . and feel poetry, and look poetry," Katharine is less able to learn the other half of the lesson: how to cope with the "web of . . . numerous interconnecting relationships" in the "giant cities." From her own position as dutiful daughter and self-abnegating friend and lover, she envies Mary Datchet's firm self-assertion, her "power of being disagreeable to [her] own family," which has yielded a room in which she can "live alone . . . and have parties" (*ND*, 59).

The distance between Katharine's mythologized, envious perception of Mary Datchet's life and its pleasant but far more complex reality suggests that more than the influence of the contemporary novel is responsible for an interesting imaginative leap in *Night and Day*. One of "Woolf's amazing political perceptions," Jane Marcus has observed, was the awareness "that the ideal of the female utopia was to be in paradise alone, to work."[16] Curiously enough, only one character attains this female utopia in *Night and Day*, although the novel's stated goal was to explore woman's conflict between social duties and the passion for serious work. While both Cassandra and, to a greater extent, Katharine plan to combine marriage and work, at the novel's close those ambitious experiments lie still in the future. Only Mary Datchet is actually alone, working.

Why was Woolf able to imagine Mary Datchet attaining her utopia, while Katharine and Cassandra are only shown dreaming of theirs? Clearly, the historical difficulty women have had in combining marriage with nondomestic work was an important reason for Woolf's imaginative constraint. In *Moments of Being* she admits that, although Bloomsbury evenings of cocoa and conversation revealed new possibilities for shared intellectual enterprise among men and women, she still felt that if one practiced the "very low down affair" that was marriage, "one practised it . . . with young men who had been in the Eton Eleven and dressed for dinner" (*MB*, 169)—young men, in short, who were more like William Rodney than Ralph Denham, who were sure to curtail any unconventional aspirations for privacy and work in their wives and daughters.

There was another reason why Woolf was able to imagine Mary

Datchet attaining a solitary dedication to work, one having to do not with Woolf's own personal experience at 22 Hyde Park Gate but with the literary model she chose for approaching that experience. When she framed Mary Datchet's story, she seems to have understood that—like so many male articulations of human experience—the classic city novel did not easily or entirely express the lives of women, either in the time of its creator, Henry Fielding, or in her own time. When one is writing of a woman, the elements of that classic city novel shift: country and city, work and leisure, emotional and economic "improvement," even the concept of a "good match" come to have very different meanings and consequences. Katharine Hilbery's story reflects this difference somewhat, in its departures from the model. Although its shape echoes the classic city novel's spiral journey into and away from the city, as does its resolution in a successful marriage, the values determining Katharine's choice of a husband invert those customary in the classic model, and Katharine herself frequently seems more beleaguered and bewildered than adventuresome and autonomous. Her experiences at her family's country seat, Stogden House, seem to prompt not exploration but resignation, confirming "the belief that to be engaged to marry some one with whom you are not in love is an inevitable step in a world where the existence of passion is only a traveller's story . . . told so rarely that wise people doubt whether the story can be true" (*ND*, 216). Furthermore, even when Katharine shakes off the regressive influence of country life and the resignation to a loveless match that it counsels, plunging instead into adventures and experiments in the city, she does so against the grain of both cultural norms and (at first) personal inclination. London initially echoes her experience of familial and social constraint; to young women, urban rambles are more likely to promise social and moral ruin (as a result of the violation of those constraints) than emotional or economic improvement. Such is the serious message underlying William Rodney's superficially silly code that "it was considerably more damning to be seen out of doors than surprised within" (*ND*, 454). I do not mean to oversimplify Katharine's complex motives and actions: far more than Cassandra, she is autonomous, independent, and concerned with questions of self-fulfillment, rather than with property or propriety. But even she seems, at the end of the novel, to succumb to society's rule, which is fittingly if uncharacteristically embodied by Mrs. Hilbery and

Ralph Denham, who agree between themselves that a wedding will take place, and that it might even take place in St. Paul's Cathedral. After this surprising reversal of the lovers' earlier agreement that "We don't wish to be married—that's all," we are rather less surprised to find Katharine deferring to Denham's preference on the question of their future home. If his character promised affirmation of her autonomy, the form of the fiction in which that character dwelt promised to limit that affirmation to the customary domestic retreat of the novel's conclusion (*ND*, 466, 489, 502).

Virginia Woolf could imagine Mary Datchet attaining the urban utopia of privacy and work because, in Mary's story, she avoided the flaws of the classic city novel as a vehicle for female characters. Several factors made it difficult for a woman to attain her utopia by that journey from country to city and back again. First, the story invests its protagonist with a degree of autonomous agency that has rarely been available to women, thus implicitly excluding female characters as protagonists. Second, its resolution in a "good match" and a return to the country would, for women, have meant surrender of whatever powers of self-determination had been acquired in the city. Finally, for women to assert themselves in choosing to engage in urban adventures (as the story requires of its protagonist) would most likely have resulted not in a triumphant, enlightened return to the rural bosom of the family, but in permanent estrangement from that family or in moral ruin, perhaps even death. Virginia Woolf herself would trace the realistic consequences of a woman's attempt to adapt this masculine plot to her life in her tale of the fictional Judith Shakespeare, whose desire to write drew her to London, yet who ended up not a celebrated playwright but pregnant, unmarried, and ultimately dead by her own hand.[17]

Mary Datchet's story turns the spiral journey inside out, transforming the elements of the classic city novel and, incidentally, adapting modernist urban images to feminist themes as well. Drawn first into London by her "determination to obtain education" and her "power of being disagreeable to [her] family," Mary expands her schooling in self-determination and emotional honesty during a rural retreat at Disham, where she is tempted momentarily by Ralph's dishonest offer of marriage (*ND*, 49, 59). Instead of taking the opportunity to return to the country by accepting a proposal of marriage she knows to be spurious, Mary chooses to remain a single woman in the city. If the climax of Katharine's story is her discovery of "the existence of passion" in her feelings for Ralph Denham, Mary's tale turns on the subtler realization that there "are different ways of loving," that her feelings for Denham have paled beside her more lasting passion for work (*ND*, 216, 447). A socially sanctioned (if self-consciously experimental) happy marriage provides the resolution of Katharine's story; Mary's tale, in contrast, features a socially anomalous conclusion: her dedication not to a man, but to work "for the good of a world that none of them were ever to know" (*ND*, 506).

Although the dramatic vertical contrast of Chapter 34, in which Katharine and Ralph pause to gaze at the light burning high above in Mary's window, endorses Mary's decision, it also removes it from the experience of the engaged couple (who can only wonder, "Is she alone, working . . . What is she working at?") and of the reader as well (*ND*, 505). Mary's story transcends the terms established by the classic city novel and so makes possible its own utopian ending. Resolution is transformed into an acceptance of continuing struggle; the "good match" into a harmonious blending of work and self, rather than lover and self; the country-city-country spiral into a trajectory culminating in the triumphant possession of a city room of one's own in which to work. So identified is Mary with London that, by the novel's end, the city's electric glow seems the same as the light in her window, symbolizing the vitality of women working in that public arena. Although she was unable in 1919 to unite the two stories, to imagine the love that Katharine enjoys in harmonious daily balance with the work to which Mary has dedicated her life, Woolf still achieves a victory of sorts with this excursion into the contemporary novel in *Night and Day*. While she began with the intention of copying from "plaster casts," she triumphantly transcended her discipleship in the story of Mary Datchet, surpassing her model in the ending she imagines.

Throughout my discussion of *Night and Day* I have been approaching Katharine Hilbery's story as a representation of Woolf's own as she was writing the novel. I have taken my cue from Woolf's choice of the art-student metaphor in describing the novel's composition (in her letter to Ethel Smyth) and from the important metatextual scene in Chapter 7 in which Katharine

Hilbery is forced to choose between two fictional forms. Adopting this approach once more, I want to consider the novel's opening for what it reveals of Woolf's strategies in *Night and Day*. Marooned at the tea table, a young woman is struggling to assimilate a difficult newcomer to a comfortable conversation between old friends. The group has been considering the fate of a cousin who has married and moved to Manchester: Will it be possible for her to find a "retired schoolmaster or man of letters" from whom she can learn Persian, and so to create for herself some intellectual companionship? When her opinion of the situation is requested, the young woman replies "at random," "I should think there would be no one to talk to in Manchester" (*ND*, 10, 11).

Of course, neither Katharine Hilbery's opinion nor her means of expressing it in this particular social situation *is* random. Rather, this initial interchange reveals Katharine's strategy for coping with the problems she faces in *Night and Day*. Trapped in a stuffy drawing room where she must observe social propriety and play the role of Angel in the House, Katharine longs for the freedom to study mathematics. In speaking of her cousin she in fact speaks of herself: she might as well be in Manchester, for she has no one to talk to in the Chelsea drawing room where the novel opens. Yet Katharine has had the same social training as her creator, and she knows that to complain of her solitude would strain the conversation even more. So Katharine gives veiled public voice to her private anxiety: that she may never find a man with whom she can learn to speak the exotic language of authentic feeling (both for him and for her work) rather than the customary banalities of teatime gossip. By chance, there is a man present just as she speaks who can hear what she is actually saying beneath her social manner, as Ralph Denham's musings make clear: "It struck him that her position at the tea-table, among all these elderly people, was not without its difficulties, and he checked his inclination to find her, or her attitude, generally antipathetic to him" (*ND*, 13). Soon he is urging her to break free from her familial constraints, and then he is breaking free of his own to find himself in love with her.

The elements of this initial scene resonate beyond Katharine Hilbery's character to reveal the anxiety that Woolf faced as she began to write *Night and Day*, and the strategies she evolved to allay it. Like Katharine, she worried that she would be unable to assimilate the difficult newcomer, her novelist self, to the comfortable conversation between old friends that was the English novelistic tradition.[18] Only recently married and newly moved from London to a suburb that was as far from being "an offshoot of London" as any provincial city, Woolf shares with the imaginary Manchester cousin the anxiety that she will be unable to find intellectual companionship. Finally, there was the further anxiety that work itself would be impossible if there was "no one to talk to" (*ND*, 11). So Woolf adopted the strategy of her heroine, using her training in social decorum to express her most deeply held feelings while protecting herself from the charge that she has failed in her social duties by breaching a code or by offending others. Like Katharine Hilbery in the novel's opening scene, Woolf uses the city in *Night and Day* to approach an issue indirectly. By adopting, transforming, and transcending her traditional literary model—the classic city novel first framed by the father of the English novel, Henry Fielding—she was able to address the question of woman's struggle to work while avoiding a risky incursion into the socially and psychologically "dangerous ground" of direct self-expression.

CHAPTER FIVE

THE CARNIVAL AND FUNERAL OF *MRS. DALLOWAY'S* LONDON

Since her days at 22 Hyde Park Gate, London had seemed to Woolf a public world of intellectual work, whether it limited women to the marginal role of passive spectators or permitted them active involvement in its cultural pursuits. In her earliest years, as *Night and Day* testifies, Woolf saw retreat from the city as the primary solution to the conflict between social and intellectual duties in a woman's life.[1] Yet in 1924, when she and Leonard Woolf bought 52 Tavistock Square and returned to London from a ten-year suburban exile, Woolf was beginning her most celebrated London novel. *Mrs. Dalloway* would approach the relationship between work and social life from a new angle. While London society was the chief lure in the decision to return to the city, "society" had taken on a dramatically different, expanded meaning to Woolf, as a diary entry of June 1923 reveals:

> For ever to be suburban. L. I don't think minds any of this as much as I do. . . . There is, I suppose, a very different element in us; my social side, his intellectual side. This social side is very genuine in me. Nor do I think it reprehensible. It is a piece of jewellery I inherit from my mother—a joy in laughter, something that is stimulated, not selfishly wholly or vainly, by contact with my friends. And then ideas leap in me. Moreover, for my work now, I want freer intercourse, wider intercourse, & now, at 41, having done a little work, I get my wages partly in invitations. [*D*, II: 250–51]

This diary entry reveals Woolf's new interest in the social side of London life, which she now saw as tinged with maternal associations and thus as an environment nurturing both her work and her life.

Several circumstances contributed to Woolf's new perspective on London. First, she had known significant success as a writer during her nearly ten years of residence in suburban Richmond, publishing *Night and Day* (1919), *Kew Gardens* (1919), *Monday or Tuesday* (1921), and *Jacob's Room* (1922). Possibly her intellectual accomplishments made her more eager to explore the social side of life, less likely to resent the intrusion of what seemed obligatory "womanly" duties into her chosen work as a writer. Having established, in *Night and Day* and in her critical essays, her ability to write within the literary and critical tradition of her forefathers, Woolf now gladly turned to the maternal heritage she had earlier avoided. On the anniversary of her mother's death, 5 May 1924, she recalled her "impressions of that day," decided "enough of death — its life that matters," and dedicated herself to just the sort of life her mother had valued: the social side of London. She vowed to "write about London, & how it takes up the private life & carries it on, without any effort" (*D*, II: 300–301). So, in the above-quoted diary entry of June 1923, she expressed her new awareness of the intellectual importance to her of London's social life; her image has a metaphoric subtext revealing her new sense of self as both writer and woman, pregnant with her work, having been fertilized by the stimulating intercourse available in London. "And then ideas leap in me. Moreover, for my work now, I want freer intercourse, wider intercourse" (*D*, II: 250).

While the female, social, private side of London life newly preoccupied Woolf as she was composing *Mrs. Dalloway*, she remained concerned with London's male, professional, public side. Contemplating the novel's impending publication, she speculated: "Very likely this time next year I shall be one of those people who are, so father said, in the little circle of London Society which represents the Apostles . . . on a larger scale. Or does this no longer exist? To know everyone worth knowing. . . . just imagine being in that position—if women can be" (*D*, II: 319). As this passage suggests, Woolf anticipated that her literary accomplishment in *Mrs. Dalloway* would win her a social position analogous to that in the cloistered masculine world of the Apostles Society in Cambridge. Yet that fantasy raises several questions with which Woolf was concerned in *Mrs. Dalloway*: What does it feel like to be an insider in society? Can a woman be an insider? Does the social organization epitomized by the Apostles Society—"an ideal community, a secret elite . . . a kind of superior fraternity" of "insiders"—still exist?[2] Although in this diary entry Woolf does not specify what might have destroyed the exclusive circle of London society which she imagines herself penetrating upon publication of *Mrs. Dalloway*, we can speculate that she is thinking of World War I, which not only devastated an entire generation of young men but also brought an end to the entire system of social relations they had known. Both the Great War and the sexually segregated society of the wartime and prewar eras—when men were manly and women womanly—are of major significance to *Mrs. Dalloway*, for the novel explores the roots of war and sexual oppression in the sexually polarized society of early modern London.

Woolf described her plans for the novel in insistent dualities: "I want to give life & death, sanity & insanity; I want to criticise the social system, & to show it at work, at its most intense" (*D*, II: 248). Yet careful study of the novel suggests that she wanted to do more than merely juxtapose two opposed ways of living; rather, she wanted to transcend the very habit of thinking in dualities, and to criticize a society based upon such habitual polarization. The novel examines two domains—the private world of women like Clarissa Dalloway, and the public world of men like Peter Walsh and Richard Dalloway. More than that, it calls into question the social polarization that divides female domain from male, private world from public. And *Mrs. Dalloway* goes beyond a critique of the private/public distinction to see its relationship to militarism. In linking a consideration of the relationship between women's domestic role and men's public role to the question of the origins of war, furthermore, the novel anticipates several of Woolf's later essays, most notably *A Room of One's Own* (1929), *Three Guineas* (1938), and "Thoughts on Peace in an Air Raid" (1941), all of which consider some facet of the relationship between woman's ancillary, nurturant social role and man's aggressive drive.

These concerns were not originally apparent in the short story from which the novel grew. "Mrs. Dalloway in Bond Street," written while Woolf was still exiled in suburban Richmond and first published in 1923 in *Dial*, offers a portrait of a woman smoothly integrated into London society.[3] Like its successor, the story is set in Westminster, Whitehall, and Bond Street, but it limits itself to anatomizing the flawed bourgeois civilization surrounding its title character. In a narrative that undercuts Mrs. Dalloway's smugly self-centered perspective on the city around her, the story juxtaposes her thoughts with sketches of the surrounding city in order to reveal the impending changes in class and gender relations seething beneath the smooth surface of London society.

Like the earlier short story, *Mrs. Dalloway* uses urban scenes to explore and embody the privileged world of prewar and wartime London, to portray and criticize a society segregated by class and gender. But while composing the novel Woolf introduced the character of Septimus Smith, the shell-shocked veteran of the Great War, and thus opened up the larger question of the relationship between social polarization (by sex and class) and war between societies. The French feminist theorist Hélène Cixous has recently argued that at the root of any insistently polar way of thinking that depends upon "dual, *hierarchized* oppositions" lies "a male privilege," revealed "in the opposition by which it sustains itself, between *activity* and *passivity*." She further argues that struggle is an implicit part of the duality sustaining male superiority: "the movement by which each opposition is set up to produce meaning is the movement by which the couple is destroyed. A universal battlefield. Each time a war breaks out."[4] This conflict between activity and passivity, which Cixous argues is reflected in all aspects of human experience, "whether we are reading or speaking, through literature, philosophy, criticism, centuries of representation, of reflection,"[5] appears in vivid specificity in the dilemma of Septimus Smith. The two systems of "hierarchized oppositions" (to borrow Cixous's phrase) clash in the experience of that shell-shocked veteran, to replicate the "universal battlefield" that links sexual oppression to militarism, male privilege to war.

While Woolf expanded the novel's focus from the story's single protagonist to three major characters—Clarissa Dalloway, Peter Walsh, and Septimus Smith—she continued to use the urban environment and in particular the city street to initiate consideration of her chosen themes. Not only does Woolf use the city as a public world to which the three characters have differing responses (for example, Clarissa feels "invisible" as she walks up

Bond Street, while both Peter and Septimus feel prominent to different degrees as they move through the city), but she also uses aspects of the physical environment to introduce thoughts into the characters' streams of consciousness (for example, when the sight of Gordon's statue initiates Peter Walsh's impulse to follow the attractive woman he sees in Trafalgar Square) and as a realistic corrective to the characters' fantasies (for example, when we can compare Septimus's perceptions of the sky-writing airplane's message with the reality of "Glaxo Kreemo"). Consideration of the novel's three focal street scenes—Clarissa's opening walk up Bond Street to buy flowers for her party (*MD*, 3–19), Peter's stroll from Clarissa's home in Westminster to Regent's Park (72–83), and Septimus's hallucinatory ramble down Bond Street to Regent's Park (20–31)—reveals that all three characters are defined by the streets through which they pass. The buildings, people, and events of their common urban surroundings establish their characters and social circumstances for themselves, for each other, and for the reader; furthermore, the three street scenes compactly present in these early pages the novel's major issues, and they anticipate its conclusion. Finally, what emerges with careful study of these three street scenes is Woolf's reliance on the urban scene to raise two issues of paramount importance to her: the consequences of the public/private dichotomy, and the origin therein of both sexual oppression at home and war abroad.

Clarissa Dalloway's walk up Bond Street in the novel's opening pages establishes a crucial fact about her character: Clarissa thinks of herself not as an important figure, but as part of the background. Woolf controls syntax, style, and theme to emphasize Clarissa's feeling of merging with her environment in the pages charting Clarissa's progress from her house in Westminster to Mulberry's in Bond Street. The narrative interweaves Clarissa's thoughts as she strolls through London, with the surroundings prompting and amplifying them: "For having lived in Westminster—how many years now? over twenty,—one feels even in the midst of the traffic, or waking at night, Clarissa was positive, a particular hush, or solemnity; an indescribable pause; a suspense (but that might be her heart, affected, they said, by influenza) before Big Ben strikes. There! Out it boomed" (*MD*, 4–5). As this passage demonstrates, Clarissa confuses internal (individual) events with external (general) occurrences; she cannot distinguish the pause between heartbeats from the silence before Big Ben strikes, the heart beating from the bell ringing. In fact, she seems unable to separate the beloved city around her from her love for life itself:

> Heaven only knows why one loves it so, how one sees it so, making it up, building it round one, tumbling it, creating it every moment afresh; but the veriest frumps, the most dejected of miseries sitting on doorsteps (drink their downfall) do the same; can't be dealt with, she felt positive, by Acts of Parliament for that very reason: they love life. In people's eyes, in the swing, tramp, and trudge; in the bellow and the uproar; the carriages, motor cars, omnibuses, vans, sandwich men shuffling and swinging; brass bands; barrel organs; in the triumph and the jingle and the strange high singing of some aeroplane overhead was what she loved; life; London; this moment of June. [*MD*, 5]

There is a social consequence to Clarissa's tendency to merge with her surroundings. Rather than feeling individual importance as the well-groomed wife of a socially prominent member of Parliament, she accepts kinship with all citydwellers based on their common love of "life; London; this moment of June." This transcendence of class boundaries, affirming a community including even the "veriest frumps" and drunks "sitting on doorsteps," suggests in fiction what Woolf expressed also in her essays—that the urban environment, by its disparate, varied nature, nurtures egalitarian social relations. Clarissa's highly empathetic response to other people, a result of her experience of fluid, shifting city life, makes her unwilling to judge or categorize them:

> She would not say of any one in the world now that they were this or were that. She felt very young; at the same time unspeakably aged. She sliced like a knife through everything; at the same time was outside, looking on. She had a perpetual sense, as she watched the taxicabs, of being out, out, far out to sea and alone; she always had the feeling that it was very, very dangerous to live even one day. Not that she thought herself clever, or much out of the ordinary. . . . She knew nothing; no language, no history; she scarcely read a book now, except memoirs in bed; and yet to her it was absolutely absorbing; all this; the cabs passing; and she would not say of Peter, she would not say of herself, I am this, I am that.

> Her only gift was knowing people almost by instinct, she thought, walking on. If you put her in a room with some one, up went her back like a cat's; or she purred. [*MD*, 11]

Yet Clarissa's self-declared unwillingness to "sum up" others does not prevent her from feeling an almost instinctive dislike or liking for people. There is, for example, the woman she admired most, Lady Bexborough, "who opened a bazaar, they said, with the telegram in her hand, John, her favourite, killed" (*MD*, 5). And there is Miss Kilman, her daughter's history teacher and unmistakably the woman she admires least:

> for Miss Kilman would do anything for the Russians, starved herself for the Austrians, but in private inflicted positive torture, so insensitive was she, dressed in a green mackintosh coat . . . she was never in the room five minutes without making you feel her superiority, your inferiority; how poor she was; how rich you were; how she lived in a slum without a cushion or a bed or a rug or whatever it may be, all her soul rusted with that grievance sticking in it, her dismissal from school during the War—poor embittered unfortunate creature! For it was not her one hated but the idea of her . . . for no doubt with another throw of the dice, had the black been uppermost and not the white, she would have loved Miss Kilman! [*MD*, 16–17]

Several differences between these two women, both of whom Clarissa thinks about during her walk to the flower shop that June morning, help us to establish the values informing her life through the qualities of which she approves. First, Lady Bexborough pleases her by keeping private experience compartmentalized, while Miss Kilman irks her by confusing a private grievance with a public wrong. Then, while both women have been severely injured by the War—one losing her son and the other losing her profession—their styles of response to that injury are dramatically different. Lady Bexborough rises above it, to attend to her social duty; Miss Kilman loses all social sensitivity under the pressure of her growing bitterness. Clarissa clearly approves of one set of qualities—compartmentalization and separation of private world and public world—which she does not herself practice. Yet the other aspect of Lady Bexborough, her attention to her social responsibilities, anticipates Clarissa's behavior in *Mrs. Dalloway*'s culminating pages, when she cuts short her musing over the suicide of Septimus Smith in order to return to her party. One final point may be made about the comparison between Miss Kilman and Lady Bexborough as potential examples of female behavior for Clarissa Dalloway; in thinking about Miss Kilman, Clarissa realizes that, with another throw of the dice, things could be entirely different. She expresses this in terms of one set of oppositions—hatred changing to love—yet the image suggests another, more fundamental opposition—identity and difference. I am suggesting that, although Clarissa nowhere actually articulates it, beneath her realization that "with another throw of the dice . . . she would have loved Miss Kilman" lies the even more important recognition that with another throw of the dice she would have *been* Miss Kilman.

Not only does a sense of social plurality and equality result from Clarissa's empathetic union with her surroundings, leading her to feel potential kinship even with such people as Miss Kilman, but a spiritual posture results as well. Once again, the vision—here of an afterlife—is shaped by the urban environment and is introduced during the novel's opening pages, on Clarissa's Bond Street walk. Clarissa imagines human lives being linked and perpetuated by the city around her: "somehow in the streets of London, on the ebb and flow of things, here, there, she survived . . . she being part, she was positive . . . of the house there . . . part of people she had never met" (*MD*, 12). Identifying herself with the city around her, Clarissa extends that identification to others, too, imagining such an atmospheric afterlife even for Peter Walsh although, as we shall see, his whole character proclaims not passive merging with his surroundings, but active intrusion into them.

Clarissa's walk up Bond Street establishes several important facets of her character and experience for readers of *Mrs. Dalloway*, then: her tendency to confuse inner and outer, self and other; her tendency to empathize with other people, whether of her social class or not, rather than distinguishing herself from them; her refusal to categorize herself or other people; her paradoxical dislike for people who (like herself) confuse public and private realms; her possession of a spiritual vision of human relatedness and endurance firmly grounded in the daily reality of the city around her. All of these qualities seen together reveal that Clarissa Dalloway is the classic female product of a patriarchal culture, with the strengths and weaknesses of that position: great ability to bond with others (particularly women) but a diffuse sense of identity; a mind infused with the instrumentalist, misogynistic values of her patriarchal culture yet in conflict with her instincts and actions, which reflect the desire for intimacy and fusion born of her female psychic structure.[6]

The most significant, and most characteristic, aspect of Clarissa Dalloway that is introduced in her walk up Bond Street is the natural extension of this conflict as well as the novel's motivating force: her love of party-giving. Unlike most of the men in the novel, who see themselves as important figures (Peter Walsh as a colonial administrator and a lover, Richard Dalloway as a legislator), Clarissa thinks of herself as merely background and does not attempt to project herself into the world. Rather, she effaces herself, concentrating instead on creating an atmosphere in which other people can shine. As Clarissa is drawn out into London to buy flowers for her party, her plans for the evening's festivities color her perception of the city around her:

> And everywhere, though it was still so early, there was a beating, a stirring of galloping ponies, tapping of cricket bats; Lords, Ascot, Ranelagh and all the rest of it; wrapped in the soft mesh of the grey-blue morning air, which, as the day wore on, would unwind them, and set down on their lawns and pitches the bouncing ponies . . . the whirling young men, and laughing girls in their transparent muslins . . . and she, too, loving it as she did with an absurd and faithful passion, being part of it, since her people were courtiers once in the time of the Georges, she, too, was going that very night to kindle and illuminate; to give her party. [*MD*, 6]

Like her sense of herself, of others, and of life after death, Clarissa's plans for her party are intertwined with their urban setting. Furthermore, her parties are at once conventional and subversive. While they express patriarchal society's relegation of women to the private sphere, in their function as "an offering; to combine; to create" they promise to transform not only that private sphere but also the larger public world (*MD*, 185). Clarissa's plans to invite "So-and-so in South Kensington; some one up in Bayswater; and somebody else, say, in Mayfair" promise to bring together not just different people, but different sectors of the city, perhaps even different classes (*MD*, 184–85). So, at the party with which the novel ends, the shabbily genteel Ellie Henderson mingles with Lady Lovejoy and the prime minister (*MD*, 253–61). Clarissa's parties become a private method of transforming public life from its characteristically male dimensions (marked by "denial . . . of relatedness in general") to a more characteristically female world marked by "both the desire and capacity for fusion."[7]

We have seen that Woolf began to feel a new interest in her maternal heritage just as she was composing *Mrs. Dalloway*, and that she linked her mother's joy in social life with her own newly felt appreciation of the pleasures of London society. Clarissa's choice of parties as her vehicle for self-expression and her form of contribution to social betterment similarly reflects and is determined by her maternal heritage—the culturally defined role as a woman in modern patriarchal society. As contemporary feminist theory has established, this role is the result, in part, of a distinctly female psychic structure resulting from the historical and sociological fact that women mother, as well as the related fact of male sexual oppression. Clarissa's stroll through Westminster and up Bond Street in the novel's opening pages reflects her position as a woman unambiguously integrated both into her feminine role and into her society, unquestioningly accepting her confinement in the private sphere and completely identified with the competitive, instrumental values of its patriarchal rulers, even to the point of self-denigration:

> Oh if she could have had her life over again! she thought, stepping on to the pavement, could have looked even differently!
>
> She would have been, in the first place, dark like Lady Bexborough. . . . slow and stately; rather large; interested in politics like a man; with a country house; very dignified, very sincere. Instead of which she had a narrow pea-stick figure; a ridiculous little face, beaked like a bird's. That she held herself well was true; and had nice hands and feet; and dressed well, considering that she spent little. But often now this body she wore (she stopped to look at a Dutch picture), this body, with all its capacities, seemed nothing—nothing at all. She had the oddest sense of being herself invisible; unseen; unknown; there being no more marrying, no more having of children now, but only this astonishing and rather solemn progress with the rest of them, up Bond Street, this being Mrs. Dalloway; not even Clarissa any more; this being Mrs. Richard Dalloway. [*MD*, 14]

Clarissa's odd sensation of invisibility ("there being no more marrying, no more having of children now") is, of course, an accurate rendition of patriarchal society's view of women: unless they are performing their "proper" physical functions of copulation or procreation, they are invisible in that society which grants women no public role. Yet what is important to understand about Clarissa Dalloway is that she *embraces* that invisibility and enjoys her relegation to the private sphere, whether she expresses that enjoyment in her impatience about politics ("she could feel nothing for the Albanians, or was it the Armenians? but she loved her roses") or her preference for solitude in an attic bedroom, reading about the retreat from Moscow, to a conjugal bed with her husband (*MD*, 182, 46). Clarissa's experience anticipates that to which Woolf would bid farewell in *A Room of One's Own*: the sense of social belonging and harmony experienced by the "typical" woman, while walking down Whitehall. In that later essay the haunts of London's patriarchal power shock the woman into a "sudden splitting off of consciousness," and she discovers herself to be not insider but outsider—not powerful agent but powerless spectator (*AROO*, 101). Until the conclusion of *Mrs. Dalloway*, in contrast, Clarissa accepts—even enjoys, up to a point—her position as an insider in society by virtue of her marriage to Member of Parliament Richard Dalloway. Party-giving is not simply her chosen contribution to society, it is her only gift: "Nothing else had she of the slightest importance; could not think, write, even play the piano. She muddled Armenians and Turks . . . and to this day, ask her what the Equator was, and she did not know" (*MD*, 185). Clarissa has learned to value herself as an accessory to her husband—for her presentable appearance, her suitability as a consort, her capacity for childbearing—but otherwise to value more highly the "manly virtues" embodied by her friend Lady Bexborough.

As the fashion center of London, Bond Street reiterates the lesson of Clarissa's female heritage: women achieve power by virtue of their relationships to powerful men, and their identities are consequently determined by the physical features that will draw men to them:

> "That is all," she said, looking at the fishmonger's. "That is all," she repeated, pausing for a moment at the window of a glove shop where, before the War, you could buy almost per-

> fect gloves. And her old Uncle William used to say a lady is known by her shoes and her gloves. He had turned on his bed one morning in the middle of the War. He had said, "I have had enough." Gloves and shoes; she had a passion for gloves; but her own daughter, her Elizabeth, cared not a straw for either of them. [*MD*, 15]

Uncle William is no more. Clarissa's musings suggest, furthermore, that gone also is that prewar society in which women and men had distinctly different social roles: while she has a "passion for gloves" and puts her energies into party-giving, her daughter Elizabeth cares "not a straw" for gloves or for shoes and dreams of having a profession. The difference in their social roles is echoed by the different districts of London through which they travel: Clarissa walks through Westminster and up Bond Street, traditionally haunts of male political and female social power, while her daughter takes an omnibus up the Strand, a newly booming center of male and female commercial and professional life: "It was quite different here from Westminster, [Elizabeth] thought, getting off at Chancery Lane. It was so serious; it was so busy. In short, she would like to have a profession. She would become a doctor, a farmer, possibly go into Parliament, if she found it necessary, all because of the Strand" (*MD*, 207). The contrasting perspectives on London of Clarissa and Elizabeth Dalloway reveal the changing status of women in postwar England. While for Clarissa, as for her creator Virginia Woolf, London "takes up the private life and carries it on, without any effort," for Elizabeth, London encourages dreams of a public life (*D*, II: 301).[8] As she rides through the city on the omnibus, the buildings she passes suggest to her the appeal of a professional life:

> The feet of those people busy about their activities, hands putting stone to stone, minds eternally occupied not with trivial chatterings (comparing women to poplars . . .) but with thoughts of ships, of business, of law, of administration, and with it all so stately (she was in the Temple), gay (there was the river), pious (there was the Church), made her quite determined, whatever her mother might say, to become either a farmer or a doctor . . . It was the sort of thing that did sometimes happen, when one was alone—buildings without architects' names, crowds of people coming back from the city hav-

The Strand in 1892 when Woolf was ten, just a bit younger than Elizabeth Dalloway (from General Lew Wallace, ed., Scenes From Every Land *[Springfield, Ohio: Mast, Crowell & Kirkpatrick, 1893], p. 25).*

> ing more power . . . than any of the books Miss Kilman had lent her, to stimulate what lay slumbrous, clumsy, and shy on the mind's sandy floor to break surface . . . an impulse, a revelation, which has its effects forever, and then down again it went to the sandy floor. [*MD*, 207–8]

What is apparent in the contrast between Clarissa Dalloway's view of London and that of her daughter is the relationship between woman's experience of the city and her conception of herself. While Clarissa feels invisible, part of the background of her society during her travels through London, Elizabeth is both visible and highly capable: "Suddenly Elizabeth stepped forward and most competently boarded the omnibus, in front of everybody" (*MD*, 205). Furthermore, the contrast between the mother's and the daughter's views of the city reveals that the choice of a meaningful occupation is determined by one's sense of self as either passive background or active figure—which, in turn, is shaped by the extent of one's compliance with the maternal heritage of patriarchal society. Clarissa feels herself as background and spends her time giving parties; Elizabeth, rebelling against "whatever her mother might say," feels an important figure in society and contemplates a profession. Elizabeth's aspirations highlight her mother's dedication to the private world of female concerns, just as Clarissa's London walk emphasizes her ancillary position as an insider in the male, public world. Moved to explore the positive and negative aspects of her maternal heritage, Woolf created in Clarissa Dalloway the embodiment of the traditional female role.

While Clarissa's London walk establishes her sense of herself as background to other, more important (and male) figures, which has determined both her relations to others and her way of creating meaning in her own life, Peter Walsh's urban itinerary reveals his sense of himself as an active, even daring figure.[9] If Clarissa is welcoming, atmospheric, inclusive in her relations with other people (as befits her female psychic structure), Peter is above all intrusive. His walk up Victoria Street, down Whitehall, through Trafalgar Square and along Cockspur Street, Haymarket, Piccadilly, and Regent Streets takes him through the haunts of masculine imperial and sexual power, where parliamentarians and admirals strolled, and where streetwalkers dallied.[10] His itinerary emphasizes that he achieves prominence through dominating those of a different race or gender; as the reader soon learns, Peter has been in India, where he ruled "a district twice as big as Ireland" (*MD*, 72). There he fell in love with young Daisy, the twenty-four-year-old wife of a major in the Indian Army. Although she has promised "she would give him everything! . . . everything he wanted!" he already seems to be tiring of her (*MD*, 238).

When Peter begins his London stroll, he has just come from visiting Clarissa Dalloway upon his return from India. In her Westminster drawing room he has enacted a domestic drama of male dominance, taking upon himself the role of Prince Charming to rescue the unwilling Sleeping Beauty from her secluded city bower.[11] Yet Peter's "rescue" was anything but altruistic. Rather, it fulfilled (if only briefly) his desire to act the hero by intruding upon Clarissa's privacy, to define the woman he "rescues" in ways which satisfy his need for dominance, impact, and prominence. The Prince Charming role adopted by Peter Walsh embodies a perspective on women that sustains male dominance: "It is clear that in dreaming of himself as donor, liberator, redeemer, man still desires the subjection of woman; for in order to awaken the Sleeping Beauty, she must have been put to sleep;

Trafalgar Square, haunt of masculine imperial and sexual power (from General Lew Wallace, ed., Scenes From Every Land *[Springfield, Ohio: Mast, Crowell & Kirkpatrick, 1893], p. 21).*

ogres and dragons must be about if there are to be captive princesses . . . To conquer is still more fascinating than to give gifts or to release."[12]

When Peter leaves Clarissa's drawing room to walk through the streets of London, the connection emerges between his desire for dominance over women and his lack of success as a colonial administrator for the British Empire. (He had "gone to India; come a cropper; made a mess of things. . . . had come back, battered, unsuccessful" [*MD*, 161–62].) As Lady Bruton and her friends suspect, there is indeed "some flaw in his character" (*MD*, 162). Peter's response to a procession of uniformed boys, who are carrying a wreath for ceremonial placement on the empty tomb on Finsbury pavement, reveals that he is drawn to the exercise of imperialist power although he lacks the self-discipline of the ideal soldier: "It is, thought Peter Walsh, beginning to keep step with them, a very fine training" (*MD*, 76). After a moment of empathy with the young soldiers, Peter thinks wryly that only their innocence makes such discipline possible: "They don't know the troubles of the flesh yet, he thought, as the marching boys disappeared in the direction of the Strand — all that I've been through" (*MD*, 77). Not for Peter the disciplined military procession, which bespeaks the renunciation of ego and personal desires. Rather, while the boys take one route, he glories in his freedom to choose from a multitude of routes: "[He] stood at the opening of endless avenues, down which if he chose he might wander" (*MD*, 78).

Woolf's use of streets here to symbolize possible directions in life recalls the essential trope of travel books which is, according to Paul Fussell, the image of life as a journey: "Travel books exercise and exploit the fundamental intellectual and emotional figure of thought, by which the past is conceived as back and the future as forward. They manipulate the whole alliance between the temporal and spatial that we use to orient ourselves in time by invoking the dimension of space. That is, travel books make more or less conscious an activity usually unconscious."[13] Yet the geographic and historical specificity of Woolf's street iconography transforms a literary convention into an acute psychological and political portrait. By describing Peter Walsh's surroundings in detail, Woolf conveys his sense of self, his relationship to others, and the texture of his life. The statues around Peter as he walks through London, like the streets they line, have both actual and symbolic, realistic and literary impact: as a literary character, he responds to them in his meditations and is defined by them; as readers, we respond to their actual resonance and intuit their symbolic meaning for an understanding of Peter Walsh.

Peter defines himself in response to his urban surroundings. Like "all the exalted statues, Nelson, Gordon, Havelock," lining his route from Whitehall into Trafalgar Square, he desires individual prominence in the eyes of others rather than anonymous dedication to a collective goal. Not for him, he has decided, the corpselike discipline of the young soldiers (*MD*, 77). Like the avenues that radiate from Trafalgar Square, Peter's current existential freedom is manifest in his ability to choose from among a number of paths. Fittingly, it is in Whitehall, "under Gordon's statue, Gordon whom as a boy he had worshipped," that Peter catches sight of a lovely young woman and decides to follow her (*MD*, 77). As the allusion embodied by Walsh's proximity to the statue indicates, the encounter with the young woman is framed to replicate Peter's earlier "encounter" with the statue's subject, General Gordon: to provide the same opportunity for worship and the same romantic love of solitary adventure. The young woman is important to Walsh for her adaptability to his sexual fantasy: "[She] became the very woman he had always had in mind; young, but stately; merry, but discreet; black, but enchanting" (*MD*, 79). Walsh's dream woman reflects the same desire for dominance earlier reflected in his encounter with "Sleeping Beauty" Clarissa Dalloway: "[The] ideal of the average Western man is a woman who freely accepts his domination, who does not accept his ideas without discussion, but who yields to his arguments, who resists him intelligently and ends up by being convinced. The greater his pride, the more dangerous he likes his adventures to be: it is much more splendid to conquer Penthesilea than to marry a yielding Cinderella."[14] So, typically, Peter's careless diversion turns to careful pursuit when the obstruction of other pedestrians makes the young woman a more elusive prey. Her resistance to his chase is exciting, elevating him in his own eyes: "he was an adventurer, reckless, he thought, swift, daring, indeed . . . a romantic buccaneer" (*MD*, 80). Peter acquires his swashbuckling self-definition through the young woman's mocking and, he imagines, admiring glance. He articulates himself as an important figure by intruding into her privacy. As the adventure continues, he fantasizes his importance throughout London, feeling himself "singled . . . out, as if the random uproar of the traffic had whispered through hollowed hands his name, not Peter, but his private name which he called himself in his own thoughts" (*MD*, 79). While Peter thinks of himself as a significant, exciting figure, this street scene reveals the origin of that self concept in woman's role as mirroring milieu for him, available to reflect him back to himself "at twice [his] natural size" (*AROO*, 35).

Just as the relationship between man as figure and woman as mirror revealed in the pattern of city streets in *A Room of One's Own* is narcissistic rather than authentically mutual, here Peter's encounter with the young woman (appropriately enough in Trafalgar Square, dominated by Nelson's phallic column) is tinged with the loneliness of masturbatory fantasy. As he follows her, "stealthily fingering his pocket-knife," Peter thinks of the young girl as merely an object of "finery and whimsy," as easily replaced as any consumer product in the stores they pass (*MD*, 79, 80). When Peter can follow her no longer, in fact, he easily finds another woman of the same type: "silk-stockinged, feathered, evanescent" (*MD*, 82).

Ironically, some of the young woman's appeal to Peter lies precisely in her difference from Clarissa: "She was not worldly, like

Clarissa; not rich, like Clarissa" (*MD*, 79). While Clarissa's sophistication makes her remarkable, such women as Peter follows are not only interchangeable, but they are also more accessible because of their commonness. In an image compactly expressing his sense of the young woman whom he follows, Peter Walsh mentally categorizes her house as "one of those flat red houses with hanging flower-baskets of vague impropriety" (*MD*, 81). Peter's careful distinction between Clarissa Dalloway and the young woman he follows recalls in a minor way the major and pervasive split in Western culture between Madonna and whore (or monster), the former distinguished by a chaste position in the private realm, the latter by public immorality, depravity, perhaps even bestiality.

Mrs. Dalloway is far from being a novel "about" sexual behavior, much less about sexual pathology, yet it is concerned with the impact of gender and sexuality upon the professional, political, social, and spiritual lives of women and men. For both Peter Walsh and Clarissa Dalloway the quality of sexual life reflects the quality of those more general social relations. Clarissa is castigated by Peter for being "cold, heartless, a prude," yet in reality her "frigidity" toward men reflects her position—revealed in her walk up Bond Street—as passive background to the active male figures in her life. The label "frigid," generally applied only to women, itself reflects woman's restricted social position, as the psychoanalyst Roy Schafer has pointed out: "*Frigidity* means extreme coldness; it is a word specifically suited for describing a milieu. . . . Although a milieu may be said to have effects, it cannot be said to act. Only people act. It follows . . . that the woman is by nature an inactive or passive object."[15] The implications of the label "frigid" highlight the contradictions of woman's position in Western culture: while frigidity is a socially unacceptable quality, the passive sense of self that the condition bespeaks is seen as entirely appropriate: "Strength, force, drive, and power are not for her; nor are intent, initiative, interaction, and control."[16] Yet precisely these qualities are necessary for genuine sexual pleasure for both men and women.

Just as Clarissa's "frigidity" is revealed to be a reflection of her more general sense of self as milieu during her Bond Street walk, so Peter Walsh's walk through London reveals not only his particular sexual problem but also the larger flaw in social relations that his sexual difficulty reflects. What emerges in the episode in which Walsh follows the young woman through London is his tendency to split the object of his emotional regard from the object of his sexual interest. In its narrowly sexual manifestation, this bespeaks "*selective impotence*," the condition of "being limited to completing the sexual act with only certain types of women; typically . . . 'degraded' women in relation to whom the man may exclude tender, affectionate, and respectful feelings."[17] Of course, in using the term "impotence" to describe Peter Walsh I am speaking metaphorically. The label suggests what Peter's street scene reveals: that he can experience his own importance only in response to women whom he can, at least in fantasy, dominate. Furthermore, Peter's desire for domination may be displaced to an interest in the imperialist politics he abjures with his conscious mind. For, as Schafer has observed, "men and women manifest these sexual concerns in areas of life, such as physical, occupational, intellectual, and social fitness and worthiness. Although these areas seem far afield from sexuality, unconsciously they are more or less invested with sexual significance."[18] Peter even seems to be aware of the irony that he should be interested in the continuation of British rule: "Coming as he did from a respectable Anglo-Indian family which for at least three generations had administered the affairs of a continent (it's strange, he thought, what a sentiment I have about that, disliking India, and empire, and army as he did), there were moments when civilisation . . . seemed dear to him as a personal possession; moments of pride in England . . . [in] girls in their security" (*MD*, 82).

The sexual difficulties of Clarissa and Peter, revealed during their solitary walks through London, bespeak a flaw in society as a whole that lies at the root not only of their social discomforts but also of Septimus Smith's suffering. Just as "frigidity" implies an image of the female self as mirroring milieu for man, so "impotence" implies an ideal image of the male self as powerful figure, even if in this case he departs from that ideal. The terms together embody the process of social polarization with which Woolf was concerned in *Mrs. Dalloway*: the opposition between the public, active, male realm and the private, passive, female realm. In establishing Peter and Clarissa as opposites, not only in gender but in sense of self and in relation to society, Woolf showed "society at work, at its most intense" (*D*, II: 248). With the introduction of Septimus Smith, the shell-shocked veteran in whose painful experience such sexual and social polarities clash, Woolf created a powerful criticism of the social system. While Peter and Clarissa dramatize the workings of society in their enactment of the male/female, public/private dichotomy, Septimus demonstrates its tragic flaw—that such polarized sex roles and limitations on female activity and male passivity breed military aggression.

A third and final street scene, Septimus Smith's walk from Bond Street to Regent's Park, reveals the tragic effect of a society that functions by oppositions, splitting the active, public, male realm from the passive, private, female realm. Septimus is a living endorsement of Clarissa's refusal to categorize people—"She would not say of anyone in the world now that they were this or were that"—because he confounds the customary gender roles, social positions, and psychological states (*MD*, 11). He is tender, emotional, artistic; when he meets his friend Evans during the War, he comes to love him just as earlier he had loved Miss Isabel Pole. When we first see him in Bond Street, Septimus is plagued by a confusion of public and private realms that, although a symptom of his insanity, compactly represents the true nature of his conflict with society. A car stalled in traffic initiates a meditation culminating in a vision of Septimus's ultimate—although mysterious—significance to the world:

> Everything had come to a standstill. The throb of the motor engines sounded like a pulse irregularly drumming through an entire body. The sun became extraordinarily hot because the motor car had stopped outside Mulberry's shop window. . . . And there the motor car stood, with drawn blinds, and upon them a curious pattern like a tree, Septimus thought, and this gradual drawing together of everything to one centre before his eyes, as if some horror had come almost to the surface and was about to burst into flames, terrified him. The world wavered and quivered and threatened to burst into flames. It is I who am blocking the way, he thought. Was he not being looked at and pointed at; was he not weighted there, rooted to the pavement, for a purpose? But for what purpose? [*MD*, 20–21]

In this world of transformed causality, public and private realms are confused: the car not only causes the sun to become hotter, by stopping outside Mulberry's shop window, but it also signals by its incipient incineration Septimus's exalted public station. The image combines Peter Walsh's classically masculine sense of prominence and importance with Clarissa Dalloway's typically feminine sense of union with her surroundings. Similarly, the sky-writing airplane's advertisement for a type of toffee, "Glaxo Kreemo," seems to Septimus an exquisitely beautiful private communication from some unspecified source "signalling their intention to provide him, for nothing, for ever, for looking merely, with beauty, more beauty!" (*MD*, 31). Hallucinating, Septimus finds that private experiences—like his love for Miss Isabel Pole or for Evans, or his inability to love his wife, Rezia—give rise to grand, eternal, public truths: "Communication is health; communication is happiness." "Men must not cut down trees. There is a God. . . . Change the world. No one kills from hatred" (*MD*, 141, 35). In his madness Septimus resists the polarization of private and public, female and male worlds enforced by his patriarchal society.

The implied connections between those statements are worked out in Woolf's late essay, "Thoughts on Peace in an Air Raid" (1941), where she traces the relationship between sexual oppression and war. In that essay, which, as Brenda R. Silver has discovered, was bolstered by a reading of Freud's *Group Psychology and the Analysis of the Ego*, Woolf expanded Freud's insights "into the group mind and group prejudices by questioning what happens if they are extended to sex prejudice and applied to war."[19] One passage from Woolf's reading notes particularly confirms a reading of the essay that finds Woolf arguing for the abolition of polarized gender roles as a step toward ending war. Silver notes that the passage follows one in which Woolf associates "woman's coming of age economically in 1918 with her simultaneous awareness of man's fighting aspect," namely, "This was true of the 1914 war. The present war is very different. For now the male has also considered his attributes in Hitler, & is fighting against them. Is this the first time in history that a sex has turned against its own specific qualities?"[20] While by World War II men saw the "subconscious Hitlerism" latent in masculinity itself, such insights were rare in a man during the Great War, Woolf's analysis suggests.

Sixteen years before Woolf wrote "Thoughts on Peace in an Air Raid" she created Septimus Smith, who in his insanity saw the "insane truth"—that a society that rigidly separated the public male world from the private female world contributed to sickness, hatred, and war. In his illness Septimus expresses the source of his pain through his symptoms—the sense that all divisions are breaking down. Yet, because the convergence of worlds he perceives is only illusory, no such liberation from the terrible legacy of those roles is available. Although he imagines himself to be the focus of the Bond Street traffic jam, perhaps even its cause, in fact the narrative reveals that he is merely one of many pedestrians thronging Bond Street on a busy shopping morning. And although Septimus imagines himself to be immortal and hallucinates a "gradual drawing together of everything into one centre before his eyes," in fact the only immortality seems to belong to the city street itself, and to the "separation of private from public domain"[21] that it symbolizes. When the face in the car is a matter of history and Septimus and his fellow onlookers are merely "bones with a few wedding rings mixed up in their dust and the gold stoppings of innumerable decayed teeth," Bond Street will remain, although dwindled to "a grass-grown path," the incarnation of the society so painful to him (*MD*, 23).

Since London is largely responsible for Septimus's agony, inasmuch as it organizes and maintains the system of opposition that so troubles him, it is not surprising that the city relentlessly mirrors his pain and confusion. Peter Walsh sees processions of youthful soldiers and attractive, vulnerable young women on his walk through London, and he is consequently reminded of his enjoyable—if largely fantasied—dominance by race and gender. Even Clarissa Dalloway, although enjoying no individual experience of power as she moves down Bond Street, participates with empathetic enthusiasm in the power of a surrogate: like the Queen in the passing car, Clarissa thinks, she too will give her party (*MD*, 24–25). But Septimus Smith sees around him only more evidence of his agonizing sense of turmoil, confusion, and emotional suffocation: lines of lunatics humiliatingly on public display; placards telling of men buried and women burned alive; dead men walking and dogs metamorphosing into men (*MD*, 135–36, 36, 105, 102).[22] An agonizing combination of stasis and movement, death and life, the private world of his mind and the public world of postwar London, Septimus's vision of the city painfully echoes the system of oppositions Woolf saw—and determined in *Mrs. Dalloway* not just to portray, but to question—

in her society. Furthermore, in his name, history, and present experience Septimus embodies the same dichotomous society that has created, and now destroys, him, the very "London [that] has swallowed up many millions of young men called Smith; thought nothing of fantastic Christian names like Septimus with which their parents have thought to distinguish them" (*MD*, 127). When Septimus's love of literature, of Miss Isabel Pole, or ultimately of Evans comes in contact with his role as a clerk in Sibley's and Arrowsmith's, as a football player, or as a soldier, two opposed systems of values meet. The resulting mental conflict recapitulates the "universal battlefield" that, as Cixous has pointed out, results whenever two hierarchized oppositions come together. The "manly" value always wins out: just as Mr. Brewer recommended football to his young clerk as a way of building up his masculinity, so once Septimus becomes a soldier he develops the "manliness" Mr. Brewer sought, and he is "promoted"—first as a soldier, then in his peacetime work as well. His public role (soldier, clerk), which embodies typically masculine virtues, predominates over his private, more passive, typically feminine role (poet, student). Struggling after the war to understand the processes that moved him to aspire to create and to love literature, and then to volunteer for the destructive duties of a soldier, to love and then to renounce all love for Evans, to feel deeply and then to deny all feeling, Septimus must confront within himself the same system that Woolf wanted to anatomize and criticize in *Mrs. Dalloway*. Yet once again the system "wins": the unemotional, unfeeling soldier predominates. Finally Septimus kills himself—according to "their idea of tragedy, not his or Rezia's. . . . Holmes and Bradshaw like that sort of thing" (*MD*, 226).

Ironically, then, Septimus's suicide is in fact "one of the triumphs of civilisation" (*MD*, 229). The phrase, of course, belongs to Peter Walsh, who smugly misapprehends the meaning of the urgent ambulance rushing past him, bearing to the hospital the badly mangled body of Septimus Smith:

> One of the triumphs of civilisation, Peter Walsh thought. It is one of the triumphs of civilisation, as the light high bell of the ambulance sounded. Swiftly, cleanly the ambulance sped to the hospital, having picked up instantly, humanely, some poor devil; some one hit on the head, struck down by disease,

> knocked over perhaps a minute or so ago at one of these crossings, as might happen to oneself. That was civilisation. It struck him coming back from the East—the efficiency, the organisation, the communal spirit of London. [*MD*, 229]

The irony in Walsh's thoughts extends to his praise of the "communal spirit of London," for as we know, Septimus feels "quite alone, condemned, deserted, as those who are about to die are alone" (*MD*, 140). The only community involved with his suicide is the one that helped cause it—a community in which we can include Peter Walsh. Like the doctors whom Septimus consulted in vain, Peter maintains and affirms in his own life the distinction between private and public experience that has caused Septimus to split his love for Evans from his behavior as a soldier, his grief at Evans's death from his "more appropriate" soldierly stoicism, and ultimately to take his own life. Dr. Bradshaw practices "proportion," submerging Lady Bradshaw in the private home until her will sinks slowly, "water-logged," into his; Dr. Holmes congratulates himself for his ability to "switch off from his patients on to old furniture," a skill that betrays their equal importance in his view; Peter Walsh maintains the split between woman and lady endemic to Western culture in his fantasy encounter with the young girl whom he follows through London, objectifying her in order to obtain a satisfying image of himself. Even the benign Richard Dalloway, although clearly better intentioned than the doctors attending Septimus or than the intrusive Peter Walsh, still makes the pernicious distinction between wife and whore, private and public, smiling at the "female vagrant" he passes in the park, "not that they would ever speak," while reserving for Clarissa both flowers and the intention to tell her "that he loved her, in so many words" (*MD*, 152, 138, 78–81, 176).

We can think of all four men as responsible for Septimus's suicide—either realistically or metaphorically—because they are all to some degree invested in the system of values which valorizes assertive masculinity. That masculinity, tragically learned in the war, prompted Septimus to value stoic instrumentalism over emotional expressiveness, hence to deny his grief at Evans's death, and thus finally, having devalued all of his previous sources of significance in life, to confront the terrible possibility that "the world itself is without meaning" (*MD*, 133). However, Woolf also presents Clarissa Dalloway as feeling responsible for Septimus's suicide, which is initially a more surprising judgment: "Somehow it was her disaster—her disgrace. It was her punishment to see sink and disappear here a man, there a woman, in this profound darkness, and she forced to stand here in her evening dress" (*MD*, 282).

How can Clarissa, who has passed all her days in the private, self-effacing female sphere "like a nun who has left the world" (*MD*, 42), have contributed to Septimus Smith's suffering? To understand this, we need to consider Clarissa's final meditation on Septimus's death: "She felt somehow very like him—the young man who had killed himself. She felt glad that he had done it; thrown it away. . . . He made her feel the beauty; made her feel the fun" (*MD*, 283–84). Of course, Clarissa affirms the freedom Septimus claims for himself with death: the freedom to define a self unconstrained by the conventions separating public from private experience, conventions that ordain "proportion" and practice "conversion."[23] Yet beneath this overtly affirmative speech lies a deeply ironic, sinister undertone. Clarissa's thoughts seem to assert a relationship between Septimus's death and her newfound ability to take pleasure in the beauty and fun of her party. Clarissa's very enjoyment of the party is sinister, for among her guests that night are Dr. William Bradshaw and the prime minister of England, the proximate and distant causes of Septimus's suicide—Bradshaw because he first failed to understand the overwhelming guilt with which Septimus struggled as a survivor of the Great War and then callously required Septimus to leave his wife for a state-mandated country rest cure; the prime minister because, in his official capacity, he declared that war. Though Clarissa's limitation to the private role of social hostess reflects her victimization by the same system of social polarization that troubled Septimus, to the extent that she accepts her limitation to private life and enthusiastically entertains representatives of the powerful public world she endorses that system of oppositions. Clarissa is responsible for Septimus's death because, as "the perfect hostess," she has supported the polarized society that caused it.

In his insanity Septimus not only dramatized in his symptoms the confusion of inner and outer, private and public experience; he also foretold the effects of his escape from that coercive social pressure, seeing himself as "the scapegoat, the eternal sufferer" (*MD*, 37). In his role as victim of the patriarchal society Clarissa celebrates, Septimus dies so that Clarissa may live on—to give more parties. Thus Septimus acts as scapegoat not only for Clarissa, but for her society as well. And just as "the receiver of this burden possesses consubstantiality with the giver,"[24] Clarissa feels "somehow very like him—the young man who had killed himself" (*MD*, 283). Septimus has assumed Clarissa's burden; they are connected by his sacrifice.

What is the burden that Clarissa transfers to Septimus? As Clarissa tries to understand the motivation for his suicide, the language in which she contemplates his death recalls the most vivid moment in her own past—a rapturous kiss on the terrace at Bourton: "Then came the most exquisite moment of her whole life. . . . Sally stopped; picked a flower; kissed her on the lips. . . . And she felt that she had been given a present, wrapped up, and told just to keep it, not to look at it—a diamond, something infinitely precious, wrapped up, which, as they walked . . . she uncovered, or the radiance burnt through, the revelation, the religious feeling!" (*MD*, 52–53). Clarissa's love for Sally Seton has been buried in her past, by her capitulation to the demands of heterosexual society, the "catastrophe" of marriage, and her lifelong role as "Mrs. Richard Dalloway" (*MD*, 50, 14). Yet, thinking of Septimus's suicide, Clarissa finds in that act an affirmation of the capacity for authentic human communion free of conventional roles ("corruption, lies, chatter"): the same capacity that she had enacted in "the purity, the integrity, of her feeling for Sally" (*MD*, 50). "A thing there was that mattered; a thing, wreathed about with chatter, defaced, obscured in her own life, let drop every day in corruption, lies, chatter. This he had preserved. Death was defiance. Death was an attempt to communicate; people feeling the impossibility of reaching the centre which, mystically, evaded them; closeness drew apart; rapture faded, one was alone. There was an embrace in death" (*MD*, 280–81). Yet Septimus's death has an ironic significance, for the gesture with which he asserts his freedom gives Clarissa Dalloway a renewed acceptance of her conventional role. Having contemplated his death, Clarissa thinks "She must go back to them. . . . She must go back. She must assemble" (*MD*, 283–84). Rather than subverting the social order by his death, Septimus supports it, for, as Kenneth Burke has pointed out, "the delegation of one's burden to the sacrificial vessel of the scapegoat is a giving, a socialization, albeit the socialization of a loss, a transference of something, deeply within, devoutly a part of one's own self."[25]

Septimus's suicide consolidates the society he leaves behind, creating a greater sense of belonging at Clarissa's party. First, his death provides the occasion for the self-congratulatory chatter and lies of Lord and Lady Bradshaw, who can mourn his suffering ("a very sad case," Lady Bradshaw murmurs to Clarissa Dalloway) while at the same time advertising Lord Bradshaw's eminent qualifications as a physician to treat such cases (*MD*, 279). Furthermore, the topic not only provides a link between Lady Bradshaw and Mrs. Dalloway, but it also reinforces their subjugation to the patriarchal hierarchy of values, drawing them together by virtue of "a common femininity, a common pride in the illustrious qualities of husbands and their sad tendency to overwork" (*MD*, 279). Lastly, Septimus's death reinforces the existing patterns of political corruption, as Lord Bradshaw finds the topic ideal for lobbying the parliamentarian Richard Dalloway "about that Bill . . . which they wanted to get through the Commons" (*MD*, 278). As a "*symbolic* suicide (on the page)," Septimus's death "is an *assertion*, the *building* of a rôle and not merely the abandonment of oneself to the disintegration of all rôles."[26] Therefore Septimus's suicide made possible an exploration of the experience of women fully integrated into patriarchal society. In his death, both within the novel and in terms of its author, Septimus paradoxically confirms the society that has destroyed him.

Clarissa imagines Septimus as having "plunged holding his treasure," and images of treasures and jewels reverberate throughout *Mrs. Dalloway*. From the diamondlike kiss with which Sally Seton surprised Clarissa as they walked on the terrace at Bourton, to Clarissa's looking-glass image of herself as "one centre, one diamond, one woman who sat in her drawing-room and made a meeting-point, a radiancy no doubt in some dull lives," to her joy in party giving which, when her husband criticizes it, she loses like "a person who has dropped some grain of pearl or diamond into the grass," these images of jewels and treasures link moments when Clarissa experiences the radiant, atmospheric sense of self unique—in patriarchal society—to the private, female sphere (*MD*, 52, 55, 182). All of these recall the strikingly similar metaphor with which Woolf described herself while she was planning *Mrs. Dalloway*, as she newly felt the attraction of London society: "This social side is very genuine in me . . . It is a piece of jewellery I inherit from my mother" (*D*, II: 250).

Although, when she was writing *Mrs. Dalloway*, Woolf accepted the piece of jewelry she had hitherto avoided since her days of enforced social outings at Hyde Park Gate, that acceptance was not always wholesale. One of her most fanciful short stories, "The Duchess and the Jeweller," tells of a self-made jeweler whose taste for the inner circles of aristocratic society leads him to disregard his shrewd commercial judgment and to overvalue a number of counterfeit pearls brought to him by an old acquaintance, the Duchess of Lambourne (*AHH*, 94–102). Woolf herself showed no such compulsion to overvalue the jewelry (metaphoric or actual) that she received from her family. Speaking metaphorically, we can surmise that this skepticism may account for the curious tension between exaltation and defensiveness in her diary entry concerning her inherited social side: her joy in London society, she rather fiercely maintains, is neither reprehensible, false, wholly selfish, nor vain. The very vehemence of her protest suggests the opposite possibility. Similarly, Woolf was quick to dispose of the actual jewels she received from her family, perhaps understanding that no inheritance is without a tax of some sort. From her mother she received an opal ring, which reminded her always of her mother's hand "as it moved across the page of the lesson book when she taught us"; from her half-brother George Duckworth she received a "Jews' harp made of enamel with a pinkish blob of matter swinging in the centre," eternally linked in her mind with the distressing lessons in female social behavior he pressed on her, ostensibly according to her late mother's wishes (*MB*, 81, 150). Woolf gave the opal ring to Leonard and sold the enamel brooch for a disappointing "few shillings," but she kept the ring her father gave her "on her twenty-first birthday, just a month before he died. 'Father gave me a ring—really a beautiful one, which I love—the first ring I have ever had.'"[27] As Leon Edel has speculated, "It was as if there were a marriage and also a laying on of hands, a literary succession."[28] Like Septimus Smith (and unlike Clarissa Dalloway), Woolf asserted in her choice of jewels the freedom from lessons in proportion and social convention—her freedom to work.

Yet if Woolf gladly saw actual jewels pass from her reach, when she had done a substantial body of work she began to celebrate the joy of London society once again. In her diary entry for 9 January 1924, the day when she purchased 52 Tavistock Square, she returns to the jewelry metaphor to celebrate that wonderful world inherited from her mother. "London thou art a jewel of jewels, & jasper of jocunditie—music, talk, friendship, city views, books, publishing, something central & inexplicable, all this is now within my reach, as it hasn't been since August 1913" (*D*, II: 283). Ending her long exile from London, and from the maternal heritage that would have made London life impossible for her as a writer, Woolf chose to echo William Dunbar's poem "In Honour of the City of London":

> London, thou art the flour of cities all.
> Gemme of all joy, jaspre of jocunditie,
> Most myghty carbuncle of vertue and valour. [*D*, II: 283; n5]

Yet, just as she had learned to do in *Night and Day*, Woolf subverted the traditional (masculine) image of the city to express her new female aesthetic. While Dunbar praises the city for "valour," its "worth or worthiness in respect of manly qualities or attributes," the resonance of Woolf's jewel imagery transforms Dunbar's traditional panegyric into a celebration of London's feminine, even maternal attributes.[29] Jewellike, central, and inexplicably significant, the city recalls both Clarissa Dalloway's evocative presence in the lives of her friends and the presence of Julia Stephen as her daughter remembered her: "Of course she was central. I suspect the word 'central' gets closest to the general feeling I had of living so completely in her atmosphere that one never got far enough away from her to see her as a person" (*MB*, 83).

The slight claustrophobia lurking beneath that otherwise affirmative description recalls the issue always connected to maternal identification: the struggle for individuation. While Woolf celebrated her mother's pervasive presence, this passage suggests, she may also have longed—at least unconsciously—for the freedom to live in another atmosphere, not only in order to create an independent identity, but also to come to a more accurate estimate of her mother "as a person" (*MB*, 83). Similarly, if Woolf celebrated London's pervasive presence, its "central & inexplicable" character, in 1924, the trajectory of her career as a writer suggests that she also needed to experience another atmosphere in order both to become a mature writer and to see for herself the complete nature of the city. Her ten-year sojourn in the suburbs appears to have given her the ability and desire to examine the traditional female side of city life. Finally, while her defiant assertion of the hereditary right to the "jewel" of London society reveals her maternal identification and her willingness to consider the strengths and weaknesses of woman's traditional role, those qualities may have been achieved by earlier disavowals of maternal identification, of the traditional female role, and even of the city itself.

Alone among all the characters in *Mrs. Dalloway*, Septimus Smith unequivocally refuses the demands of social convention. Enacting by his suicide a rebellion against lessons in proportion and conversion, Septimus functions as a scapegoat not only for Clarissa but also for her creator. Considering Septimus in light of Woolf's own life, we may infer that he defuses the anxiety and antagonism Woolf felt toward the traditional role expectations she inherited from her mother and was taught by her half-brother; embodying that role, he enables Woolf for the first time to consider it fully, without either blind idealization or rote rejection. As a scapegoat, Septimus makes it possible for Woolf to present the full spectrum of London society; as an outsider, he enables her to experience the role of the insider in Clarissa Dalloway. And then he plunges, "holding his treasure" (*MD*, 281).

"Communication is health; communication is happiness," Septimus Smith muttered in his madness (*MD*, 141). Septimus's gnomic phrases do more than merely alert the reader to his insanity; they also embody Woolf's important advance as a writer and feminist theorist in this complex novel of social analysis. Here for the first time Woolf engaged in a dialogue between her maternal and her paternal identifications: here she presented not only a fuller social picture, but one revealing the distortions in individual and collective experience resulting from such a polarization of identifications. She was able to make such an advance into dialogue because she relied so heavily on the city—particularly its streets—to initiate consideration of the themes embodied in her social portrait. "The urban street provides physically, probably uniquely, for a scale and range of communications vital to the life of society."[30] In *Mrs. Dalloway* Woolf uses street scenes to juxtapose Septimus Smith, Peter Walsh, and Clarissa Dalloway in such a way that the reader must consider their interrelatedness, must connect (if only momentarily) what would otherwise remain disconnected: private and public, female and male society, Clarissa's function as hostess and Septimus's function as soldier. The creation of such associations, according to one architect and urban theorist, has always been the central function of the city street: "It is the urban street that from the first origins of settlements has acted as principal place of public contact and public passage, a place of exchange of ideas, goods and services, a place of play and fight, of carnival and funeral, of protest and celebration. Its place in the web of associations that have sustained human society is therefore paramount."[31]

Drawing its form and theme from the city streets in which it first originated, in "Mrs. Dalloway in Bond Street," *Mrs. Dalloway* examines the "web of associations" that has formed patriarchal society. Like the city streets in which it is grounded, the novel is a creature of opposites: carnival and funeral, protest and celebration. While *Night and Day* derived from Woolf's departure from London a response to the conflict between work and society in a woman's life, *Mrs. Dalloway* drew from Woolf's return to London the courage to consider the relationship of woman's traditional social role to the nature and structure of British society.

CHAPTER SIX

FLUSH'S JOURNEY FROM IMPRISONMENT TO FREEDOM

Writing in 1933 to Lady Ottoline Morrell, Woolf dismissed her most recent novel as "a joke." *Flush*, she explained, had its origins in her fatigue after finishing *The Waves*: "I lay in the garden and read the Browning love letters, and the figure of their dog made me laugh so I couldn't resist making him a Life" (*L*, V: 161–62). Furthermore, she admitted she wanted "to play a joke on Lytton . . . to parody him" (*L*, V: 162). Indeed, the last paragraph of the novel "as originally written was simply Queen Victoria dying all over again—Flush remembered his entire past in Lyttons best manner" (*L*, V: 232). Yet when Lytton was no longer "there to see the joke," having died on 21 January 1932, some of the impetus for *Flush* as a comic biography seems to have died as well. While this, Woolf's second fantasy biography of her mature years (after *Orlando*), began as a light-hearted spoof on biographical conventions governing the Victorian doubledecker biography as well as the Stracheyesque modern version, it ultimately framed a serious critique of the values organizing London's social and political life.

Four years before *Flush*, Woolf published *A Room of One's Own*, her analysis of the woman writer's position in patriarchal society. There she told the story of Judith Shakespeare, the Bard's fictitious sister, whose poetic gift came to an early, violent end. In *Flush* she returned to the theme of *A Room of One's Own*, offering an alternative vision of the woman writer in modern urban society. Central to *Flush* is a physical and psychological journey from imprisonment in London to freedom in the foreign cities of Pisa and Florence: archetype for the woman writer's development from a view of urban culture as patriarchal and restrictive to an awareness of the city's liberating potential and a determination to enjoy that liberation.

The plot of *Flush* is a simple one, the story unwinding in the margins of the far more celebrated love story of Elizabeth Barrett and Robert Browning. After a country youth during which he raced across meadows, chased rabbits and foxes, and fathered puppies although still a puppy himself, the cocker spaniel Flush is introduced to an urban confinement in Wimpole Street, when he becomes the cherished pet of the invalid poet Elizabeth Barrett. With her, Flush learns to endure a confinement of intense monotony, whether in the sickroom with its dismal disguises born of propriety ("Nothing in the room was itself; everything was something else") or in the city parks, where strict leash laws are administered by terrible men in shiny top-hats (*F*, 28). Just as Flush has become accustomed to the constraints of this sheltered city life, he is kidnapped by dog thieves and held hostage in Whitechapel, the slums that exist cheek by jowl with the opulence of Wimpole Street. When suddenly exposed to the terrible underside of London life, Flush begins to question his old beliefs in order, kindness, civilization. The "gods of the bedroom" tumble and, with them, the patriarchal authority ruling the Barrett household is defeated (*F*, 109). Flush escapes the prison of London when Miss Barrett, secretly married, leaves her father's home for the transforming freedom of Pisa and Florence. When an outbreak of fleas forces Flush to be shorn, his liberation is complete. No longer wearing his fine, glossy red spaniel coat, Flush is indistinguishable from any mongrel; he becomes a citizen, free to roam anonymously through the streets of the classless Italian cities. A valedictory visit to London tests—and confirms—Flush's transformation. The city immediately appalls him by its hostility to freedom, and when he hears the cautionary tale of Nero (the Carlyles' dog), who leaped to his death under the intolerable strain of Cheyne Row life, Flush is finally moved to cast his lot forever with classless outsiders. He gladly returns to Florence, there to die a beloved elder of the motley street community.

I have said that *Flush* contains the woman poet's archetypal psychological and physical journey, yet my summary of the novel presents the tale of a male cocker spaniel who moves from London confinement to Florentine freedom. As Quentin Bell has observed, "*Flush* is not so much a book by a dog lover as a book by someone who would love to be a dog" (QB, II: 175). And, we might add, by someone who imagined her loved ones as dogs. In 1932, while she was writing *Flush*, Woolf tried to convince Vita Sackville-West to sell the manuscript of *Orlando* by promising her another mock biography: "I will write another book and give you the MS. instead—about turning into a rusty, clotted, hairy faithful blue-eyed sheepdog" (*L*, V: 41). Woolf's implicit analogy between Orlando's transformation into a woman and the promised new book's tale of a transformation into a sheepdog uncovers *Flush*'s subtext. Flush operates as a stand-in for the woman writer: for the woman poet who was his historical mistress; for the woman poet to whom Woolf's previous mock biography was dedicated; and for the woman writer who was his creator.

Despite Woolf's disclaimer to Ottoline Morrell, the personal and general resonances of Flush's tale make the novel "a joke" only in the deep psychological sense, as unconscious truthtelling. Flush's biography contains several important parallels between his experience and that of the woman writer. First, although clearly canine, he has an uncanny resemblance to his human mistress, the poet Elizabeth Barrett. The two share a mirror relation in which curls match curls, eyes shine at answering eyes, and two spirits are united in the awareness of "a likeness between them."

> As they gazed at each other each felt: Here am I—and then each felt: But how different! Hers was the pale worn face of an invalid, cut off from air, light, freedom. His was the warm ruddy face of a young animal; instinct with health and energy. Broken asunder, yet made in the same mould, could it be that each completed what was dormant in the other? She might have been—all that; and he—But no. Between them lay the widest gulf that can separate one being from another. She spoke. He was dumb. She was woman; he was dog. Thus closely united, thus immensely divided, they gazed at each other. [*F*, 31]

Not only does Flush physically resemble his mistress, but his social position as a house pet parallels hers as a woman in Victorian society. Of course, Woolf is satirizing the biographer's obsession with names and origins when she begins this comic biography with the speculation that the name of Flush's breed, "spaniel," may have originated in the Basque word "españa," signifying an edge or boundary, but she is also alerting her readers to the most significant fact about her subject: Flush's marginal position, and its human analog. Animals are routinely relegated to a marginal position in modern urban society, and as "angel in the house" women have suffered a similar marginalization.[1] If the zoo animal or house pet acts as an endorsement of man's power to colonize or dominate wild nature, so, too, the middle-class domestic woman in the parlor demonstrates the sexual and economic potency of the men around her through her clothing, her accomplishments, and her conspicuous leisure time. How much more vividly, then, does an invalid woman demonstrate the health and strength of the men around her, who apparently support her passive existence without receiving any benefit in return! (The benefit, of course, is the self-aggrandizement of such a "generous" act.) Flush occupies a marginal position in human society, and in his marginality he resembles his invalid mistress, elegantly imprisoned in her bedroom in Wimpole Street, the center—as Woolf's description makes clear—of patriarchal society.

London—particularly the Wimpole Street/Whitechapel nexus—demonstrates in *Flush* the marginalization and oppression of Barrett (and, by implication, of all women) through the parallel marginalization and oppression of Flush the spaniel.[2] Both quarters of the city express values that have strikingly different meanings for Flush and his mistress than for the men around them. Like the catalog of Flush's sensory impressions upon entering the Wimpole Street bedroom for the first time, the narrator's ironic description of Wimpole Street itself emphasizes that disjunction of male and female values.

> Wimpole Street . . . is the most august of London streets, the most impersonal. Indeed, when the world seems tumbling to ruin, and civilisation rocks on its foundations, one has only to go to Wimpole Street; to pace that avenue; to survey those houses; to consider their uniformity; to marvel at the window curtains and their consistency; to admire the brass knockers and their regularity; to observe butchers tendering joints and cooks receiving them; to reckon the incomes of the inhabitants and infer their consequent submission to the laws of God and man—one has only to go to Wimpole Street and drink deep of the peace breathed by authority in order to heave a sigh of thankfulness that, while Corinth has fallen and Messina has

> tumbled, while crowns have blown down the wind and old Empires have gone up in flames, Wimpole Street has remained unmoved . . . for as long as Wimpole Street remains, civilisation is secure. [*F*, 23–24]

This survey of Wimpole Street reveals a phallocratic world of material uniformity, consistency, and authority, just as it appeared to Flush and Miss Mitford when in the early summer of 1842 Flush first entered No. 50. It is a world in which one admires the regularity of brass knockers and watches butchers tendering joints to accepting cooks, a world where the greatest irritant is "the perpetual presence on the sideboard of bananas," as Flush later discovers (*F*, 147). Yet this passage admits that Wimpole Street—indeed, London itself—is still only a city, like Corinth and Messina before it. We feel a tremor like the foreshocks of the earthquake that tumbled Messina to ruins, for the sexual and ironic substructure of this passage reveals that Wimpole Street's authority rests on phallic power, and that if such power is evaded—if one no longer submits to the "laws of God and man"—Wimpole Street itself will crumble (*F*, 24). *Flush* records this crumbling process: the disobedience toward God and man; the evasion of phallic power; the escape from patriarchal Wimpole Street.[3]

In order to move beyond Wimpole Street, from a world of uniformity, consistency, and authority into a world valuing creativity, spontaneity, and multiplicity, one must come to recognize and to renounce the values Wimpole Street embodies. Flush's stay with Barrett gives him that recognition, and his kidnapping prompts that renunciation. Upon entering Barrett's sickroom, Flush feels like "a scholar who has descended step by step into a mausoleum and there finds himself in a crypt, crusted with fungus, slimy with mould, exuding sour smells of decay and antiquity," or "an explorer into the buried vaults of a ruined city" (*F*, 27). By linking the image of the sickroom to images of a ruined city and a mausoleum, Woolf makes Flush's experience of being shut off from social intercourse, forced to see the world and its inhabitants as names only and to live only inwardly, seem both ghoulish and archaic; by implication, so, too, are the values of the tyrannical father who enforced such "almost conventual seclusion."[4] Flush's first impression of Barrett's bedroom invokes the resistance to, and destruction of, other great civilizations: Antigone's entombment by Creon; Pompeii's mass burial. Similarly, Woolf's mock celebratory description of Wimpole Street suggests that, for Flush as for his mistress, paternal tyranny will perish when phallic power is overthrown.

Similar as they are in appearance and social position, Flush and Elizabeth Barrett also share a rebellious response to paternal tyranny. Woolf links their joint rebellion by the figure of a thief, "a man in a cloak . . . a cowled and hooded figure . . . like a burglar" (*F*, 60). This image first evokes Robert Browning, whose presence at Wimpole Street Flush initially resents. Yet if Browning is a thief of Barrett's affection it is in the tradition of Robin Hood, for he moves Barrett to rebel against her father's tyranny, just as an encounter with genuine thieves moves both Barrett and Flush to question the structure of patriarchal society which for so long they had accepted unthinkingly. In exposing him to another economic and social situation, Flush's kidnapping does for him what the struggle to win him back does for his mistress: it moves him to question the legitimacy of stable, consistent, orderly Wimpole Street. *Flush* enacts the process of renouncing fatherhood for motherhood; London (Capital of the Patriarchy, as Jane Marcus has described it) for Florence (City of Maternal Love); insiders for outsiders.

In *Flush*, as throughout Woolf's work, spatial relationships often embody significant nonspatial realities. It is not surprising that the gang that steals Flush has as its base of operations a sector of London "not a stone's-throw from Wimpole Street," and that the spatial proximity reflects a comfortable economic symbiosis between the two social environments. "St. Giles's stole what St. Giles's could; Wimpole Street paid what Wimpole Street must" (*F*, 86, 89). Furthermore, when Flush is removed from the comfortable sickroom in Wimpole Street to the dark, dank, dirty quarters of "The Rookery," he discovers that the two environments are linked by more than merely mutual economic dependence. His imprisonment comes to seem an echo of Barrett's position on the invalid's sofa, as she attempts to negotiate Flush's release only to find herself thwarted not only by Mr. Taylor, head of the gang of Whitechapel thieves, but by the men around her in Wimpole Street. Although Taylor's motivating principle is greed, while Barrett's father, brother, and lover are all motivated by the most high-minded moral conviction, the effect of each type of male domination is the same: "It was almost as difficult for her to go to Flush as for Flush to come to her" (*F*, 98).

> Her father and her brother were in league against her and were capable of any treachery in the interests of their class. But worst of all—far worse—Mr. Browning himself threw all his weight, all his eloquence, all his learning, all his logic, on the side of Wimpole Street and against Flush. If Miss Barrett gave way to Taylor, he wrote, she was giving way to tyranny; she was giving way to blackmailers; she was increasing the power of evil over right, of wickedness over innocence. [*F*, 98–99]

Although the battle lines at first seem drawn between Wimpole Street and Whitechapel, between the upper and lower classes, the confident generalizations of father, of brother, even of lover soon reveal the "class" whose interests such arguments really serve. Males have banded together against females and other marginal creatures—against Barrett and Flush. Speaking as and for men, the various males in Elizabeth Barrett's life apply masculine logic to the problem of the kidnapping, ignoring both Flush's feelings in captivity and Barrett's own. The Whitechapel episode is a temptation scene; forced to choose between winning the approval of her male counterparts and saving Flush, Barrett is also being asked, symbolically, to choose between two systems of morality—one masculine and impersonal, the other feminine and personal. Tempted to give in, to admit her ignorance of "law and justice," and to trade the life of her spaniel for the good opinion of her father, brother, and lover, still Barrett resists male domination. Instead, she fires back to Browning a letter, inquiring what he would have done "if the banditti had stolen her; had her in their power; threatened to cut off her ears and send them by post to New Cross?" (*F*, 101).

With that letter the connection is made between Wimpole Street and Whitechapel, between Flush's imprisonment and Barrett's, between Woolf's comic biography of a cocker spaniel and her implicit, deeply serious portrait of a woman writer's development. Whereas Wimpole Street links Flush and his mistress on the basis of their imprisonment and their movement toward rebellion against paternal tyranny, Whitechapel links them by parallel threats to their very existences. In her description of this seedy area bordering on opulent Wimpole Street, Woolf draws upon Thomas Beames's *The Rookeries of London* (1850), one of the many mid-Victorian volumes that conjured up "the most lurid vision of the metropolis," with titles such as *The Sorrows of the Streets*, *Ragged London*, *London's Shadows*, and *Sinks of London Laid Open*.[5] Yet the portrait of Whitechapel in *Flush* subverts several of the commonplaces of the Victorian histories of which Beames's volume is a characteristic, although minor, example. From Mayhew's celebrated *London Labour and the London Poor* (1851–1852) to *The Bitter Cry of Outcast London* (1883), the London slums were presented as symbolic of urban poverty itself. Mayhew's "comprehensive" study of the poor was in fact quite narrowly focused on "street people," emphasizing their distinctive, repellent, even physically and psychologically regressive features, with the result that a subgroup of the London population was portrayed as "a race apart."[6] Mayhew's vision characterized much writing on the East End until the very end of the Victorian era. It was portrayed as unfamiliar territory—another country, even another world.

Yet whereas the popular image of the slums was as a city of the poor worlds away from the city of the rich, the reality was just the opposite. The squalid underside of Wimpole Street opulence lay just around the corner, readily accessible to anyone "active and able-bodied and fond of walking" (*F*, 86). This proximity might have happy consequences—for when the "slum backed on to the mansion . . . there was always the chance that the rich individual would step round the corner and save a poor individual"[7]—yet the reality was probably more often a studious indifference to slums and slumdwellers on the part of the rich. This indifference lasted only as long as the slums posed no physical threat to the well-being of wealthier neighbors. Just as the distinction between the two worlds of Victorian London served to account for the public indifference to poverty and to downplay public responsibility for suffering, so the "discovery" of poverty by middle-class journalists and writers often served only to push through social reforms designed to serve the wealthy. Thomas Beames presents a good, if extreme, example: although he is "surprised . . . shocked" when "he [takes] it into his head to go walking about London," the sights, language, and smells he encounters cast "doubts upon the solidity even of Wimpole Street itself," moving him not to reconsider the hierarchical structure of social and economic relations, but to desire to shore up their solidity even more.

> Splendid buildings raised themselves in Westminster [Beames found], yet just behind them were ruined sheds in which human beings lived herded together above herds of cows—"two in each seven feet of space." He felt that he ought to tell people what he had seen. Yet. . . . [that] was a task, as Mr. Beames found when he came to attempt it, that taxed all the resources of the English language. And yet he felt that he ought to describe what he had seen in the course of an afternoon's walk through some of the most aristocratic parishes in London. The risk of typhus was so great. The rich could not know what dangers they were running. [*F*, 86–87]

While Beames's perceptions of Whitechapel are informed by his sense of class superiority, they contain not only his concern with the physical risk the slums pose for wealthy nearby families but also a subterranean allusion to the later risk of revolutionary class conflict that would face all Victorian wealth.

The Whitechapel episode in *Flush* presents another sort of conflict as well: between men and women. With her letter to Browning, Elizabeth Barrett extends the Whitechapel conflict from class to sex. Whether or not Woolf's parallel was intentional, the phrasing of the Whitechapel scene recalls one of the most notorious murders of the nineteenth century: the savage butchery of five Whitechapel prostitutes by Jack the Ripper. These murders, committed from August to November 1888, took place within one square mile in Whitechapel. The murderer slit the throats of his victims, eviscerated them with surgical precision (leading to the speculation that he was a doctor, a butcher, or a professor), and in one instance mailed part of a victim's kidney to the police. The *London Times* on 2 October 1888 reported a communication from the murderer that echoes Woolf's phrasing of Barrett's letter:

> Two communications of an extraordinary nature, both signed "Jack the Ripper," have been received by the Central News Agency, the one on Thursday last and the other yesterday morning. The first was a letter bearing the E.C. postmark in which reference was made to the atrocious murders previously

Illustrated Police News *picture of how Catherine Eddowes's kidney was sent through the post to the Whitechapel vigilance committee with a note in "The Ripper's" writing (from Felix Baker and Peter Jackson,* London: 2,000 Years of a City and Its People *[New York: Macmillan Publishing Co., Inc., 1974], p. 327).*

> committed in the East End, which the writer confessed in a brutally jocular vein to have committed, stating that in the "next job" he did he would "clip the lady's ears off" and send them to the police. . . .[8]

These infamous murders directed the popular imagination to Whitechapel and the whole East End, creating an image of the quarter as "violent and outcast" and prompting George Bernard Shaw to remark, "If the habits of duchesses only admitted of their being decoyed into Whitechapel backyards, a single experiment in slaughterhouse anatomy on an aristocratic victim might fetch in a round half million [pounds] and save the necessity of sacrificing four women of the people."[9] In Barrett's letter Woolf implies what Shaw only hints at: that, for women, whether one is poor or middle-class changes only the nature of one's oppression, not the fact of its existence.

As their parallel experiences during Flush's kidnapping make clear, both Flush and his mistress are equally subject to the wills of the men around them, whether the lawless Mr. Taylor or the lawful Mr. Browning. Although Shaw challenged Victorian complacency by linking the Jack the Ripper murders to the nature of the Whitechapel environment, thus expanding the notion of responsibility from one well-known, elusive psychopath to an entire class of people, he did not go as far as Woolf did. In this section of *Flush*, extending the arm of oppression from class to gender, she implies that the social system that produced the admirably controlled, ordered, and authoritarian civilization of Wimpole Street also produced the terrifyingly uncontrolled, chaotic, and seemingly anarchic violence characterized for an entire generation by the Jack the Ripper murders.[10] Furthermore, Woolf's parallel phrasing and choice of details remarkably similar to those of the Ripper murder case imply that the link between the two seemingly diametrically opposed London environments—Wimpole Street and Whitechapel—was misogyny and sexual oppression. The novel anticipates contemporary feminist understanding of rape and pornography, presenting the kidnapping of Flush (and, by implication, the Ripper murders) as but a special instance of a general situation: the domination and oppression of women and other marginalized groups within patriarchal culture. Flush's kidnapping and imprisonment, with its horrible motif of the threatened package of his head and paws, implicitly recalls the murders of Jack the Ripper. And Flush's value to patriarchal society is analogous to woman's value, as Barrett discovers when she tries to win him back against the wishes of the men around her: his value, like hers, depends upon the worth the master assigns.

For both Barrett and Flush, the experience of Whitechapel results in an irreversibly changed vision of the world. Barrett has only to see again, in memory, the faces of the men in that slum quarter, has only to think that there "lived women like herself; while she lay on her sofa, reading, writing, they lived thus," to find her imagination "stimulated . . . as the 'divine marble presences,' the busts on the bookcase, had never stimulated it" (*F*, 104). For her, the Whitechapel experience has produced a sense of sisterhood with the slum women, a sisterhood that women of the upper and middle classes attained less frequently later in the century, as the charity visitors to slum districts like Whitechapel were frightened away by Jack the Ripper. While, before her Whitechapel experience, Barrett had written playfully of "a Greek nymph in some dim grove in Arcady," read with the help of a "Greek lexicon," and undertaken all of her writing under the watchful eyes of her epic poet predecessors, the new discovery of female solidarity supersedes that earlier identification with the male epic tradition (*F*, 46, 55, 176). In fact, Woolf implies that Flush's kidnapping provided the basis for Barrett Browning's feminist epic, *Aurora Leigh*, which interweaves the story of a woman poet's development with the experiences of Marian Earle, a woman of the slums:

> Readers of *Aurora Leigh*—but since such persons are nonexistent it must be explained that Mrs. Browning wrote a poem of this name, one of the most vivid passages in which (though it suffers from the distortion natural to an artist who sees the object once only from a four-wheeler, with Wilson tugging at her skirts) is the description of a London slum. Clearly Mrs. Browning possessed a fund of curiosity as to human life which was by no means satisfied by the busts of Homer and Chaucer on the washing-stand in the bedroom. [*F*, 175–76]

For Flush, too, the Whitechapel episode results in a reordered cosmology: "The old gods of the bedroom—the bookcase, the wardrobe, the busts—seemed to have lost their substance. This room was no longer the whole world; it was only a shelter; only a dell arched over by one trembling dock-leaf in a forest where wild beasts prowled and venomous snakes coiled; where behind every tree lurked a murderer ready to pounce" (*F*, 109). Whether "the gods" are male epic poets or strict human fathers like Mr. Barrett, whose voice evokes in Flush the terror and horror a savage feels when "couched in flowers . . . he hears the voice of God," they lose their authority when challenged by the new perspective on life gained in the experience of Whitechapel (*F*, 51). Paradoxically, victimization enlightens both Barrett and her dog, leading to their liberation. Although Flush seems anything but free in the days following his rescue (he spends his time trembling by the sofa), and although Barrett's manner is as quietly deferential as ever, tremors of change shake the foundation of Wimpole Street life. The earthquake comes one September morning when, secretly married to Robert Browning, Elizabeth Barrett Browning carries Flush off to Italy, "leaving tyrants and dog-stealers behind them" (*F*, 117).

The contrast between Wimpole Street and Whitechapel is a distinction without a difference, for it masks a deeper similarity in gender relations; each region operates under the rule of the patriarchs, whether Mr. Taylor or Mr. Barrett. However, a comparison of London to Pisa and Florence provides a genuine contrast; where London meant sheltered, invalid women and dogs led on chains, Florence and Pisa offer Flush and Barrett Browning a new and heady freedom. Moreover, the Italian societies are marked by equality between genders and classes. Pisa introduces Barrett Browning to the pleasure of city streets where "pretty women could walk alone," and of a society in which "great ladies first emptied their own slops and then went to Court 'in a blaze of undeniable glory'" (*F*, 123). "Fear was unknown in Florence; there were no dog-stealers here and . . . there were no fathers" (*F*, 126). Florence, the maternal city, is appropriately free from patriarchal tyranny; Flush and his mistress replace the habit of fear with an experiment in growth. An index of the freedom they find appears in the fact that the two old fellow captives begin to drift apart, to experience and to interpret things differently. Although in London they were linked by their mutual oppression and imprisonment, in Florence they are autonomous, in judgments and deeds. For Barrett Browning the sense of Florentine freedom crystallizes in street marches, where people carry banners saluting "Liberty," while for Flush it is the more mundane pleasure of a night spent "traced in love" with a spotted spaniel bitch (*F*, 130).

The Italian cities astonish Flush by their absence of class distinctions: "In London he could scarcely trot round to the pillar-box without meeting some pug dog, retriever, bulldog, mastiff, collie, Newfoundland, St. Bernard, fox terrier or one of the seven famous families of the Spaniel tribe. To each he gave a different name, and to each a different rank. But here in Pisa, though dogs abounded, there were no ranks; all—could this be possible?—were mongrels" (*F*, 120). While at first Flush felt like a "prince in exile" in this new classless society, he becomes steadily more and more democratic, and when he arrives in Florence "the last threads of his old fetters [fall] from him" (*F*, 121, 125). In his "moment of liberation" Flush realizes: "Where was 'must' now? Where were chains now? . . . Gone, with the dog-stealers . . . four-wheelers and hansom cabs! with Whitechapel and Shoreditch! . . . He was the friend of all the world now. All dogs were his brothers" (*F*, 125).

An attack of fleas completes Flush's introduction to this world beyond Whitechapel and Wimpole Street. Spaniels wear their pedigree on their backs, and Flush's coat "meant to him what a gold watch inscribed with the family arms means to an impoverished squire whose broad acres have shrunk to that single circle" (*F*, 142). Flush's shearing represents a symbolic feminization, bringing a greater social and geographic mobility and a new identification with outsiders. This appears most clearly with examination of the explicit parallel between this episode in *Flush* and a similar episode in Woolf's own life. Flush's creator was shingled in 1927, shortly before beginning his biography; she described the event in her diary, celebrating the greater convenience and lessened social anxiety that resulted: "I am short haired for life. Having no longer, I think, any claims to beauty, the convenience of this alone makes it desirable. Every morning I go to take up brush & twist that old coil round my finger & fix it with hairpins & then with a start of joy, no I needn't. In front there is no change; behind I'm like the rump of a partridge. This robs dining out of half its terrors" (*D*, III: 127). With tongue in cheek, Woolf wrote of this as "the most important event in my life since marriage," yet as usual there is truth in her joking. The shingling seems to have freed her from her social anxieties precisely because with it she renounced all claims to distinction, to beauty. A similar willingness to be obscure and ordinary colors Flush's ultimate response to his shearing, although the intermediate stages are more painful:

> As Robert Browning snipped, as the insignia of a cocker spaniel fell to the floor, as the travesty of quite a different animal rose round his neck, Flush felt himself emasculated, diminished, ashamed. What am I now? he thought, gazing into the glass. And the glass replied with the brutal sincerity of glasses, "You are nothing." . . . But as he gazed, his ears bald now, and uncurled, seemed to twitch. It was as if the potent spirits of truth and laughter were whispering in them. To be nothing—is that not, after all, the most satisfactory state in the world? . . . To caricature the pomposity of those who claim that they are something—was that not in its way a career? [*F*, 143]

Flush discovers the pleasures of anonymity; "emasculated," he is now free to go where he wishes, to associate with whomever he pleases. He possesses a new philosophy: "'Flush,' Mrs. Browning wrote to her sister, 'is wise.' She was thinking perhaps of the Greek saying that happiness is only to be reached through suffering. The true philosopher is he who has lost his coat but is free from fleas" (*F*, 144). This new philosophy is put to the test immediately by a return to London, during which Flush reassesses the city from a perspective newly sympathetic to women and outsiders. Contemptuous of national boundaries and class distinctions, Flush finds in the imperial pride and hierarchical social arrangements of London "a certain morbidity" (*F*, 147). "The confinement, the crowd of little objects, the black-beetles by night, the bluebottles by day, the lingering odours of mutton, the perpetual presence on the sideboard of bananas—all this . . . wrought on his temper and strained his nerves" (*F*, 147). The return to Italy drives his judgment home: while cities like Pisa and Florence make possible a life of emotional freedom, Victorian London offers only stagnation and confinement. Two images rule Flush's London visit: the thought of Nero, the Carlyles' dog, leaping from the top window in despair at the strain of life in Cheyne Row, and the knowledge that the "front door was always locked. He had to wait for somebody to lead him on a chain" (*F*, 147–48).[11]

Bidding farewell to her London home near the end of *Flush*, Elizabeth Barrett Browning asserts with remarkable understatement, "Nothing had been changed. Nothing had happened all these years . . . Yes, she said, it seemed to her that the house wanted cleaning" (*F*, 149–50). Woolf renders a profound criticism of patriarchal society here in the most humble terms, through the eyes of a woman thinking about housecleaning. For Woolf, the image of the charwoman had always possessed a subversive potential, however; in her essays on "The Docks of London" and "Great Men's Houses," written at roughly the same time as *Flush*, she used the charwoman to link the oppression of women and of the working poor in the space of patriarchal London, while later in *The Years* the same figure would give her a heroic symbol for woman's transforming political importance.[12] It is significant, then, that in her essay on Barrett Browning, Woolf asserted that "the only place in the mansion of literature that is assigned her is downstairs in the servants' quarters" (*CR*, II: 183). In *Flush* Woolf implies that only from a spatially and politically marginal position in the social household can any serious housecleaning be done. From the liminal position of exile—for Flush, from the human race; for Barrett Browning, from the world of patriarchal London—this comic biography indicts London society of the Victorian era for its restrictions, its hypocrisies, its unholy alliances that oppress women and other marginal groups (embodied by the thief or hooded man, who links "proper" Wimpole Street with "depraved" Whitechapel, Mr. Barrett with Jack the Ripper). Yet, in its glimpse of Elizabeth Barrett Browning's life in Pisa and Florence, *Flush* also offers the picture of a very different sort of city life, one whose union of maternity and literary creativity recalls the modern London enjoyed by Flush's predecessor, Orlando, in Woolf's earlier comic biography.[13] For Flush and his mistress, the urban environment intensifies both the penalties and privileges of marginal status. To Ethel Smyth, Woolf described *Flush* in 1932 as "just a little joke to boil my years pot" (*L*, V: 140). This novel is far more than a joke, however, for in its union of the oppressive and liberating aspects of urban experience, as in its use of an urban setting to link sexual and class oppression, *Flush* anticipates the serious family chronicle, *The Years*.

CHAPTER SEVEN

WOOLF'S DEVELOPING URBAN VISION IN *THE YEARS*

None of Woolf's other novels has so dramatically incongruous a moment of origin as *The Years*: "I have this moment [20 January 1931], while having my bath, conceived an entire new book—a sequel to A Room of Ones Own—about the sexual life of women: to be called Professions for Women perhaps—Lord how exciting! This sprang out of my paper to be read on Wednesday to Pippa's society" (*D*, IV: 6). By November 1932 Woolf saw the incipient work as a "novel of fact" in the tradition of *Night and Day*, but her plans for it implied a far more ambitious treatment of some familiar themes than that earlier work: "Its to be an Essay-Novel, called the Pargiters—& its to take in everything, sex, education, life &c; & come . . . across precipices from 1880 to here & now—" (*D*, IV: 129).

The intertwined issues of a woman's sexual and professional lives had preoccupied Woolf since *Night and Day* (1919), where she documented Katharine Hilbery's struggle to escape woman's traditional "profession" as helpmate in order to work in her chosen profession—mathematics. In *Night and Day* Woolf presented sexual and professional life as ultimately unreconcilable for women in patriarchal London; she resolved the conflict by portraying Mary Datchet as living a chaste London professional existence, while Katharine Hilbery escaped with her lover to country seclusion, there to study mathematics. By the time she wrote *The Years*, in contrast, Woolf was prepared to consider the full scope of female life in the city.

As Woolf originally planned it, *The Years* was to combine several "excerpts" from a longer novel, tracing a typical English family from 1880 to 2032, with a number of interpolated essays exploring the issues raised by those "chapters" from the longer novel. Woolf abandoned her experiment in the combination of fact and fiction, however, after completing only five fictional extracts and six factual essays. In a massive revision in February 1933 she excised the "interchapters," or essays, and concentrated thenceforth wholly on fiction. Not only did Woolf eliminate the six essays, but in at least two later revisions she excised several further sections, first cutting several pages from what would have been a longer "1910" chapter, and then deleting "two enormous chunks" from the "1917" and "1921" chapters.[1] The development of this novel from *The Pargiters* (her title for its original version[2]) to its published form as *The Years* reveals a pattern of revision characteristic of Woolf's fiction: a consistent movement away from direct denunciation of British society for its belligerence and sexism to the indirect dramatization of her criticism. Although Woolf's plans for the novel changed drastically between her first conception of it in 1931 and its published form in 1937, many of the themes from those omitted essays remain, dramatized in fiction.

Woolf's working title for this ambitious rethinking of the family chronicle emphasizes her difficulty in directly addressing her chosen topic, "the sexual life of women," or—as she put it to the London/National Society for Women's Service—in speaking "the truth about her body" (*P*, xxxx). "Pargiter," as Jane Marcus has shown, resembles "pargeter," an entry in the *English Dialect Dictionary* of Joseph Wright, whose love letters Woolf had been reading with pleasure while she composed her early draft of the novel. "Parget" means both to cover up, to whitewash, to lie *and also* to patch up, to build, and to beautify. Both connotations of "parget" figured in Woolf's composition of *The Pargiters*, later *The Years*.[3] Concerned to tell the truth about "the sexual life of women," a truth that included social and political oppression as well as different ways of struggling for sexual and professional freedom, Woolf turned once more to a strategy of indirection. *The Years*, like *Night and Day*, opens with an episode around the tea table, and the form of indirect expression that Woolf acquired in her "tea-table training" is crucial to her composition of the novel (*MB*, 129).[4]

A Room of One's Own, Woolf claimed in a diary entry of January 1931, was the significant precursor of *The Years*; the essay and the novel have in common not only their concern for women's treatment as a sex, but their reliance on the city—as image and setting—to convey women's situation indirectly. In *The Years* women's war for sexual and professional equality is waged on the battlefield of London, where men and women struggle with each other for control of the streets. Woolf traces from 1880 to "Present Day" the fortunes of the Pargiter family, of "number fifty-six Abercorn Terrace, one of [those] large old fashioned houses with flights of steps in front and long gardens behind which are still to be found between Ladbroke Grove and Bayswater" (*P*, 10). Although the novel focuses on Eleanor, the unmarried daughter of Colonel Abel Pargiter, who remains at Abercorn Terrace to act as his housekeeper after her mother dies, it introduces us to other members of this large, late Victorian upper-middle-class family as well. The male Pargiters occupy a variety of positions in patriarchal society—Edward is an Oxford don, Morris a suburban lawyer, Martin an African explorer turned London bachelor, and North a demobilized soldier still looking for a suitable profession. The female Pargiters also exemplify a range of relations to the institutions of British society. In addition to keeping house for her father, Eleanor occupies herself with charitable projects, collecting rents for a philanthropic society in Lisson Grove, planning "Rigby Cottages," and sitting on various committees. Her rebellious cousin, Kitty Malone, who as the daughter of an Oxford don dreamed of freedom as a farmer in the north of England, has capitulated by making a socially advantageous marriage to Lord Lasswade; she sympathizes secretly with the suffrage movement while living (during her husband's lifetime) as a wealthy society hostess in Grosvenor Square. Delia, whose cause had been Irish home rule, marries a beefy Anglo-Irish gentleman and settles in the Irish countryside; one of their few visits to London prompts the family party of the novel's concluding chapter. There is Milly, who married Hugh Gibbs and lives in the country—she preoccupied with her children, he with his hunting. And Rose, whose childhood experience of a drunken man's exhibitionism has motivated an adult commitment to militant suffragism. Rose's cousin, slum-dwelling Sara Pargiter, is a quasi-Cassandra whose apocalyptic world view is often eerily accurate. Maggie, Sara's sister, has escaped conventional London ways for a happy, egalitarian marriage to (ironically) a French munitions manufacturer, and family life in "one of the obscure little streets under the shadow of the Abbey" (*TY*, 279). Finally, there is

Peggy Pargiter, Eleanor's niece, who after her country childhood is now a doctor, having followed training that took its deadening toll on her spirit and senses—training for which Woolf would later attack the professions in *Three Guineas* (1938). A political novel in the feminist and pacifist senses, *The Years* traces the changes that befall the many Pargiters, male and female, as England moves from empire to a nation threatened by fascism, and as women move from the protected prison of the Victorian home to the freedom of the modern city streets, there to struggle with men for their rightful public place.

Two settings predominate in the novel's early pages: London's upper-middle-class Abercorn Terrace and upper-middle-class Oxford. Both cities are shown to be full of intellectual and professional opportunities for the boys and men who live there—Martin Pargiter gets his sixpence for being at the top of his class, and Edward Pargiter his case of fine old port to help him prepare for the Greek fellowship exam—but cities are stifling for the girls and women trapped in their drawing rooms. Imprisoned at the tea table whether in London or Oxford, the women are confined to an endless round of errands, boring social functions, and obligatory family gatherings. In addition to these contrasting views of male and female upper-middle-class London and Oxford, we are also given glimpses of another section of each city: London's Lisson Grove and the Robsons' house in Oxford, "down Ringmer Road, past the gasworks" (*TY*, 66). To the Pargiter women who experience it, life in those working-class districts seems preferable to their own: freer, more honest, and with more scope for intellectual and sexual experimentation. From "1880" to "Present Day," *The Years* traces two parallel developments reflecting this feeling: women's movement into public life from the private sphere, and their corresponding drift from family life in the upper-middle-class districts of Victorian London and Oxford to independent life in the working-class districts of modern London. The published version of the novel uses this spatial shift between middle- and working-class districts of London as one of several indicators of the fact that woman's sexual and professional life is shaped by oppressive male society and liberated only by a movement out of that society into a more egalitarian, feminist one created by women in their new working-class milieux.

In the course of *The Years* the Pargiter women also become increasingly involved in the institutions of the city in which they live, reflecting not only their increasing maturity and social prominence, but more importantly the changing times. In 1891 Eleanor plans Rigby Cottages; in 1910 she sits on what is probably a suffrage committee with her cousin Kitty; by 1917 she reflects ruefully (in the deleted passage) on how *she* would have used the money available to munitions buyers—to rebuild Rigby Cottages. By the "Present Day," Eleanor has visited India, lives by herself, and has a group of friends who span several generations and many nationalities. Rose sees the inside of a prison for her militant suffrage work and is later decorated for her war work (*TY*, 420). Even Sara ultimately takes a job in the public sphere, as a journalist (*TY*, 342).

To appreciate Woolf's developing use of urban themes, images, and settings we can chart her treatment of London in the novel's drafts—her discussion of street love in *The Pargiters*; her revision of Cleopatra's Needle as symbol of the feminist civilization to come, in an excised portion of "1910"; and her contrasting visions of wartime and postwar London in "two enormous chunks" deleted from the novel's galley proofs. Then, turning to the published version of *The Years*, we can assess the impact of these extensive revisions upon the texture of the finished novel. By studying her treatment of two urban images—the pillar box and the bridge—we can trace her new use of the urban setting to reflect, in style as well as theme, the novel's anti-authoritarian political philosophy and to convey two sides of woman's urban experience in the modern period: the fellowship of oppression and the fellowship of feminist struggle.

"Street Love"

In *The Pargiters* Woolf shows us a city "artificially partitioned off" into sex-lined zones, each with its own form of love (*P*, 36). Her analysis of this partitioned city permeates the entire volume but is concentrated particularly in the "Second Essay," where she links spatial zones to the different kinds of love operating in the lives of the Pargiters. As Woolf describes these zones, to women and children belongs the drawing room, with its varied forms of open and concealed love: Captain Pargiter's love for his children, Delia's and Milly's different sorts of love for Eleanor, Bobby's love for Miriam Parrish, and Eleanor's love for Morris. To the men belong the streets, with their largely male force that Woolf calls street love, which is "different from the other loves inside the drawing room," and which both controls the streets and besieges the private home "on all sides" (*P*, 38).

Woolf's analysis of street love—the frank, aggressive, even hostile display of predominantly male sexuality that she dramatizes in *The Pargiters* and in the "1880" chapter of *The Years*—uncovers the powerless situation of the Pargiter women, suggesting through its treatment of London the underlying analysis of sexual politics that was Woolf's aim. Discussing street love, she illuminates the novel's central topic, the "sexual life of women" (*D*, IV: 6). Yet she does so not by producing the exposé that such a phrase might suggest, but by turning the topic inside out to show how the social life of women is determined by their lack of sexual freedom—by the restrictive structures of their lives—just as the social opportunities of men are determined by their lesser restrictions.

As Woolf describes it, street love affects the Pargiter boys, in 1880, by introducing them to sexuality in the person of a jeering prostitute at a lamppost, and so initiating them into the "fellowship of men together," with its "great many rights and privileges," its territorial claims, and its proscriptions against both friendship with women and love with men (or by oneself) (*P*, 54). Yet because they have been, from early childhood, allowed more freedom in the city than their sisters—Edward Pargiter, for example, had been "free from a very early age to walk about London alone; and the knowledge that he acquired from the streets was soon supplemented by the boys at school"—the Pargiter boys find street love both more familiar and more controllable than do the Pargiter girls. Furthermore, since they are only very rarely its passive objects, they find it infinitely less threatening (*P*, 81).

In contrast, the fact of street love had a major influence on the girls and women of the time, Woolf asserts:

> Eleanor and Milly and Delia could not possibly go for a walk alone—save in the streets round about Abercorn Terrace, and then only between the hours of eight-thirty and sunset. An exception might be made in favour of Eleanor, when she went to Lisson Grove; but even she, whose mission was charitable, was expected either to take a cab, or to get one of the girls at the Settlement to see her into the omnibus, if she went to a meet-

> ing or concert after dark. For any of them to walk in the West End even by day was out of the question. Bond Street was as impassable, save with their mother, as any swamp alive with crocodiles. The Burlington Arcade was nothing but a fever-stricken den as far as they were concerned. [*P*, 37]

As Woolf describes it, the all-pervasive threat of street love alters the face of London for the Pargiter girls, turning it from a civilized environment of familiar landmarks (Bond Street, the Burlington Arcade) into a fever-infested, trackless swamp. The implicit analogies here are between patriarchal civilization and a primeval, uncivilized jungle; between sexually driven men and life-threatening crocodiles or fever-carrying mosquitoes. Woolf's image, although reminiscent of Joseph Conrad's classic modernist vision of the "heart of darkness," is also informed by a realistic awareness of the actual dangers of male sexuality to late-Victorian women, which changes it from a mere figure of speech to a vivid statement of the threat to women's very lives posed by sexual molestation, pregnancy out of wedlock, and sexually transmitted venereal diseases.

The threat of street love in one of its most basic forms—prostitution—had motivated the passage of the Contagious Diseases Acts several decades earlier. These measures were intended to protect the military from venereal disease. Yet they and the restrictions on free female movement created in response to street love were misguided, for the Contagious Diseases Acts enforced the ineffectual and oppressive measure of investigating and, if necessary, treating prostitutes while wholly ignoring their customers. Similarly, attempts to deal with rape and pregnancy by keeping women "innocent" and restricting their movements ignored the real cause of both problems. The struggle to repeal the Contagious Diseases Acts, waged in the 1860's, grew out of a conviction that they wrongly enforced a double standard of sexual morality. As Josephine Butler argued, "It is unjust to punish the sex who are victims of a vice, and leave unpunished the sex who are the main cause, both of the vice, and its dreaded consequences."[5] Similarly, the suffrage struggle, which would later engage several Pargiter women, was frequently yoked to a campaign for male chastity, as in the Pankhursts' purity campaign of 1913, with its slogan, "Votes for women, purity for men."[6] Woolf's image of London transformed into a jungle by street love embodies her critique of the uncivilized deeper nature of patriarchal society, as well as evoking some of the sources of the Pargiter women's later commitment to the suffrage movement.

Not only did street love change the landmarks of London in the 1880's, revealing the city's men to be predatory, infection-laden creatures, but it altered the physical and psychological experience of London women as well. The spirited Pargiter girls did not always obey the rules; occasionally they did what was forbidden, going to Bond Street or the Burlington Arcade alone. Then, to make matters worse, they lied about it to their father. The restrictions upon their physical and social liberty created, in turn, a sort of psychological restriction manifest in the need to cover up, to lie to others about their activities, to lie even to themselves, whether about a forbidden jaunt alone or so trivial an event as a peek from the window at a young man come calling down the street. "[The] feeling, since it was never exposed, save by a blush, or a giggle, wriggled deep down into their minds, and sometimes woke them in the middle of the night with curious sensations, unpleasant dreams, that seemed all to come from this one fact — that Abercorn Terrace was besieged . . . by what may be called street love" (*P*, 38). In *The Pargiters* Woolf explains that this return of the repressed has a complexity better embodied in a fictional scene than in an essay, and she offers the episode of Rose Pargiter's nighttime trip to Lamley's—which becomes a significant episode in the first chapter of *The Years*—as a representative childhood experience. This episode not only exemplifies the psychologically coercive and crippling effects of street love upon little girls, but also offers a clue to the sources of Rose's adult passion for the suffrage movement.

One evening in 1880 Rose Pargiter ventures out to Lamley's in violation of the strict rule that girls must never go out alone after dark. She wants to buy ducks and swans to float in her bathtub. Hurrying down Melrose Avenue to the shop, she passes a man whose face frightens her: "'The enemy—the enemy!' Rose cried to herself . . . playing the game" (*P*, 42). Yet, as her return trip reveals, there is nothing playful about this encounter at the pillar box. Instead, it represents one of many serious urban rituals through which women are taught their "proper place" in a patriarchal society. "When she reached the pillar box there was the man again. He was leaning against it, as if he were ill, Rose thought, filled with the same terror again. . . . There was nobody else anywhere in sight. As she ran past him, he gibbered some nonsense at her, sucking his lips in & out; & began to undo his clothes" (*P*, 43). The man's frightening exhibitionism at the pillar box elicits shock and guilt from Rose, preventing her later from telling Eleanor what she has seen. She is reduced to saying she is worried about a "robber" when she wakes from her nightmare, and to receiving from her sister the ironically unconsoling answer, "Theres Papa, & theres Morris. . . . They'd never let a robber get into this house" (*P*, 48). To Rose, however, Papa and Morris provide little comfort. Not only are they male, and thus implicated in the street love this scene embodies, but, as Rose's thoughts reveal, her father seems to advocate the same sexual double standard that underlies the threat of street love and was embodied, more than two decades earlier, in the Contagious Diseases Acts. "Papa would kill him she said. And yet [*if Papa knew what she had seen,*] [*she could never tell Papa what she had seen—never;*] she felt he would [*think her*] be very angry with her if he knew [*what she had seen.*] <*the truth*>" (*P*, 48).

In her guilty response to the experience at the pillar box, Rose demonstrates the complex effects of street love upon Victorian girls: it defuses their anger at their victimization by overlaying it with guilt for participating (albeit involuntarily) in a sexual experience, and, by linking that particular experience to sexuality in general, it also poisons the sources and inhibits the expression of their own natural sexuality. Such childhood repression could have a lasting effect upon the adult as well, as the "Fifth Essay" of *The Pargiters* explains. Kitty Malone, for instance, who was sheltered throughout adolescence from any experience of sexuality, lost contact not only with the outer world from which she was protected but with her inner world as well. Kitty's sexual response had been muted by the restrictions imposed upon it in response to the threat of street love:

> From her earliest childhood, ever since she was allowed to come down into the drawing room in a starched white frock, she had been taught a very strict moral code, which in childhood prevented her from kicking up her legs in the presence of the other sex; and as she grew older, prevented her from being alone in the room with them, from standing at an open window in her nightgown, from saying anything or doing anything which could suggest even remotely that she felt physi-

cally or ideally attracted by them. So that when, at the age of sixteen, George Carter had kissed her behind the haystack, the pleasure was great, but she knew she was committing an awful crime; and when, at the age of twenty, Alan Hammond had proposed to her, and Lord Lammermuir had admired her, she felt much less, physically, than they did—for the physical side of love had been so repressed not only in her, but in her mothers and grandmothers, that it was much weaker, even in a girl of perfect physique like Kitty, than in a young man like Tony Ashton who was physically less perfect, but sexually much better developed, since no restrictions had been placed either on him or on his fathers or grandfathers that were comparable in severity with those that had surrounded Kitty almost since birth. [*P*, 109]

Since sexual response is dependent upon the escape into freedom that each of the Pargiter women longs to make, and is muted as her freedom is constrained, they paradoxically direct their sexual energy toward people whose lives seem—even if fallaciously—to have been lived free of patriarchal restrictions.[7] Kitty Lasswade is drawn to Lucy Craddock for this reason, and is attracted in different ways to the entire Brooks family, particularly the eldest son: "Oh to be free; to be herself; on her own; to earn her living; to be a farmer . . . & then to—the thought did strike her . . . though probably it was a [th] very wrong & immodest thought—& then to fall in love with Jo, & be . . . the wife of a man with a shaving in his hair who mended hen coops, while she [bred] bred pigs in Yorkshire!" (*P*, 148). Kitty's sexual fantasy follows from her fantasy of freedom—to live as she wishes, by herself, and to earn her own living. The women of *The Pargiters*, and later of *The Years*, eroticize liberty because, for them, liberty *is* sexuality: oppression of the former results in repression of the latter.

Cut off by street love both from the outer world of London and Oxford and from much of the inner world of their female experience, the Pargiter women suffered a diminished range of possibilities. Single life was difficult, because in most cases women were unable to earn a living wage, and to a single woman chastity was essential:

plainly it was unthinkable for a middle- or upper-middle-class woman to have a relation with a man which might lead to her bearing an illegitimate child—a disgrace which a woman could

> scarcely survive, socially, or practically either; for the whole cost of the child's upbringing (in 1880) would fall solely upon her; and she was disabled by law from earning enough money to provide for herself, let alone for another human being. [*P*, 52]

Because of the supreme importance of chastity, they were unable to go to parties or even to visit friends without a chaperone. Thus their chance for enjoyment or occupation was reduced to finding the single socially acceptable route out of their father's home into a less straitened existence: marriage. Competition in the marriage market was, consequently, intense, as was revealed in the hostility Eleanor sensed between Delia and Milly when a friend of their father's invited him to bring one of them (without specifying which one) to dinner to meet his visiting son. "Neither spoke, but from the hardness of Delia's lips & the tremor with which Milly moved a tea cup, unnecessarily, she was aware . . . that each was acutely jealous of the other . . . <It is true that neither of them> knew Roger Blake . . . but he was a young man & in their circle young men were rare" (*P*, 15). Rivalry between women—even between sisters—inevitably resulted, in such a restricted social environment.

The Pargiters reveals the maddeningly circular effect of street love upon women: to keep from them economic, social, and legal equality with men. Women were denied the vote, and hence the opportunity for education and a profession, because they must remain chaste, protected from the dangerous forces of street love. Female chastity was essential, in turn, because women did not have the vote and hence could not change the law that prevented them from earning enough money to support the children who might result from sexual freedom. Street love thus lay at the root of the limitations on both women's sexual and professional lives. As a determining aspect of the milieu of late-Victorian London, street love provides a vivid spatial representation of woman's secondary status.

Turning from fact to fiction in the massive revisions of 1933, which changed *The Pargiters* to *The Years*, Woolf omitted her discussion of street love, along with all of the other factual material. Still, a legacy of themes remains in the published volume: in Eleanor's and Rose's worries about being followed through the streets by drunken men; in the sexual double standard as it variously affects the lives of Delia, Colonel Pargiter, Martin Pargiter, and even Charles Stewart Parnell; in Peggy Pargiter's innocently charged question to her Aunt Eleanor, "Was it that you were suppressed when you were young?"; and, most of all, in Rose Pargiter's developing commitment to the suffrage movement, which was as much an outgrowth of her individual experience of childhood fear at the pillar box as it was of the general struggle of women to repeal the Contagious Diseases Acts and, by attacking the sexual double standard, to improve the lot of women (*TY*, 335).

Whereas "1880" was the era of street love, "1910" saw the beginning of a retreat from those patriarchal Victorian mores of which street love was an instance. Woolf expressed this change in her treatment of one urban monument in a scene deleted from the "1910" chapter of *The Years*.[8] The passage takes place on 6 May 1910, a spring evening. Year, month, and day all mark crucial turning points for the Pargiter family, for women, and for the nation as a whole. The patriarchal households once headed by Colonel Abel Pargiter and his politician brother, Digby, are beginning to dissolve: Digby's death has brought about the sale of his house and the dispersal of his children, and within a year the death of Colonel Pargiter will force a similar decampment. "[On] or about December, 1910, human character changed," Woolf asserted in "Mr. Bennett and Mrs. Brown," but the spring of that year saw an even more specific change in the behavior of women (*CDB*, 96). After the general election, the Women's Social and Political Union adopted a calmer posture toward the government in an attempt to encourage Parliament to pass the Conciliation Bill, which would have guaranteed limited female suffrage.[9] During the spring and summer of 1910, militant suffrage demonstrations ceased and a peaceful, more unified mood prevailed. Finally, 6 May 1910 marked the end of a reign, as King Edward VII died and the crown passed to George V.

A scene from the early drafts of "1910" captures not only the sense of an ending, characterizing this period both in British history and in the Pargiters' private lives, but also a sense of private and social beginnings. Elvira (later Sara) Pargiter and her sister Maggie frame a letter to their cousin Rose, who has visited them earlier that day. Their conversation reveals that their minds still turn on the issues Rose's presence raised for them: women's rights and duties in a patriarchal society, and women's means for achieving a feminist society. Central to their discussion—and to the letter that they hope will result from it—are images for two different civilizations: the rural image of a "trunk of stone" lying in a desert, which marks the ruins of patriarchal civilization, and the urban image of Cleopatra's Needle, a London monument which, in their use of it, comes to symbolize the feminist society of the future.

The first monument appears in Elvira's account of the suffrage meeting she attended earlier that day with Rose, where the topic of discussion was whether or not to use violence in their struggle for the vote: "Oh, but a meeting's a very queer thing, Maggie. It's beautiful. Like a trunk of stone lying in pale greenish light in a desert."[10] Elvira's simile recalls Shelley's broken monument to Ozymandias, a similarly incomplete stone shape of a man also standing in the desert. Its inscription reads: "My name is Ozymandias, king of kings: / Look on my works, ye Mighty, and despair!"[11] Yet, ironically, "Nothing beside remains. Round the decay / Of that colossal wreck, boundless and bare / The lone and level sands stretch far away."[12] In its revelation of a desert where once a populous royal city thrived, Elvira's simile expresses the suffragist faith that one day the patriarchal civilization currently oppressing women will have left no more trace than the kingdom of Ozymandias. Further, she hopes that, with patriarchal power expelled, women can create a feminist civilization whose duration and influence will make the old one seem "but a rose leaf on top of what's to come. Our civilisation, Maggie, is but the thickness of one green leaf on the top of all Cleopatra's Needle; what's to come."[13]

At first, Elvira's image seems merely to combine imperialism with nationalism, British rule with the authoritarian reign of Cleopatra, one form of oppression with another. For, like the monuments in the published version of *The Years*, Cleopatra's Needle is preeminently a British imperialist figure of conquest. This needle-shaped stone on London's Victoria Embankment was presented by Egypt to the British Empire in 1878. Celebrating British dominion over Egypt, it is named for a powerful queen who was far from a feminist monarch. Yet when Elvira's image is considered in its context—the brief, sisterly conversation in which it appears—Woolf's subversive reframing of this London monument becomes apparent, for Cleopatra's Needle suggests a quite different group of associations.[14]

Needle-shaped, named for a queen, this London monument is a domestic transformation of the phallus, evoking the fellowship of women born from private household labor, like the needlework with which Maggie is absorbed while she and Elvira discuss their dreams for a feminist society. In linking domestic work to radical discourse, here as elsewhere, Woolf reflects her determination not to "take it for granted that life exists more fully in what is commonly thought big than in what is commonly thought small" (*CR* I, 155). She eavesdrops on sewing rooms and washhouses as another writer might loiter near the House of Lords—in search of significance. But there is a further and more important reason for Woolf's frequent attention to domestic activities in her fiction: she felt that women's household drudgery, while clearly a product of oppressive patriarchal culture, served feminist aims in two ways. First, because of its very banality, domestic labor guarantees privacy. Throughout her works Woolf shows women appreciating the safety from male interruption provided by household work. Even Clarissa Dalloway's alarm at being surprised sewing by Peter Walsh attests to the privacy such work usually affords. Second, when women enjoy such privacy—and at few other times—they are, ironically, free to engage in criticism of the male society that has banished them to kitchen, washhouse, or sewing room.

To say that Woolf understood how the experience of isolated domestic work could create solidarity among women is not, of course, to suggest that such work always nurtures a feminist outlook in Woolf's fiction. We need only remember the shrine built by Crosby, the Pargiters' servant, to "Almighty, all-powerful Mr. Martin," whose laundry she continues to do even after she is pensioned off by the family, to see that drudgery may also encourage hero worship (*TY*, 230). Yet the issue here, as so often in power relationships, is identification. If the domestic drudge identifies with her oppressors, her condition will nurture only alienation—from her peers even more than from her exploitative master. Both Kitty Lasswade and Crosby experience that alienation in *The Years*, although they occupy opposite ends of the social scale. Kitty is oppressed by her disinheritance; Crosby, by her labor. Crosby scorns the other inhabitants of her rooming house; Kitty despises rich society women. Both feel more at home with the masculine, privileged society that has used and then banished them—Crosby to her single room in the suburban lodging-house, Kitty to a cottage on her son's country estate.

If the domestic drudge profits from her experience, however, she learns to trust and to identify with her peers. In time, the result can be the sense of fellowship that Woolf imagined as the source of a "Society of Outsiders" in *Three Guineas* (*TG*, 113). As she imagined such a society drawn together by insights born from oppression, it would struggle to transform not only the individual life, but the whole of human relations, by breaking down class and sex barriers. So simple an act as choosing an unusual fabric for one's dress may be a form of insurrection worthy of the Society of Outsiders: in her fifties, Woolf still remembered with anguish George Duckworth's criticism of an evening dress she had made as a young girl, "of a green stuff bought erratically at a furniture shop . . . because it was cheaper than dress stuff; also more adventurous." Duckworth took one look at her and told her to "tear it up," sensing "some kind of insurrection; of defiance of social standards" (*MB*, 130). Duckworth's intuition was correct, of course: Woolf's adventurous green dress defied the standards of fashion, which dictated what women should wear and how they should behave. The allusion to seamstresses in the image of Cleopatra's Needle bespeaks faith in the power of just such feminist insurrection born from female fellowship: faith that a king will someday fall to a queen, and that patriarchal civilization will be succeeded by an egalitarian feminist one.[15]

The transition from patriarchal to feminist rule is given further shape, in the course of Elvira's conversation with Maggie, in the juxtaposition of two processions. Elvira thinks first of "an interminable and wonderful procession, from one end of time to the other, The Pargiters."[16] Then Elvira subverts this familiar Woolfian image of the patriarchal family as a caravan crossing the desert, as she imagines a future moment when women will bid farewell to the seemingly eternal legacy of patrilineality—and to the social desert it has created: "Here we are, following the procession through the desert, with nothing but a clump of trees on the horizon, and the spears of savages and hyenas howling; and now we are come to this rock; this formidable and craggy mountain; and rubbing our eyes and taking a look round, we . . . wave our swords in the air, blow them a kiss and make off [on a track of our own.]"[17] The image of a female procession away from patriarchy and patrilineality invokes the goals and tactics of the suffrage movement, which subverted the procession to its own ends. Formerly royal or ecclesiastical (but always patriarchal), when practiced by the suffragists in huge marches, a procession led not to a throne or an altar but to a podium where speakers would press for a feminist society built on a very different model from the competitive, privileged one of Colonel Pargiter and his forefathers. In this society, Elvira and Maggie imagine, "We'll live like reasonable human beings. We don't want gold lace, and Eton and Harrow and muskets."[18]

Woolf deleted the memorable phrase "a track of our own," with its ringing echo of *A Room of One's Own*, from the second draft of this passage, just as she later deleted the entire passage discussing the transition from a patriarchal to a feminist society (envisioned as "Cleopatra's Needle") from the "1910" chapter of *The Years*. In so doing, she followed her characteristic pattern of revising away from direct denunciation of social ills to a more indirect dramatization of them, a pattern that we may lament, but that we must also understand.[19] While in *The Pargiters* Woolf used the concept of street love to anchor a discussion of the effect of the sexual double standard and the threat of venereal disease, rape, and unwed pregnancy upon the social, psychological, economic, and legal position of women in Victorian society, by the time she wrote the first draft of "1910" she had moved her most radical critique of patriarchy from such direct discussion into two opposed images: the trunk of stone marking the ruins of male civilization in the desert, with the "interminable and wonderful procession" of the patriarchal family which leads to it, and—in opposition—the monument of Cleopatra's Needle, symbolic of the feminist civilization women can attain by breaking off "on a track of our own."

London: 1917 and 1921

By the time Woolf read the galley proofs of *The Years*, she apparently had come to feel uncomfortable with even the greater degree of indirection she employed after compacting the essays of *The Pargiters* into fictional material, for in revision she omitted not only the passage celebrating the feminist civilization to come but also "two enormous chunks"—part of the "1917" chapter and all of what would have been the "1921" chapter.[20] The episodes she deleted used portraits of modern London to convey her social analysis: in "1917" she implicitly explored the causes of World

War I, and in "1921" she suggested the sources and remedies for woman's secondary position in society. What emerges with study of these two episodes is Woolf's presentation of social criticism through her portrait of the urban milieu, and her dramatization of the relationship between militarism and the oppression of women.

The first "enormous chunk," set in 1917, uses a panoramic portrait of modern London to suggest the social climate responsible for World War I, shifting its focus from Crosby, the Pargiters' pensioned-off servant, to Bert Parkes, the "traveller in men's underwear," to sentimental spinster Miriam Parrish, to an unnamed passenger in a train, and finally to the novel's protagonist, Eleanor Pargiter. In a series of vignettes ranging from park to train to theater district to a suburban high-rise block of flats, Woolf indicts British society for its obedience to authority, its sentimentality, and above all its failure to make connections between the private and public spheres. While the characters in this episode fail to see any relationship between events in their private lives and the war raging abroad—with the exception of Eleanor, who comes close to making that connection—the many juxtapositions inevitable in city life impose those connections on the reader's awareness.

The passage begins with an accidental encounter between Crosby, who is leading the indolent children Alf and Gladys on a walk to Kew Gardens, and a "company of young men in khaki" who are marching down Richmond High Street to the beat of a drum. The conjunction of the two processions suggests an underlying resemblance between the apparently unrelated groups—the obedient wartime children with their leader, and the grimly disciplined soldiers—and so establishes the theme of the entire section: the relationship between private life and the war that is occupying public attention. As Woolf presents a series of sketches of people who refuse to question the conventions of wartime England, she reveals the prevalence of surface decorum and sentimentality: in the park, as Crosby erroneously imagines the young man, woman, and child seated near her to be a family; on the train, as the passengers refrain from discussing the news blaring from every newspaper: "THREE BRITISH CRUISERS SUNK"; as the traveler pained by the meaninglessness of wartime life sees himself reflected in the window, expressionless as the others; and as the passengers unite in sympathetic admiration of the uniformed officer and his girlfriend, "having a last night together before he goes to the Front" (*B*, 230).

Woolf presents a chilling portrait of London as a city of vital machines and deathly human automata:

> Advertisements were popping in and out. The names of the theatres were framed in blue and red lines; there was a bottle of beer that poured and stopped, then poured again. The sky glared as if a red and yellow canopy hung down over it. . . . There was the Coliseum with its globe on top of it. Long queues stood in the street, moving slowly as if they were being gradually swallowed by a snake. The people were moving on step by step. Some of them were eating bananas; others were reading newspapers; men were turning somersaults and playing horns; but the queue moved slowly; then stopped; then moved on again, as if the snake had swallowed another mouthful. [*B*, 230]

This image of wartime London has both historical and prehistoric or mythic overtones. The description of the Coliseum converged upon by a procession of dulled citizens, moving in a horrible parody of festivity, evokes imperial Rome on the brink of its collapse. Although eating, reading newspapers, turning somersaults, and playing horns, the people in this scene seem not celebrants but sleepwalkers, and their destination not a circus, a play, or an athletic event (which one might expect in a Coliseum), but a mass sacrifice.

The ancient resonances of the passage suggest, moreover, the nature of that sacrifice: the deadly collusion that Woolf would label "subconscious Hitlerism," the collaboration between military men and mothers in the making of war (*DM*, 245).[21] The controlling image for London in this section from "1917" is the uroboros—the snake that eats its own tail—traditionally an image for the rapacious mother who devours her own children.[22] Implicitly, this image of uroboric, sleepwalking London extends the guilt for the war from military men in the public world to mothers in the private home. The newspapers read so obsessively throughout this episode make the connection, even if the uncommunicative populace reading them fails to: juxtaposed with "THREE BRITISH CRUISERS SUNK" they report "The wife of a postman at Andover had been brought to bed of triplets" (*B*, 229). Moreover, the image of the uroboros emphasizes the horribly circular nature of this relationship: as long as women continue willingly to bear cannon fodder, the warmaking will continue.

While the image of the city as devouring mother stresses women's share in the responsibility for war, the corresponding guilt that men—even seemingly innocent men—must bear for warmaking becomes apparent later in the same episode from "1917," as Eleanor Pargiter and Miriam Parrish emerge from their evening at the theater, bid each other farewell, and Eleanor makes her way home to her high-rise flat in a safe suburb. In this passage Eleanor's emotional state is shaped by the city through which she moves, just as in 1880 Rose's emotions were affected (permanently, in fact) by her frightening experience at the pillar box. From the self-doubt that Eleanor feels on emerging from the theater, she shades into dependent sentimentality, patriotism, nostalgia, and finally guilt-laden conventional femininity; her changing moods correspond to her urban surroundings. When she first comes out into the street, she has to "readjust all her ideas" (*B*, 231). Under "the influence of the play," she had "been completely taken in": "Until five minutes of the end, she had believed that the innocent man was the villain" (*B*, 231). In fact, Eleanor was right. The "innocent man" *is* one of the villains of this war; his sexual tyranny at home is intimately related to the political tyranny abroad, as the scene which follows Eleanor's insight suggests. Yet, as she makes her way through wartime London to her suburban flat, Eleanor abandons her own intuitions and independent judgments to become an echo of her fellow citizens: patriotic, sentimental, and conventional.

Woolf choreographs Eleanor's trip home so that her emotions echo or are echoed by her surroundings. When first she emerges from the theater, she overhears a bit of conversation between two professional men: "Ah, but it's not a time for picking and choosing" (*B*, 231). Weaving this simple statement into her developing mood of self-doubt, Eleanor feels guilty for not yet being able to support her country's cause. She feels that she is picking and choosing, trying to tell the innocent man from the guilty one. The concern with moral responsibility suddenly seems "childish" to her, when compared to the pragmatic patriotism of the professional men. Eleanor's desire to feel similarly patriotic affects her perception of the street down which she walks: able to ignore the details that distract her by day, by night she finds it "larger and more dignified. . . . clear blue and spacious" (*B*, 231). Suddenly she thinks back to the moment four years earlier when the war was announced: "the maid came out on the terrace, she thought, and said, Soldiers are guarding the line with fixed bayonets! . . . And I said to myself, Not if I can help it, she thought" (*B*, 231). Eleanor's memory is ambiguous: it is unclear whether she resisted the thought of England in danger, or the idea of her country's willingness to go to war. Whatever her thoughts four years ago, however, in 1917 she suddenly feels a surge of patriotic emotion ("There it was . . . the familiar feeling"), appropriately, just as her itinerary has taken her down "Cockspur" and up the Haymarket (*B*, 231). That area of London, once the haunt of prostitutes, was off limits to all respectable women; in its role in embodying the split between female sexuality and feminine decorum, it embodies a domestic instance of the sex role division that was also responsible for the chivalric soldier ideal, as Woolf dramatized in *Mrs. Dalloway*. Furthermore, Eleanor's rush of patriotism while walking up the Haymarket is succeeded by a mood of fearful dependent conventionality, suggesting a link between patriotism (with its glorification of the "masculine" virtues) and conventions of proper feminine behavior, which result in women's sexual, economic and social oppression: "She had meant to walk; but she felt a sudden disinclination to walk by herself. It would be better to be with other people, she thought. Other people, she thought, getting into the omnibus, stop one from thinking. They're a help" (*B*, 231). To readers familiar with Eleanor's active and inquiring mind, this sudden desire to stop thinking compellingly demonstrates that she is entrapped by inauthentic feelings: patriotism, conventional femininity, conformity. Further proof comes when Eleanor lapses into a sentimental fantasy as the omnibus passes her father's club, imagining that the woman sitting opposite with her young child has been visiting her husband, a wounded soldier "in one of the City hospitals" (*B*, 232). Yet Eleanor cannot sustain her little story herself; she finds it "unsatisfactory" and abandons it when the woman leaves the omnibus.

Guilt-ridden, nostalgic, fearful, sentimental, Eleanor is finally relieved to find herself alone in the safe suburban night, where her surroundings serve as a final mirror for her mental state: "The houses were all small middle-class villas. . . . All looked equally demure as she passed them; blind and safely curtained for the night" (*B*, 232).[23] Like the houses around her, Eleanor has become demure, blind, safely (mentally) curtained against any realization of the evils of past or present. Instead, she has indulged herself, during her trip home, in a nostalgic evocation of the "clear blue and spacious" days gone by, has induced in herself a patriotic mood, and has fed that feeling with a sanitized fantasy of a wounded soldier and his visiting wife and child, a fantasy devoid of any suffering or pain. At last Eleanor fittingly takes refuge in her suburban flat, surrounded by the defining possessions of her family home—"her mother's picture over the writing-table; and the cabinet full of china"—there to feel "dry, isolated, in a high, safe place" (*B*, 233).

Having returned to her high-rise flat in the safe London suburb, however, Eleanor at last comes close to making the connection between militarism and the enforcement of conventional female roles that the city around her has reflected. Warming herself at the "little white skulls" of the gas fire, she glances at the city paper and sees the name "Ranken" among the list of "casualties" of the naval battle. Thinking of Captain Lionel Ranken, she begins a train of thought that suggests that his death—in fact, all war deaths—are anything but the product of "Crass Casualty."[24] She remembers Captain Ranken opening the door for her at Celia's one summer: "For a second she felt a wish to put out her hand and stop him as he opened the drawing-room door. But how could I have stopped him? she asked herself" (*B*, 233). An earlier draft of this passage makes more explicit Eleanor's momentary understanding of the relationship between Ranken's chivalrous behavior and his death in battle. In that draft Eleanor listens to some men on the street who are discussing the war, and she considers, "If she as a girl had always read the papers; if she had followed the course of politics; if she had twenty years ago formed a society & headed a procession & gone to Whitehall, & said, if you don't stop what you're doing. . . ."[25] Eleanor's thought implies that, by refusing to let men do things for them (whether opening a drawing-room door or "managing" politics), women could stop wars.

Although Eleanor has come close to glimpsing the relationship between her powerlessness and her responsibility for the war raging abroad, she cannot resolve that conflict—at least not in so many words: "But what's the use of thinking? she said to herself angrily" (*B*, 233). Yet her actions suggest that on some level she has made the connection between war and the oppression of women, and, furthermore, that she has understood that she will be responsible for the deaths of men like Captain Ranken as long as she acquiesces in a social system that demands chivalry from men and passivity from women. Her final action in this scene is to flaunt one of the conventions that had so frustrated Kitty Malone almost forty years earlier: defying the rules of modesty, she bathes before an uncurtained window.

One could read this passage as a hypocritical self-purification, continuing the theme of blamelessness that Eleanor's thoughts have already established, when she thinks about whether she could have kept Colonel Ranken from his death, and about how much good she could have done at Rigby Cottages with half the money being spent upon munitions, only to conclude, "What's the use of thinking?" However, the expansive beauty of this scene, with its implicit contrast between Eleanor's moonlit nakedness and Kitty Malone's earlier obedient withdrawal from the window because "Anybody might see in," makes Eleanor's bath seem not a hypocritical self-purification but a ritual of dedication. Like the charwomen of "The Docks of London," Eleanor dedicates herself to cleaning up the mess men have made—in this case, the war. She cleanses herself both of the sentimental stories she has told herself in the course of the evening and of the male politics they reflect, "all phantasies and moonshine," as Woolf put it herself, "only mudcoloured moonshine" (*L*, II: 582).

In this deleted portion of "1917," the image of wartime London suggests what Eleanor Pargiter's thoughts and actions ratify—that women must stop male warmaking by breaking off from patriarchal society on processions of their own; processions like those formed by the suffragists, who marched not only for the vote, but for freedom from compulsory maternity and domesticity; processions like that imagined by Elvira in the early draft of "1910," leading away from the desert of patriarchal society to the feminist civilization of the future marked by Cleopatra's Needle. Above all, processions *unlike* that deadly uroboric procession of sleepwalking Londoners in the "1917" section, shuffling onward to the death that awaits them in a civilization dedicated to war. Although Woolf ultimately deleted this from the novel's final version, her concern with the relation of pacifism to feminist issues, like her character Eleanor's commitment to finding a way to "live more naturally . . . better," remains as the thematic center not just of "1917," but of *The Years* (*TY*, 296).

In the second "enormous chunk," which would have formed the transitional chapter, "1921," Woolf shows how the changing face of London reflects the changing social position of women between 1917 and "Present Day." While in "1917" traces of the impact of street love still existed in the emphasis on male chivalry and feminine decorum, by 1921 there are signs of a further loosening of these constraints. Both Kitty Lasswade and Eleanor Pargiter have finally become free women, since Kitty's husband and Eleanor's father have died. The two women's contrasting reactions to London amplify the theme introduced at the end of the passage from "1917": the relationship between a society's treatment of women and its national and international politics. Although they have shared the same restrictions born of street love since their childhoods, these two women plan very different forms for their free adult lives. Woolf suggests that there is a causal relationship between the future each woman can imagine for herself and her present experience of being a woman in the modern city.

The "1921" chapter follows a vignette from what became "1918": Crosby is struggling down Richmond High Street at the moment when peace is declared, and she catches sight of "Mr. Edward and Miss Kitty" in a car in a traffic jam. She wishes futilely that "somebody had been with her, to whom she could have pointed them out" (*B*, 237). The chapter then follows Kitty and Edward as they walk in Richmond Park, goes on to recount a teatime conversation about London between Kitty and Eleanor, continues by observing London through Eleanor's eyes as she strolls through the streets contemplating herself and her family, and records Eleanor's solitary meal in a rather garish city restaurant. The passage closes with Eleanor's nervous walk through the dark streets to her tube stop.

The opening vignette begins with what seems a drastic change —the end of World War I. However, as the passage reveals, peace actually has a minimal impact on British society: "The war was over—so somebody told [Crosby] as she took her place in the queue at the grocer's shop" (*B*, 237). Not only wartime scarcity, but also wartime habits of thought still prevail in the chapter that follows. Kitty's walk through Richmond Park with her cousin

Edward emphasizes the continuing dominance of traditional social forms. So hedged round are they by the restrictions of propriety, property, and power that their stroll only parodies the freedom and discovery of a real walk. The motorcar defines their itinerary: the chauffeur drops them off at one gate and meets them at the other. Their conversation dwells on property—the lodge at Oxford where Kitty grew up, which Edward is about to "inherit" as "new Master"; the estate Kitty shared with her husband which, with his death, has passed not to her but to her son Dominick (*B*, 238–39). That both Edward and Dominick are usurpers is Kitty's unconscious judgment, betrayed, as they discuss these changes, in her fancy of hearing a cuckoo: the bird that lays its eggs in other birds' nests (*B*, 239). Lord Lasswade's place has also been usurped, it seems; rather than enjoying the new freedom of being unescorted, Kitty has chosen her great dog, Sultan, for a chaperone. The dog even seems to define Kitty's plans for life as a widow: "He hates London," Kitty confides to Edward, and then goes on to mention that she plans to leave the city. Like his oriental namesake, Sultan also restricts the interaction between Kitty and Edward, who at one time was in love with her. The dog claims Kitty for himself in a spray bath that, as seen through Edward's eyes, has unmistakably sexual overtones:

> He wished she had not brought the dog. It made talk so difficult. But she always had a passion, he remembered, for big shaggy dogs. . . . It was extremely difficult now to see what it had been in her that had so fascinated him. He half shut his eyes. He had been passionately in love with her. He could still remember the day. . . . But the dog had clambered out of the water and was shaking himself so that drops flew in a shower all over Kitty's skirt. She shook herself, too. She beat him off with her bare hand. He was glad on the whole that he had not married her. She was too rough, too abrupt. [*B*, 239]

Kitty's life has narrowed since her husband's death, yet she accepts this narrowing, if with a touch of regret: "so much time was wasted getting into touch with people; so little was ever said. It was her fault largely" (*B*, 239). The fault lies in Kitty's willingness to accept continued patriarchal rule after losing her husband. Sultan, rather than Lord Lasswade, now takes first place in her thoughts, but the model of male-female interaction is still the same. The exclusive right of a man to his wife's care still decrees that all other human relations come second. So, as Kitty and Edward reach the car at the walk's end, she turns her attention first to Sultan and only then considers Edward: "'Sultan's been in the water,' said Kitty, pointing to the wet dog. 'You'll have to put a rug for him to lie on. And where shall we put you down, Edward?' she asked" (*B*, 240).

Kitty reveals both her dispossession, as a widow in male-centered society, and her obstinate refusal to recognize any change in her social position or any injustice in the way society has treated her. Clinging to the forms of a bygone world, Kitty imposes her static vision of society upon the changing city around her. When, as they drive through London, Edward begins to tell her of a friend's strongest impression of the city after the war, Kitty finishes his sentence for him, true to her own denial of change. "He didn't even finish his sentence, she thought. What had he been going to say? Something about Piccadilly? Things going on, she supposed" (*B*, 241).

At tea with Eleanor, Kitty continues to reveal her antiquated social vision and her inability to reject the tenets of the patriarchal society that has so abruptly rejected her. The two women stand in sharp contrast: Kitty's perspective on life is nostalgic and pessimistic, Eleanor's dynamic and optimistic. Kitty plans to retreat from postwar London where, as she sees it, the desire for power still predominates because "it's human nature" (*B*, 243). She feels little hope for change from the "mess" men have made of things, for to her the younger generation seems the same as their parents: "the women such fools, and the men caring only for their sport, their politics" (*B*, 243). Shorn of the power she once had, however, Kitty can only imagine a future shaped around the attempt to regain it through regression to the past, and identification with the very sex and class responsible for her present powerlessness. She adopts mannish gestures, eats "like a schoolboy," and stands "in front of the fire with her arms behind her back like a country gentleman" (*B*, 241–42). With Sultan, she will retreat to a "Tudor manor house" in the north of England, to live the life of feudal isolation befitting her nickname, "The Grenadier" (*TY*, 257). Kitty's dreams for the future are now far from those she once enjoyed in Oxford. Then she had hoped only to live as a farmer, and possibly to marry "a man with a shaving in his hair" (*P*, 148). Now she has bought a house that was once a farm, but she seems unable to surrender the trappings of power and place that she has acquired through her marriage to Lord Lasswade.

Kitty and Eleanor stand together at the window for a moment, looking out onto Grosvenor Square below, and in that brief time their different perceptions of the city highlight their divergent social and political visions. Kitty's view of the city is colored by her limited sense of options, her pessimism, and the self-absorption that restricts her interest in other people. Her city features insignificant people and dominant institutions: "the little figures, foreshortened from this height, looked oddly insubstantial. . . . And all round them were the great ring of houses, red gold in the evening haze" (*B*, 243). "How I hate London!" cries Kitty, responding to that vision of the city as controlled by a few powerful, wealthy families. "How I love it," Eleanor counters (*B*, 243). Her vision, revealed in the next view from the window, shows the people below not as "foreshortened" and "insubstantial," but as fascinating, active, and detailed. Entering into the drama of the street, Eleanor seems even to read the mind of "one of those shabby-looking old women who are always to be seen in London squares," to guess that she will give a copper to the cornet-playing beggar (*B*, 243).

Eleanor's appreciation of London, which makes possible that moment of mental fellowship with the shabby old woman, reflects a social and political perspective dramatically different from Kitty's isolated, feudal nostalgia. This perspective is hinted at when Eleanor thinks of another conversation during which she and her friend, Nicholas, deplored all that Kitty's life embodies: "'People wanting power,' . . . No, she could not possibly tell Kitty what they had been talking about. Power, patriotism, love, sex and all the rest of it" (*B*, 243). Eleanor's reluctance to share her conversation suggests its content: the alienating effects of power, patriotism, and sexual repression—all major components of Kitty's past life. Unlike Kitty, Eleanor recognizes the roots of the problems people feel with intimacy—"How difficult it is to know people—how afraid we all are of each other"—in the hierarchical, patriarchal society that Kitty continues to endorse (*B*, 242).

Although both women have been shaped by this society, they differ in their responses to it—and consequently in their ability to get close to other people. Kitty still identifies with the very sources of power that oppress her ("the great ring of houses") and, as a result, finds it difficult to share her feelings even with her cousin: "She had a photograph of the house. She wanted to show it to Eleanor. It was a charming house; a little manor house, that had been used as a farm-house. She was going to alter it. But perhaps Eleanor would not be interested" (*B*, 241). Kitty assumes that her little manor house has small importance in a world of great houses. In contrast, Eleanor identifies with those who are powerless, like the "shabby old woman," and can form close friendships with those who reject power, like the foreigner, Nicholas Pomjalovsky, who in the novel's last episode repeatedly declines to make a speech (*TY*, 425). The London that Eleanor loves is a city that Kitty Lasswade has never seen, a city that Woolf was to hope, in *Three Guineas*, that women would claim for their own: "[Let] the daughters of uneducated women dance round the new house, the poor house, the house that stands in a narrow street where omnibuses pass and the street hawkers cry their wares, and let them sing, 'We have done with war! We have done with tyranny!'" (*TG*, 83).

The difference between Eleanor's London and Kitty's London is most apparent in Eleanor's walk through the city streets following her tea with Kitty. It is in the working-class quarter of the city that Eleanor feels most comfortable; she feels distinctly uncomfortable dining at the large, garish restaurant where people play at being "some rich man," some "Lady-this-or-that in the illustrated papers" (*B*, 248). In fact, as one critic has pointed out, many of the Pargiter women choose an area of London just like that through which Eleanor strolls in which to make their homes, and in so doing they shape the social and political vision of the novel, drawing it "furthest away from the paths trod out by men," the typical milieu of the family chronicle, "toward other visions and other realities."[26]

Woolf first wrote about that alternative city as background, in "Street Haunting" and *The London Scene*. In *The Years* her achievement was to people it—with Eleanor, Maggie, Rose, and Sara Pargiter—and to illuminate its goals: to "have done with war . . . have done with tyranny" (*TG*, 33). As the theologian Paul Tillich explained, a city not only could influence the character of one human being (as Woolf showed it doing to Rose Pargiter in "1880," through its restrictions in response to street love), but it could shape the very nature of human society as a whole, making it either hospitable or hostile to unfamiliar people and experiences:

> The anti-provincial experience furnished by the metropolis is typified by encounters with that which is strange. Meeting the

> strange can have two consequences. It can produce hate against the strange, and usually against the stranger, because its existence threatens the self-certainty of the familiar. Or it can afford the courage to question the familiar. In the metropolis, it is impossible to remove the strange and the stranger, because every neighbor is mostly a stranger. Thus the second alternative of questioning the familiar ordinarily prevails.
>
> There are ways, however, to avoid questioning the familiar. One is to shun the strange. All forms of totalitarianism try to avoid the strange, the problematic, the critical, the rational. To do so, they must deny the metropolitan spirit. . . .[27]

In this second "enormous chunk" Eleanor and Kitty enact the two possible responses to "meeting the strange": Eleanor asserts that she loves the city because "the people are so interesting," and Kitty, whose entire perception of life is dedicated to denying change, asserts vehemently that she hates the city. Eleanor questions man's familiar lust for power, in her conversation with Nicholas about "power, patriotism, love, sex and all the rest of it," while Kitty accepts the desire for power as "human nature" (*B*, 243). Kitty's future plans—to move from London to the north of England—represent not just a denial of the metropolitan spirit but an escape from the metropolis itself.

In acknowledging the affirmative perspective on city life revealed in Eleanor Pargiter's thoughts in "1921," it is important not to overstate the case. Eleanor's freedom to walk alone through the "foreign quarter" of London, where the shops "had French and Italian names over them . . . sold maccaroni [*sic*] . . . sold red rubber tubes," to dine alone if she wishes and to "finish her evening at a picture palace" if she so chooses, represents a considerable advance over the hedged-in life she lived as a child at Abercorn Terrace (*B*, 245, 249). Yet the position of women is not completely satisfactory in postwar London, nor have class distinctions been wholly eradicated. During her dinner Eleanor thinks with irritation of the "large company," with "branches all over London," that dictates such an opulent and unsatisfying menu in a restaurant whose decor combines "the arches of Buckingham Palace and the Alhambra" (*B*, 248). The waitress who serves her is burdened under more dishes than she should have to carry, Eleanor notices, and she smiles only automatically, and only when Eleanor tips her. The young couple on their evening out sit dully, without talking. Everywhere Eleanor meets evidence of the passive, conventional, sheeplike character of her fellow citizens. Faced with this vision of London, she mentally recants on her earlier assertion to Kitty: "She had turned to Kitty and said, 'I like people—they're so interesting.' And that was a lie, she said: the kind of lie she hated most; the becoming pose—she who had said that she did not pose. The lie that makes one out a lover of one's kind, she thought. . . . And I don't love them, she thought. . . . I hate them. There they still were, eating. There they all were, staring passively at their food. I despise them, she thought" (*B*, 249). The Londoners whom Eleanor despises respond to the unfamiliar experience of restaurant dining just as Kitty does to her unfamiliar state as a widow in London; they attempt to deny it. Insulating themselves by choosing a restaurant where the food is predictable and the decor derivative, they further hide from the experience by carrying on desultory conversations or sitting in silence.

The numbed passivity of Eleanor's fellow diners demonstrates that even citydwellers are vulnerable to the lure of the safely familiar; preferring security to the risk of unfamiliar experience, they may remove the mystery from city life—and lose their urban freedom. Paul Tillich has observed that when "the big city is sliced into pieces, each of which is observed, purged and equalized," then the "freedom of the metropolis" is endangered.[28] Eleanor's distasteful vision of the garish restaurant shows us the big city writ small: each section of the menu is sliced into pieces, which are purged of any sensuous appeal and equalized in unappetizing portions, and provided not for personal pleasure but for conspicuous consumption under the observation of the other diners. In objecting to that spirit, Eleanor demonstrates her own willingness to question the familiar, to act as what Tillich called a "prophet of attack," unsettling her fellow citizens' complacency in order to find a way to "live more naturally . . . better" (*TY*, 296).[29] Eleanor learns during her dinner that it is still frighteningly possible to choose the opposite way of life: to insulate oneself from the demands of postwar society, to "shun the strange," to take refuge in the automatism that makes this restaurant scene, like Woolf's portrait of wartime London in "1917," so chilling.

The Published Version of *The Years*: Pillar Boxes and Bridges

When Woolf deleted those "two enormous chunks" from the galley proofs of *The Years*, she was making the last of a number of revisions undertaken during more than four years of intensive rewriting.[30] Abandoned first, along with the essay portions of the novel, had been the explicit discussion of woman's social situation as shaped by street love; abandoned later, along with the "1910," "1917," and "1921" material, had been the brilliant urban image for a feminist civilization, the analysis of the causes of World War I, and the analysis of the relationship between a society's treatment of women and its international politics. However, Woolf retained in both the imagery and plot of *The Years* her interest in the political implications of one's response to unfamiliar people and experiences, as well as her highly condensed use of urban images to embody her original interest in the "sexual life of women" (*D*, IV: 6). Although she finally deleted the image of Cleopatra's Needle and the survey of London presented during Eleanor Pargiter's walk in "1921," she retained the positive implications of those later visions of a more feminist city, adding to her awareness of London's oppressive potential a consciousness of its liberating possibilities as well.

Woolf's reasons for deleting the factual sections of *The Years* were complex.[31] As she wrote in 1937 to Stephen Spender, "I've had to leave out one whole section which I could not revise in time for the press. . . . The theme was too ambitious. . . . I expect I muted down the characters too much, in order to shorten and keep their faces towards society; and altogether muffed the proportions: which should have given a round, not a thin line" (*L*, VI: 116). While Woolf clearly revised both for fear that the novel was far too long and under the pressure of her publisher's deadline, still her deletions also suggest an intentional shift toward indirection.[32]

Juxtaposing a changing city to a changing society, *The Years* conveys the nature of women's political, social, sexual, and economic lives over more than half a century, from 1880 to "Present Day" (1937). The published novel contains none of the penetrating factual analysis of women's conditions in Victorian London that makes *The Pargiters* such a fascinating social document for contemporary readers. Instead, it relies upon urban images to convey the same information in fiction, dramatically, indirectly, and—most importantly—uncoercively. In its published version *The Years* reflects "aesthetic principles that are the opposite of fascist," as Margaret Comstock has pointed out.

> It has no center or central figure around which subordinate elements can be arranged. The reader cannot possibly surrender to the glamour of a life that seems more elevated than one's own. The way the novel is written discourages a reader's inclination to "march in step after a leader"—a phrase central to *The Years*. There is no character whose life is captivating; the author's voice is unusually unobtrusive; there is not even any "beautiful prose." [*B*, 254]

Instead, *The Years* practices the politics it refuses to preach—embodying its feminist insights in its characters, its events, and (most interesting for our purposes) its urban imagery. The novel reveals the shift in women's social situation by a corresponding change in its urban setting; the Pargiter women move from the private homes of middle- and upper-class London to simple rooms in noisy streets near the Thames.

Rather than explicitly considering women's oppression in late-Victorian and modern London, in the novel's published version Woolf used aspects of the urban setting to exemplify women's situation, both by linking episodes exploring related themes, and by embodying directly the coercive or liberating forces affecting women. For example, she used the images of pillar box and bridge to illustrate the two significant sorts of female fellowship between 1880 and 1937, the pillar box marking the community of female oppression resulting from street love, and the bridge expressing the new fellowship of women based on the shared feminist vision of a better world.

The pillar-box image appeared first in Woolf's speech to the London/National Society for Women's Service, which formed the inspiration for *The Years*.[33] In that speech the pillar box marked the boundary between the private and public worlds, between the dependent position of a woman in the patriarchal home and the freedom of money and a room of one's own. To the difficulties faced by many women (among them Dame Ethel Smyth) in finding a place in the professions, Woolf contrasted her own relative ease at becoming a writer, the result, she claimed ironically, of "the cheapness of writing materials" (*P*, xxviii). All a woman need do to become a writer, she told her audience, is to follow the example of the girl in her story:

> You have only got to figure to yourselves a girl [*sitting and writing*] <in a bed-room with a pen in her hand> a girl who had plenty of pens and paper at command. Then it occurred to her to do what again only costs a penny stamp—to [*send*] <slip> an article [*on to a newspaper*] <into a pillar-box>; and to suggest to the editor of that newspaper that she might be allowed to try her hand at reviewing a . . . book. [*P*, xxix]

"Hence I became a reviewer," Woolf told her audience in 1931. Yet, as her speech went on to explain, something so seemingly uncomplicated as the walk to the pillar box with envelope in hand was actually fraught with difficulties. Not only did the aspiring writer have to grind out reviews on Mrs. Humphry Ward and her ilk, but in order to do so she had to vanquish the "villain in the piece"—not, "I grieve to say, our old friend [*Man*] <the other sex—>" but "the Angel in the house," woman's own internalized "ideal of womanhood" (*P*, xxix, xxx). The first association of the pillar box in *The Years* is to professional work—and to the struggle against male oppression and female repression that makes such work so difficult for women—just as in Woolf's speech.

In addition to standing for the obstacles confronting women when they attempt to enter the professional world, the pillar box is also associated with another boundary in *The Years*. A conjunction of phallic and imperialistic symbolism, with its pillar shape and its raised insignia of royal power, that red box first teaches Rose Pargiter the political and social implications of her sexuality. When she is terrified by the exhibitionist standing beside it, during her forbidden trip to Lamley's shop that night in 1880, Rose learns about the restrictions on women "necessary" to protect them from such manifestations of street love. While the pillar box appears first in a discussion of female self-expression (Woolf's speech describing her experiences as a woman writer), in this episode from *The Years* it is associated with prohibitions against speech, particularly speech about sexuality. The episode at the pillar box cloisters off certain areas of Rose's mind: she cannot tell her sister what she saw, and she can scarcely admit it to herself. Rose herself has become the "besieged garrison" of her adventure fantasy; the man at the pillar box, whom she rightly intuits to be "the enemy," not only holds her captive at home (through the restrictions on female movement instituted in response to street love) but has invaded, and now controls, her mind.[34]

In addition to the pillar box's associations to work and sexuality, there is a third association, to education. That issue is embodied first in a ritual Eleanor remembers on the night her mother dies. She has written to her brother Edward, and Morris offers to post her letter for her:

> He got up as if he were glad to have something to do. Eleanor went to the front door with him and stood holding it open while he went to the pillar-box . . . Morris disappeared under the shadows round the corner. She remembered how she used to stand at the door when he was a small boy and went to a day school with a satchel in his hand. She used to wave to him; and when he got to the corner he always turned and waved back. It was a curious little ceremony, dropped now that they were both grown up. [*TY*, 44]

Perhaps the ceremony has been dropped because it has served its purpose: after years of preparation, Eleanor has accepted her place in the home. That night, upon her mother's death, she takes on the role of housekeeper for her father. Also a result of that obsolete little ceremony is the suppressed emotion that troubles Morris, for the ritual embodies the system that has suppressed the lives and emotions of the female half of the family. Finally, the ceremony is responsible for the distance that has grown up between Eleanor and Morris, for it also embodies the distinction between the scantiness or nonexistence of education available to women and the thoroughness of education given to (middle- or upper-class) men. As Woolf would go on to write of this distinction in *Three Guineas*, it is a "precipice, a gulf so deeply cut" between the female and the male that she wonders whether "it is any use trying to speak across it" (*TG*, 4). Education equips Morris to enter the public world of the bar; without it, Eleanor must stay at home or do volunteer work with families like the Levys. Finally, Eleanor's sketchy self-education keeps her from asking questions about Morris's work from fear of seeming silly, and he, in turn, no longer shares his thoughts with her:

> Ought she not to have said Lord Chief Justice? She never could remember which was which: and that was why he would not discuss Evans v. Carter with her.

> She never told him about the Levys either, except by way of a joke. That was the worst of growing up, she thought; they couldn't share things as they used to share them. When they met they never had time to talk as they used to talk—about things in general—they always talked about facts—little facts. [*TY*, 34]

The gulf that separates men and women—created by limitations on women's education—makes it more complicated for them to communicate, because it discourages the speaker and makes hearing more difficult for the listener.

With its triple associations to professional, sexual, and educational oppression, in the published version of *The Years* the pillar box embodies the demarcation between the male, public world (where educational, professional, and sexual experiences are available) and the female, private world (where educational, professional, and sexual experiences are strictly curtailed, with men rationing money and social contacts). Furthermore, Woolf uses the pillar box to convey the effect of these restrictions in a passage in "Present Day." Eleanor and Peggy Pargiter take a taxi to a family party, and as the taxi passes Abercorn Terrace, Eleanor and Peggy look at the "imposing unbroken avenue with its succession of pale pillars and steps" (*TY*, 332). Thinking of her childhood, Eleanor murmurs, "Abercorn Terrace. . . . The pillar box." Although Peggy doesn't understand Eleanor's association, she soon seems to have made a similar one: "Was it that you were suppressed when you were young?" she asks Eleanor (*TY*, 335). In an image that combines the three associations of the pillar box, Eleanor remembers "A picture—another picture—had swum to the surface. There was Delia standing in the middle of the room; Oh, my God! Oh, my God! she was saying; a hansom cab had stopped at the house next door; and she herself was watching Morris—was it Morris?—going down the street to post a letter" (*TY*, 335–36). Although Eleanor had no way of knowing the pillar box's associations for her sister Rose (who had been unable to tell her of the episode of exhibitionism there), the picture of her suppression as a young girl includes those limitations that the pillar box placed upon women by dividing social life into male and female zones. In an earlier version of this scene, in *The Pargiters*, Woolf elaborated upon Delia's feelings to show the interconnections between sexual, social, and psychological freedoms.

Delia, despairing, says, "Oh, my God!" because she sees a woman wheeling a baby carriage, and that image of her own probable future makes her realize that she will never be allowed to travel to Germany to study music (*P*, 36). Eleanor's "Present Day" memory of watching Morris post the letter recalls the triad of restrictions that settled upon her with her mother's death, the event that freed Delia and the other Pargiter sisters from the home while it left Eleanor as spinster housekeeper.

While Woolf used the pillar-box image in *The Years* to embody women's limitations in late-Victorian England, she used another urban image to suggest the city's role in opening up women's possibilities. Like the pillar box, the bridge image first appeared in the talk to Pippa Strachey's group, the London/National Society for Women's Service. Discussing those obstacles to a writing profession that she had faced as a young woman, Woolf compared herself to the preceding speaker, who "built bridges and thus made a way for those who came after her." Speaking of Dame Ethel Smyth, Woolf explained, "We honor her not merely as a musician and a writer, but also as a blaster of rocks and the maker of bridges. It seems sometimes a pity that a woman who only wished to write music should have been forced also to make bridges, but that was part of her job and she did it" (*P*, xxviii). In *The Years*, as in the speech from which the novel sprang, woman's talent, and her job, is bridgebuilding. In fact, the image appears in some of the earliest childhood memories of Eleanor Pargiter, suggesting society's role in instilling the bridgebuilding talent in women. Just as the novel was nursed to life by Pippa Strachey's request that Woolf speak to her women's organization, so the fellowship of women that is one of the novel's themes is revealed in nursery rhymes sung by the Pargiters' old nurse, Pippy. The rhymes are evocative in themselves, but what is even more significant is that they vary: Pippy sings a different song depending upon the sex of her listener. While to Martin she sings "The King of Spain's daughter/Came to visit me/All for the sake of/My silver nutmeg tree," to Eleanor she sings "Sur le pont/d'Avignon," as the song continues, "l'on y danse, toute en ronde." Martin's song suggests his role of sexual and economic superiority; in it he commands the attention of the King of Spain's daughter because of his wealth, embodied by a silver nutmeg tree. The curious image is revealing: the nutmeg, called the pasha of spices, grew in rows like a harem, one male tree for every ten female trees. Male sexual and political domination are both associated with the nutmeg tree, for many (male) wars were fought for possession of lands planted with these valuable spice harems.[35] While Martin's exotic possession (the nutmeg tree) thus defines his economic, political, and sexual dominion, the woman in his nursery rhyme is defined by her powerful male relative, the King of Spain. In the fantasy world of Martin's nursery rhyme, as in reality, the woman's role is ancillary; the excitement of being visited by the King of Spain's daughter, one assumes, lies in the political implications of such a visit.

Whereas the song Pippy sings to Martin embodies a type of personal hymn to money and power, the song she sings Eleanor instead emphasizes the qualities of discontinuity, change, and movement in the circle dance on the bridge of Avignon. By the time she wrote *Three Guineas* Woolf would use the bridge image to express the impossible choice facing women, between the oppressions of the private world and the different oppressions of the public world. She imagines the

> daughters of educated men . . . between the devil and the deep sea. Behind us lies the patriarchal system; the private house, with its nullity, its immorality, its hypocrisy, its servility. Before us lies the public world, the professional system, with its possessiveness, its jealousy, its pugnacity, its greed. The one shuts us up like slaves in a harem; the other forces us to circle, like caterpillars head to tail, round and round the mulberry tree, the sacred tree, of property. It is a choice of evils. Each is bad. Had we not better plunge off the bridge into the river; give up the game; declare that the whole of human life is a mistake and so end it? [*TG*, 74]

But in *The Years* the nursery rhyme that Pippy sings to Eleanor accurately represents the experience of most of the Pargiter women, who are learning in various ways to leave the tyrannies of the private home behind them but have not yet—with the exception of Peggy Pargiter—experienced the different tyrannies of the public world. Most of the women in *The Years* choose to dance on the bridge, rather than to jump from it—sometimes in a dance of liberated sexuality, such as Rose's lesbianism or Maggie's happy marriage; sometimes in a dance of mysticism or friendship, like Sally's or Eleanor's. Building bridges beyond the private home, extending the concept of family to include friends of several generations and nationalities, Eleanor learns to live happily as an independent woman after more than half a lifetime of selfless attendance to her father's needs. Marrying a Frenchman, Renny, Maggie bridges nationalities despite her Aunt Celia's reservations: "'Everybody says he's a very nice fellow . . . But René—René,' her accent was bad, '—it doesn't sound like a man's name'" (*TY*, 206). Sara bridges the ordinary world and the spiritual world with her mystical visions, so that a simple walk to a suffrage meeting reveals a vision of human mortality:

> "And what did you do with Rose?" said Maggie . . . Sara turned and glanced at her. Then she began to play again. "Stood on the bridge and looked into the water," she murmured.
>
> "Stood on the bridge and looked into the water," she hummed, in time to the music. "Running water; flowing water. May my bones turn to coral; and fish light their lanthorns; fish light their green lanthorns in my eyes." [*TY*, 186]

Perhaps most of all, Rose—modeled on that indefatigable bridgebuilder Ethel Smyth—builds bridges between women by her work as a suffragist. In fact, a bridge image explains how Rose gained the psychological and social liberty to do suffrage work. In 1910 she descends from an omnibus to walk across one of the Thames bridges, and she catches a glimpse of herself reflected in the window of a tailor's shop:

> It was a pity, she thought . . . not to dress better, not to look nicer. Always reach-me-downs, coats and skirts from Whiteley's. But they saved time, and the years after all—she was over forty—made one care very little what people thought. They used to say, why don't you marry? Why don't you do this or that, interfering. But not any longer.
>
> She paused in one of the little alcoves that were scooped out in the bridge, from habit . . . As she stood there, looking down at the water, some buried feeling began to arrange the stream into a pattern. The pattern was painful. She remembered how she had stood there on the night of a certain engagement, crying; her tears had fallen, her happiness, it seemed to her, had fallen. Then she had turned—here she turned—and had seen the churches, the masts and roofs of the city. There's *that*, she had said to herself. Indeed it was a splendid view . . . There

House of Parliament (from General Lew Wallace, ed., Scenes From Every Land *[Springfield, Ohio: Mast, Crowell & Kirkpatrick, 1893]. p. 29).*

> were the Houses of Parliament. A queer expression, half frown, half smile, formed on her face and she threw herself slightly backwards, as if she were leading an army. [*TY*, 161]

In 1941 Woolf would argue that one of the causes of war lay in women's willingness to take on the role of "slaves," which she epitomized in the image of "painted women; dressed-up women; women with crimson lips and crimson fingernails" gazing with vain pleasure at their reflections in shop windows (*DM*, 245). "They are slaves who are trying to enslave," she wrote of such women. Yet with her reach-me-down and ready-made clothes, Rose Pargiter is no slave trying to enslave. Instead, she has ceased to care about what people think of her—thus saving not only her time, but also her autonomy. No interfering friends now suggest that she marry; instead, she is free to devote herself wholly to the suffrage cause. As Rose stands looking down on the Thames, she remembers an earlier night when she had stood on the same bridge, crying—perhaps for a failed love affair—and then chosen to devote herself to the suffrage movement. At that moment, she remembers, the splendid view from the Thames bridge—of the Houses of Parliament, where the Conciliation Bill was soon to be debated, and where the suffrage movement was very much alive albeit as a controversial issue—provided her with compensation for her pain. It was then, the bridge image suggests, that she pledged herself to work for suffrage, and so took on the mingled pleasure and responsibility of an "army" of followers. Even Rose's term for her enlistment in the fellowship of women working for a better world conveys Woolf's subtle factual grounding to the fiction *The Years*, for it echoes Emmeline Pankhurst, who in 1912 described the Women's Social and Political Union as "simply a suffrage army in the field."[36] Furthermore, in its union of suffragist concerns with a militaristic metaphor, this bridge image embodies one of the main themes of *The Years*, which Woolf later treated separately in *Three Guineas*: the relationship between war and the oppression of women.

In using a pillar box and a bridge to convey her analysis of women's changing position in late-Victorian and modern London, Woolf has chosen objects imbued with both personal and historical significance. But since her own personal experience (posting her first article at a pillar box), like historical events (from the traditional song "London Bridge is falling down" to the pillar-box bombings of the suffragists), ran the risk of being either too arcane or too quotidian to establish the pattern of references necessary for the indirect presentation of her political analysis, she has carefully embedded in *The Years* a number of significant episodes and memories in which these objects figure. As a result pillar boxes and bridges interlace the novel's characters and events in important ways. These two urban objects come to stand as central images of women's experience in this revisionary feminist family chronicle. The pillar box links the episodes of professional, sexual, and educational limitations suffered by the Pargiter women, while the bridge image (with its echo of the bridgebuilding talent of Dame Ethel Smyth) embodies women's in-between social position, as they moved from the private home to the public world.

Woolf claimed *A Room of One's Own* and *Night and Day* as the significant precursors of *The Years* in her diary entries of 1931 and 1932. While the novel's focus on women's struggle to combine sexual and professional lives in modern London obviously recalls *Night and Day* (as does its realistic style), *The Years* ultimately presents a more optimistic picture of the outcome of that struggle. To be sure, Peggy Pargiter begins the novel's concluding party in a bitterly self-conscious and disillusioned mood, yet in the course of the evening she achieves a rapprochement of sorts

London Bridge (from General Lew Wallace, ed., Scenes From Every Land *[Springfield, Ohio: Mast, Crowell & Kirkpatrick, 1893], p. 27).*

with her brother North (including his promise to bring a current girlfriend around to meet her), is praised for her intellect by her teacher in her father's hearing, and shares with her brother a vision of "living differently" (*TY*, 423). Moreover, *The Years* closes with an image of the dawn whose rhetorical thrust is unmistakably optimistic: "The sun had risen, and the sky above the houses wore an air of extraordinary beauty, simplicity and peace" (*TY*, 435).

Yet there are several ways in which this lengthy family chronicle, so clearly a reiteration of the style and themes familiar from the similarly realistic novel *Night and Day*, also recalls the slim essay *A Room of One's Own*. Like the latter work, *The Years*, too, depends upon urban images both to describe the situation of women in patriarchal London and to prescribe a feminist utopia, as variously imagined by Rose (as a suffragist), Maggie and Sara (in both the draft version and the published chapter of "1910"), or Eleanor and Peggy (in "Present Day"). Finally, just as *A Room of One's Own* relies upon a delicately choreographed convergence of man, woman, and taxicab to suggest the ideal balance of human relations, both sexes mirroring each other reciprocally, so *The Years* ends with a strikingly similar urban image expressing optimism about the future of human society. Eleanor "was watching the cab. A young man had got out; he paid the driver. Then a girl in a tweed travelling suit followed him. He fitted his latch-key to the door. 'There,' Eleanor murmured, as he opened the door and they stood for a moment on the threshold. 'There!' she repeated as the door shut with a little thud behind them" (*TY*, 434).

What emerges with study and comparison of the city's image in draft and published versions of *The Years* is a shift from a didactic to a dramatic treatment of patriarchal society, as Woolf more and more imbeds her social criticism in the lived texture of city life. Furthermore, it becomes clear that not only did Woolf's use of urban imagery change as she evolved new ways to convey the scope of women's urban experience, but her perspective on the nature of city life also broadened. From the stress on the fellowship of women created by oppression, in *The Pargiters*, she moved in the later drafts (and later chapters) of *The Years* to an appreciation of the city's role in opening up possibilities to women: from a room of one's own free from the demands of a tyrannical father (even if in a shabby lodging-house south of the river) to a taxi ride through twilight London with one's niece, a doctor. As the novel approaches "Present Day," it more and more reveals another sort of fellowship among women, exemplified by but not wholly comprised of the suffrage movement. Whereas Woolf embodies this new vision of a feminist fellowship in the deleted portions, first in her image of Cleopatra's Needle, then in the portrait of Eleanor Pargiter in the "two enormous chunks" deleted from "1917" and "1921," she gave it full expression, and in a style demanding reader participation consonant with her anti-authoritarian political vision, in her use of bridge imagery in the published novel.

While it would be an exaggeration to say that Woolf presents an exclusively positive portrait of women's position in modern London, it would be a similar distortion to overlook the optimistic elements in her vision. In her use of the city as a gauge of a culture's essential character, Woolf departs from both the political isolationism and the pessimism of *Night and Day*. Instead, she mingles two thematic and historical undercurrents in *The Years*: the threat of totalitarianism, and the possibility of liberation for women—the one so deeply pessimistic, the other so hopeful. The novel ends in a strange song, sung to the assembled Pargiters by Cockney twins who seem to exemplify the novel's double urban character. The song is both beautiful and disconcerting, for, like the city from which it springs, it is neither static, conclusive, nor coercive. Rather, inspiring questions, it moves people to turn to each other for the answers: "'But it was . . .' Eleanor began. She stopped. What was it? As they stood there they had looked so dignified; yet they had made this hideous noise. The contrast between their faces and their voices was astonishing; it was impossible to find one word for the whole. 'Beautiful?' she said, with a note of interrogation, turning to Maggie" (*TY*, 430, 431).

CHAPTER EIGHT

"I WILL NOT CEASE FROM MENTAL FIGHT"

Two diary entries from the spring of 1939 suggest the style and itinerary of Woolf's city rambles during the final years of her life.

> *January 30th, 1939*
> Took the bus to Southwark Bridge—Walked along Thames Street;—saw a flight of steps down to the river—I climbed down—a rope at the bottom—Found the strand of the Thames, under the warehouses . . . very slippery; warehouse walks crusted, weedy, worn—The river must cover them at high tide—it was now low. People on the Bridge stared Difficult walking—a rat haunted, riverine place, great chains, wooden pillars, green slime, bricks corroded, a button hook thrown up by the tide. A bitter cold wind. Thought of the refugees from Barcelona walking 40 miles, one with a baby in a parcel.

> *April 29th, 1939*
> But what are the interesting things? I'm thinking of what I should like to read here in 10 years time. And I'm all at sea. Perhaps literal facts. The annal, not the novel. Yesterday I went out in a fur coat, for it was bitter cold, to walk in London. I stopped at the [Tower?] Church; there were photographers—Soon the Bride arrived—the car glided on. There were too many cars behind. Mother & small page arrived: 2 girls in absurd little boat hats. They helped the Bride with her veil—"Can you get it over my bouquet?" She asked—very gay: rather red; very slim. Husband & best man waiting in grey trousers & cutaway coats. Old sitters in the sun watching. Camera men—a little procession—rather skimpy & cold & not very rich I thought. The old man—my age—had shabby boots. . . . Then I walked along the embankment up into the fur

> quarter behind Blackfriars—Men in white coats aparelled [*sic*] in silver fox skins—A smell of fur—Found some old City Company houses—one the Inn Keeper Company—Also a green plant bursting out of a factory . . . Bought a paper with Hitler's speech—Read it on top of Bus Inconclusive—Cut up in stop press. Everyone reading it—even newspaper sellers, a great proof of interest.

In the exploration of the worlds of workers and warehouses, of loving couples and clashing nations, these prewar diaries attest to what Brenda Silver has demonstrated: that Woolf's interest in "the relationship between hierarchy, patriarchy, fascism and war" did not end with *The Years*, her novel charting the decline of the British Empire.[1] Nor did her reliance on the urban environment to raise those issues end with that lengthy London family chronicle. In *Three Guineas* (1938), as in these prewar diary entries, each element of the city scene is selected with an eye to what it reveals of gender, class, and international relations. To understand the meaning of the city in Woolf's final years, we must begin, then, with *Three Guineas*.

Woolf thought of that essay as "a sequel to *A Room of One's Own*." Its origins lie also in the richly urban textures of *The Years*, from which the essay split off in January 1933.[2] To *Three Guineas*, as to both of its antecedents, the city is both thematically and stylistically central. The essay scathingly indicts patriarchal society for causing war, dramatically portraying male, public life in all of its possessiveness, competition, hierarchy, and ritual, as it appears to women "from the threshold of the private house."

> At first sight it is enormously impressive. Within quite a small space are crowded together St. Paul's, the Bank of England, the Mansion House, the massive if funereal battlements of the Law Courts; and on the other side, Westminster Abbey and the Houses of Parliament. There, we say to ourselves, pausing, in this moment of transition on the bridge, our fathers and brothers have spent their lives . . . It is from this world that the private house (somewhere, roughly speaking, in the West End) has derived its creeds, its laws, its clothes and carpets, its beef and mutton. [*TG*, 18–19]

Not only does *Three Guineas* use urban images to embody the sources of war in patriarchal society, but in calling women to resist war and fascism by abandoning that society the essay uses the city landscape to dramatize the power women can wield against both war and male domination. The female energy that "opposed itself to the force of the fathers" is so powerful, Woolf implies, that its use transforms the very face of London: "it was a force of tremendous power. It forced open the doors of the private house. It opened Bond Street and Piccadilly . . . it shrivelled flounces and stays; it made the oldest profession in the world . . . unprofitable" (*TG*, 138). Once women play a part in the public world, in other words, they need no longer sell their bodies for money; they need no longer decorate themselves to attract men. Whole sectors of the city that once depended for profit on such decoration or sale must now adapt to women not as objects, but as agents in public life. In its treatment of the city *Three Guineas* leads the reader to one inescapable conclusion: "that the public and the private worlds are inseparably connected; that the tyrannies and servilities of the one are the tyrannies and servilities of the other"—in short, that war and the oppression of women in the home spring from the same source (*TG*, 142).

In "Thoughts on Peace in an Air Raid," the important brief pamphlet published only two years after *Three Guineas*, Woolf went on to advance a highly condensed analysis of that common source of war and women's oppression. Borrowing from Lady Astor, she named it "subconscious Hitlerism."[3] As in *Three Guineas*, Woolf uses scenes of city life to dramatize her argument, finding the evidence of "subconscious Hitlerism" on a typical commercial street:

> subconscious Hitlerism . . . is the desire for aggression; the desire to dominate and enslave. Even in the darkness we can see that made visible. We can see shop windows blazing; and women gazing; painted women; dressed-up women; women with crimson lips and crimson fingernails. They are slaves who are trying to enslave. If we could free ourselves from slavery we should free men from tyranny. Hitlers are bred by slaves. [*DM*, 245]

Yet while Woolf is returning to her investigation of the links between pacifism and the struggle for freedom in which women, among others, are engaged, she now takes a new approach to the problem. In *Three Guineas* Woolf argued that scornful indifference to male aggression was women's best course of action, but

Bloomsbury Square in 1940 (from Pictures Collection, New York Public Library).

by the time she wrote "Thoughts on Peace" her position was more complex.[4] She argued that women and men must work together to combat "subconscious Hitlerism": in order to "switch off" man's "instinct" for aggression—by which Woolf meant an urge nurtured by centuries of socialization, "fostered and cherished by education and tradition"—women must "compensate the man for the loss of his gun" (*DM*, 247). Women must reeducate men away from aggression, Woolf argues, by creating "more honorable activities for those who try to conquer in themselves their fighting instinct" (*DM*, 247). One way this can be done, the essay implies, is for women to abandon their exclusive rights over mothering and, instead, to let men into the circle of the private home and into the emotions bred therein: nurturance, compassion, creativity, happiness (*DM*, 247–48).

"Thoughts on Peace" boldly redefines not only the social

meaning of gender but also the concept of militancy. Whereas fighting was unacceptable to Woolf when she wrote *Three Guineas*, by the time of "Thoughts on Peace" she had come to think of "fight" more broadly, in a way that made it correspond to her feminism and pacifism:

> there is another way of fighting for freedom without arms; we can fight with the mind. We can make ideas that will help the young Englishman who is fighting up in the sky to defeat the enemy . . . Are we not leaving the young Englishman without a weapon that might be of value to him if we give up private thinking, tea-table thinking, because it seems useless? . . . . "I will not cease from mental fight," Blake wrote. Mental fight means thinking against the current, not with it. [*DM*, 244]

Woolf has in this essay tellingly redefined the concept of patriotic battle, so that now to struggle *against the current of oppression*, at home or abroad, becomes a patriotic act. In revising the battle metaphor, Woolf reflected her reading of Freud's *Group Psychology and the Analysis of the Ego* in 1939. Her reading notes suggest that the work led her to think of war as a battle between aspects of the human psyche.[5] One passage associates "woman's coming of age economically in 1918 with her simultaneous awareness of man's fighting instinct," and the notes go on to elaborate this link between the growth of feminism and a new female concern over male aggression:[6] "The present war is very different. For now the male has also considered his attributes in Hitler, & is fighting against them. Is this the first time in history that a sex has turned against its own specific qualities? Compare with the woman movement."[7] Woolf calls for "mental fight" as a way to aid the Englishman because, as she sees it, the issue is largely a mental one: male aggressive instincts are at war with the creative, nurturing, healing qualities associated with the female psyche. Woolf urges women to join the battle, armed with their "private thinking, tea-table thinking," in order to teach men another way of being.

Yet the essay implies that women must join the battle not only to help men, but also to help themselves, for the fascist oppression that men are battling abroad is also the sexist oppression that women fight at home: "We are equally prisoners tonight—the Englishmen in their planes, the Englishwomen in their beds" (*DM*, 245). For both, the enemy is the same: "'Hitler!' the loudspeakers cry with one voice. Who is Hitler? What is he? Aggressiveness, tyranny, the insane love of power made manifest . . . Destroy that, and you will be free" (*DM*, 245).[8] In her notes and letters Woolf expanded on this redefinition of patriotism to include both resistance to male aggression and affirmation of the creative impulse. She wrote in her jottings for "Thoughts on Peace," "For Outsider: news. manufacture of toy soldiers for the buttonhole: to balance white feathers."[9] The terse entry suggests that toy soldiers could be given out, as a shaming symbol of one's unpatriotic addiction to power and domination, to balance the current practice of handing white feathers to men in civilian dress. And in a letter written when the bombardment of London had forced her to leave the city permanently for refuge at Rodmell, Woolf's identification with London prompted her to redefine the term "patriotism" to include a loyalty to the masculine British literary tradition that the city embodied. To her good friend Dame Ethel Smyth she wrote, "How odd it is being a countrywoman after all these years of being Cockney! For almost the first time in my life I've not a bed in London . . . You never shared my passion for that great city. Yet its what, in some odd corner of my dreaming mind, represents Chaucer, Shakespeare, Dickens. It's my only patriotism" (*L*, VI: 460). Not only did Chaucer, Shakespeare, and Dickens help to fuel Woolf's "passion" for "that great city," but, as this passage shows, London also gave her a common ground of experience that enabled her to claim a place in the literary tradition they embodied.

In "Thoughts on Peace" Woolf evokes the British literary tradition by citing William Blake. Furthermore, the city is central to the patriotic act that she draws on Blake's "Milton" to endorse: continual "mental fight":

> I will not cease from Mental Fight,
> Nor shall my Sword sleep in my hand
> Till we have built Jerusalem
> In England's green & pleasant Land.[10]

As Raymond Williams has convincingly demonstrated, Blake's urban image exists within a lengthy and rich British literary tradition: "The city had long had a symbolic dimension, most powerfully in the religious image of the Holy City, the City of God. In a variant of this mode, William Blake saw London . . . and wanted to build Jerusalem."[11] Yet whereas Blake's celestial city is modeled—as its name indicates—along the patriarchal lines of Christian revelation, the celestial city for which Woolf urges us to fight in "Thoughts on Peace" is vividly anti-patriarchal: its men have renounced both their glory and their guns, and its women have relinquished the privileges of the home—among them, their possessive "maternal instinct" (*DM*, 247).

Borrowing Blake's city image, Woolf revises it to accommodate her feminist, pacifist vision. This two-part act of assimilation and revision exemplifies the major strategy of Woolf's literary career, for a reshaping of the city's meaning—both as an actual place and as a literary image—was central to her development as an artist. In her earliest years Woolf saw the city as a competitive environment that excluded her and that stressed hierarchy, property, and patriarchy. Yet her mature work portrays the city as an environment holding out the possibility of a feminist, egalitarian society. This transformation was made possible only by Woolf's assertive appropriation and transmutation of masculine cultural and literary forms. Thus, in her early novel *Night and Day*, Woolf worked within the traditional conceptions of city life. Assimilating Fielding's model of the classic city novel, dominated by the urban spiral journey of an adventuresome young man, Woolf then rang changes on the plot and character to express her implicit critique of Fielding's urban vision. *Mrs. Dalloway* continued that revision by questioning the conventional division of urban space into a public male realm and a private female realm. There Woolf used the urban environment to explore links between the position of women such as Clarissa Dalloway in the private home and the experience of men such as Septimus Smith, Richard Dalloway, and Peter Walsh in the public worlds of war and politics. *Flush* presents several challenges to conventional views of the city. Not only is the novel an unexpectedly canine perspective on city life, thereby unsettling a human-centered value system, but in its Whitechapel chapter the novel explores the links between wealth and poverty denied in the modern metropolis. *Flush* raises the possibility that London may be not the most but instead the least civilized city, if judged in terms of its treatment of marginal beings. Furthermore, *Flush* flaunts the conventional association of maternity with an unintellectual, rural retirement, portraying instead Elizabeth Barrett Browning's happy motherhood and authorhood in Pisa and Florence. Finally, in *The Years* Woolf inverts the customary family chronicle to follow not the lives of great men but the half-lives of obscure women, tracing their experiences in the patriarchal private home and then following them as they escape to create more rewarding places for themselves in the public world.

While Woolf's career as a novelist and essayist demonstrates an increasingly flexible and often more positive outlook on the urban environment, and consequently on the position of women in patriarchal society, that optimistic belief in the human capacity for change and improvement came to an end with the beginning of World War II. Two diary entries from the first days of the war reveal a grim, medieval metropolis:

> *Monday Sept 11th (war on)*
> London after sunset a medieval city of darkness & brigandage. Mr. Connolly told by a taximan he had just been robbed & knocked over the head. The darkness they say is the worst of it.
>
> *Sunday Oct. 22nd, 1939*
> We have spent a week in London. The poster read, at Wimbledon; "The war begins . . . Hitler says, Now it's on." So as we drove to M[ecklenburgh] S[quare] I said it's foolish to come to London the first day of war. It seemed as if we were driving open eyed into a trap. The feeling was strong those first days . . . You never escape the war in London. People are all thinking the same thing. All set on getting the day's work done. Hitches & difficulties hold one up. Very few buses—Tubes closed—No children—No loitering—Everyone humped with a gas mask. Strain & grimness. At night it's so verdurous & gloomy that one expects a badger or a fox to prowl along the pavement. A reversion to the middle ages with all the space & the silence of the country set in this forest of black houses . . . People grope their way to each other's lairs. . . .

While the city's reversion from a rational, civilized environment to a primitive wilderness was profoundly disturbing to Woolf, what was shattering was the actual physical destruction of London when the bombing began. Her letters record in painful detail the deteriorating landscape of her beloved city, as first their house in Mecklenburgh Square, then the house in Tavistock Square and Vanessa's and Duncan's studios in Fitzroy Street were reduced to rubble. Holborn, all "heaps of glass, water running, a great gap at top of Chancery Lane," seemed "like a nightmare," and "Lord, what chaos in the Temple! All my lovely squares gone" (*L*, VI: 428, 429, 462). "[The] passion of my life," she wrote to Ethel Smyth, "that is the City of London—to see London all blasted, that . . . raked my heart" (*L*, VI: 431).

The impact of the London bombings upon Woolf's imagination cannot be overestimated: while the actual city crumbled, destroyed, too, was the potent image of London that had been central to her writing. As city life became impossible, as her house, her typist's office, her printing press, even the familiar squares were reduced to hulks of fallen stone and charred timbers, writing became increasingly difficult. In September 1940, Woolf wrote to Ethel Smyth that London seemed "like a dead city" (*L*, VI: 433). By the following February she noted in her diary, "No walks for ever so long," and wondered, "shall I ever write again one of those sentences that gives me intense pleasure? There's no echo in Rodmell—only waste air." Without the long walks through London to stir up her imagination, without the echo of an audience that the city provided, Woolf found it impossible to finish her last novel, *Between the Acts*. Despairing, she mailed the manuscript to her friend John Lehmann: "I've just read my so called novel over; and I really dont think it does. Its much too slight and sketchy. Leonard doesnt agree. So we've decided to ask you if you'd mind reading it and give your casting vote? . . . I feel fairly certain it would be a mistake from all points of view to publish it" (*L*, VI: 482).

Between the Acts reflects not only Woolf's personal paralysis as a writer, bereft of the city so central to her imagination, but also her wartime vision of "a reversion to the middle ages with all the space & the silence of the country." In its deep pessimism about the human condition the novel echoes Woolf's letter to Shena, Lady Simon: "No, I don't see what's [to] be done about war. Its manliness; and manliness breeds womanliness—both so hateful" (*L*, VI: 464). Against the backdrop of World War II, the novel portrays the relationship of Isa and Giles, the possessive mother and the aggressive father, and returns a despairing rebuttal to the argument of "Thoughts on Peace in an Air Raid." In its final scene we are drawn back to primeval time—before there were cities, before there were even roads—to concede that human character is so instinct dominated that change is impossible and conflict inevitable:

> Left alone together for the first time that day, they [Giles and Isa] were silent. Alone, enmity was bared; also love. Before they slept, they must fight; after they had fought, they would embrace. From that embrace another life might be born. But first they must fight, as the dog fox fights with the vixen, in the heart of darkness, in the fields of night . . . It was night before roads were made, or houses. It was the night that dwellers in caves had watched from some high place among rocks. [*BA*, 219]

In its retreat from the city to a feudal, rural world, *Between the Acts* recalls one of Woolf's earliest apprentice works of fiction, "The Journal of Mistress Joan Martyn."[12] Yet *Between the Acts* reveals that, with the destruction of the familiar urban landscape, Woolf had lost her hard-won mature vision of a utopian city in which men and women are free of the war-creating instincts of male aggressiveness and maternal possessiveness.[13] In Woolf's final novel, the characters cling to country life far from the besieged wartime city, while Mistress Joan Martyn longs for London as passionately as ever did Judith Shakespeare—or the young Virginia Woolf: "My thoughts naturally dwell upon . . . the great city which perhaps I may never see, though I am for ever dreaming of it" (*JMJM*, 254).

Joan Martyn dies in her thirtieth year, having never seen London. In contrast, for Virginia Woolf, London played a central role in a long and productive writer's life. As she exulted in a 1926 diary entry, "London itself perpetually attracts, stimulates, gives me a play & a story & a poem, without any trouble, save that of moving my legs through the streets" (*D*, III: 186). The bombardment of London in World War II made city life no longer possible for Woolf. Bereft of walks in her beloved squares, she lost the creative stimulus that the city had for so long provided. Her death in 1941, with *Between the Acts* still uncompleted, reflects the crucial place of London in Virginia Woolf's art and life.

NOTES

CHAPTER 1

1 This critique has its culmination in Woolf's understanding that warmaking abroad is related to the oppression of women at home. I examine another facet of this critique, her analysis of the institution of mothering as it functions to perpetuate male aggression, in "Mirroring and Mothering."

2 For discussion of the woman writer's identification with the paternal and maternal traditions, see Sandra Gilbert and Susan Gubar, *The Madwoman in the Attic*; Margaret Homans, *Woman Writers and Poetic Identity*; Cynthia Griffin Wolff, *A Feast of Words*; Bell Gale Chevigny, "Daughters Writing" and *The Woman and the Myth*; Louise A. DeSalvo, "1897: Virginia Woolf at Fifteen"; Helen Cooper, "Elizabeth Barrett Browning," unpublished MS.

3 For consideration of Woolf's apprenticeship to Sir Leslie Stephen, see DeSalvo, "1897: Virginia Woolf at Fifteen," and Katherine C. Hill, "Virginia Woolf and Leslie Stephen." For discussion of the "anxiety of authorship," see Gilbert and Gubar, *Madwoman in the Attic*, esp. pp. 43–49.

4 The androgynous aesthetic developed near the end of *A Room of One's Own* is problematic for a number of reasons. Not only does its stress on Shakespeare as being the "type of the androgynous, of the man-womanly mind" of the true artist threaten to eclipse the earlier importance of Judith Shakespeare, but its evocation of artistic creation also threatens to subsume the womanly side of the artistic sensibility to the manly side. The narrator imagines the writer, "once *his* experience is over," letting "*his* mind celebrate its nuptials in darkness" (my emphasis). Elaine Showalter discusses the troubling aspects of *A Room of One's Own* in her *A Literature of Their Own*. Clearly, this passage should not be understood as Woolf's final position on the proper voice or vision for women writers. For further discussion of the role of the woman writer in *A Room of One's Own*, see Jane Marcus, "'Taking the Bull by the Udders': Sexual Difference in Virginia Woolf, A Conspiracy Theory," unpublished MS.

5 Moreover, she suggests that those women thronging London's streets and shops may be writers in the raw themselves, with their Shakespearean gesticulations and their faces mirroring the shifting city scene.

6 Many passages in Woolf's essays and fiction express her conviction that the male literary tradition has overlooked women's experiences; one

of my favorites is the celebrated Chloe and Olivia passage from *A Room of One's Own*, in which Woolf explains: "All these relationships between women, I thought, rapidly recalling the splendid gallery of fictitious women, are too simple. So much has been left out, unattempted . . . almost without exception they are shown in their relation to men. It was strange to think that all the great women of fiction were, until Jane Austen's day, not only seen by the other sex, but seen only in relation to the other sex. And how small a part of woman's life is that; and how little can a man know even of that when he observes it through the black or rosy spectacles which sex puts upon his nose. Hence, perhaps, the peculiar nature of woman in fiction; the astonishing extremes of her beauty and horror; her alternations between heavenly goodness and hellish depravity—for so a lover would see her as his love rose or sank, was prosperous or unhappy" (*AROO*, 86). One of the many pleasures of this passage, for me, is its anticipation of the argument in Gilbert and Gubar's *Madwoman in the Attic*, proving that we are all, as feminist critics, Virginia Woolf's daughters.

7 See DeSalvo, "1897: Virginia Woolf at Fifteen."

8 My understanding that scenes can express the earliest sense of self and world experienced by the woman writer draws on the work of D. W. Winnicott, and on Nancy Chodorow's feminist revision of that psychoanalytic perspective known as "object relations theory," to view space itself as an important metaphoric and actual vessel for intrapsychic and interpersonal relationships from infancy onward. Object relations theory holds that, when an infant first establishes a self separate from the mother (or other nurturing person), his or her movement from continuity with the caretaker to contiguity is made possible by the establishment of an intermediate realm between child and caretaker that Winnicott calls "potential space." This fantasy-charged realm, in which the infant feels simultaneously fused with and separate from the nurturing person, is the origin of cultural experience, according to Winnicott. As his theory holds, the child dramatizes his or her sense of self through play in that realm of "potential space"—enacting the experience of being both part of and apart from the mother or nurturing person. Thus both the texture and the extent of an adult's cultural experience are determined by the original encounter, in infancy, with "potential space." The more "room" the child has, in fantasy, in which to experience the reassuring in-between state of simultaneous fusion with and separation from the nurturing one, the more freedom the adult will feel to be creative. See D. W. Winnicott, *Playing and Reality*, esp. pp. 112–21; see also Nancy Chodorow, *The Reproduction of Mothering*; Juliet Mitchell, *Psychoanalysis and Feminism*; Gayle Rubin, "The Traffic in Women"; Dorothy Dinnerstein, *The Mermaid and the Minotaur*; Meredith Skura, *The Literary Use*

of the Psychoanalytic Process; Diane Hunter, "Hysteria, Psychoanalyis, and Feminism"; Marianne Hirsch, "Mothers and Daughters."

9 Gilbert and Gubar discuss these strategies as characteristic of nineteenth-century women writers in *The Madwoman in the Attic*; in my view, they represent a far more widespread strategy, whose formulation I have found very valuable.

10 In this understanding of city life as reflecting both private and public worlds, I have learned from a number of feminist theorists and literary critics, in particular Sherry B. Ortner, "Is Female to Male as Nature Is to Culture?"; Michelle Z. Rosaldo, "Women, Culture, and Society"; Sherrill E. Grace, "Quest for the Peaceable Kingdom"; and Anthony Vidler, "The Scenes of the Street."

11 Leonore Davidoff, "Class and Gender in Victorian England," 97.

12 Carroll Smith-Rosenberg's groundbreaking study, "The Female World of Love and Ritual," helped to establish critical awareness of the different emotional and social worlds in which men and women lived. Moreover, it contained rich documentation on the implications of such split worlds, for Smith-Rosenberg argued that the gender-role differentiation characterizing mid-eighteenth to mid-nineteenth century American society "permitted women to form a variety of close emotional relationships with other women." However, while Smith-Rosenberg's essay is a major landmark in feminist theory because of its innovative approach to understanding emotional relationships by reading them against a sociocultural rather than a purely psychoanalytic backdrop, it testifies vividly to the social taboos of that era and society against lifelong homosocial object choices in its repeated dramas of female friendships ended by a woman's often unwilling marriage. It seems to me that a society structured on a male/female split and the resulting emotional and social segregation of the sexes is likely to have strong taboos against homosexual or homosocial relationships. This is clearly the case in the rigidly patriarchal and gender-differentiated world of *Mrs. Dalloway*. While both Clarissa and Septimus do feel love for Sally and Evans, respectively, what is most important for the novel's development is the social taboo against homosexuality that brings each love affair to a painful, enforced end.

13 Raymond Williams examines the social meaning of the images of country and city in English literature in *The Country and the City*, while Irving Howe offers a more general survey of "The City in Literature." For a discussion of the image of the city in eighteenth-century British literature, see Max Byrd, *London Transformed*. For a collection of essays on women writers' treatments of the city from the eighteenth century through the twentieth, in England, Europe, and America, see *Women Writers and the City*, ed. Susan M. Squier. Dorothy Brewster has de-

scribed the portrait of London in Woolf's works in *Virginia Woolf's London*. Alexander Welsh brilliantly analyzes *The City of Dickens*, and Donald Fanger considers the city's significance in Russian literature in *Dostoevsky and Romantic Realism*. Richard Sennett's writings on the city are justly celebrated, although he has yet to devote the same careful attention to woman's experience of the urban environment that he has shown to man's. While many of Sennett's volumes on the city are concerned with the urban experience itself, rather than with its literary treatment, he provides a thorough analysis of the city in literature in *The Fall of Public Man*. Malcolm Bradbury has surveyed "The Cities of Modernism," and Monroe K. Spears has explored the meaning of the urban image in literary modernism in *Dionysus and the City*. The relationship of modern writers to the city is studied by a number of critics and writers in *Literature and the Urban Experience*, ed. Michael C. Jaye and Ann Chalmers Watts, and Burton Pike surveys *The Image of the City in Modern Literature*. Marshall Berman interprets the complex relationship between literary and artistic modernism, technological modernization and the urban environment in *All That Is Solid Melts into Air*. In addition to those studies of the city's literary presence, the following treatments of the city's social and historical meaning have been most helpful to me: Carl E. Schorske, "The Idea of the City in European Thought"; Richard Sennett, *The Uses of Disorder* and *Classic Essays on the Culture of Cities*; "Women and the American City: *Signs* Special Issue," ed. Catharine R. Stimpson; *On Streets*, ed. Stanford Anderson.

14 Brenda R. Silver, *Virginia Woolf's Reading Notebooks*, 235. I have discussed Woolf's appropriation and revision of the "Defoe narrative" in "Tradition and Revision in Woolf's *Orlando*."

15 For a consideration of the modernist treatment of the city, see Bradbury, "The Cities of Modernism." Also see Jane Marcus, "Putting Her in Her Place," for a consideration of Woolf's difference from the modernists.

CHAPTER 2

1 Although Woolf was her married name, for convenience I will often refer to her as "Woolf" even when discussing events before her marriage.

2 Woolf's early diaries are currently being edited by Louise A. DeSalvo and Mitchell A. Leaska. I am grateful to them for permitting me to read a typescript of their edition.

3 René Spitz, *The First Year of Life*, 36. The quotation continues, "even in such fundamental respects as the relation between discrete neural centers on the one hand and their muscular effector organs on the other,

only very few privileged areas appear to be segregated into functional units."

4 D. W. Winnicott, "The Use of an Object," in *Playing and Reality*, 100–11.

5 Roy Schafer, *Language and Insight*, 151.

6 Neil Harris, *Humbug*, 235–53.

7 Nancy Chodorow, *The Reproduction of Mothering*, 76.

8 For a consideration of the most important feminist scholarship on the mother-daughter relationship and an evaluation of Chodorow's contribution, see Marianne Hirsch, "Mothers and Daughters." Hirsch makes the crucial point that while the insights of object-relations psychoanalytic theory have enriched feminist scholarship, they should be used with the awareness that at their center lies "a developed androcentric system, which, even if deconstructed and redefined, still remains a determining and limiting point of departure" (205).

9 Roy Schafer, *Aspects of Internalization*, 140.

10 Chodorow, *Reproduction of Mothering*, 70–71. In defensive identification, for example, the child "takes over controls previously exercised from without in order to prevent such control" (70).

11 For a further discussion of this complex issue, see Katharine C. Hill, "Virginia Woolf and Leslie Stephen."

12 Alfred Schutz, cited in Erving Goffman, *Frame Analysis*, 4.

13 For a reading of the pacifist and cultural implications of this scene in Woolf's memoirs, as well as the brother-sister relations it incarnates, see Sara Ruddick, "Private Brother, Public World."

CHAPTER 3

1 The diaries are currently being edited by Louise A. DeSalvo and Mitchell A. Leaska, and I am grateful to them for sharing their work with me.

2 The passage anticipates Woolf's tale of Shakespeare's sister in *A Room of One's Own*, as well as her continuing interest in lives of the obscure.

3 For a survey of several critics' responses to Woolf's use of the pronoun "one," see Jeremy Hawthorn, *Virginia Woolf's "Mrs. Dalloway,"* 99–101.

4 In *A Room of One's Own*, the woman walking down Whitehall shifts from "one" to "she" when her surroundings precipitate a "sudden splitting off of consciousness," and she feels no longer a privileged member of the patriarchal society around her, but instead an outsider (*AROO*, 101). Similarly, Woolf's own conflicting identifications at times resulted in flaws in diction, such as the awkwardly rendered interior monologs of

Mrs. McNab in *To the Lighthouse* and Crosby in *The Years* (*TTL*, 196–212; *TY*, 218–22). Woolf herself admitted, in the introduction (p. xxviii) to *Life as We Have Known It*, "Because the baker calls and we pay our bills with cheques, and our clothes are washed for us and we do not know the liver from the lights we are condemned to remain forever shut up in the confines of the middle classes, wearing tail coats and silk stockings, and called Sir or Madam as the case may be, when we are all, in truth, simply Johns and Susans."

5 Hélène Cixous expands on this point in "The Laugh of the Medusa": "Until now . . . writing has been run by a libidinal and cultural—hence political, typically masculine—economy; . . . this is a locus where the repression of women has been perpetuated, over and over, more or less consciously, and in a manner that's frightening since it's often hidden or adorned with the mystifying charms of fiction. . . . It is by writing, from and toward women, and by taking up the challenge of speech which has been governed by the phallus, that women will confirm women in a place other than that which is reserved in and by the symbolic, that is, in a place other than silence. Women should break out of the snare of silence. They shouldn't be conned into accepting a domain which is the margin or the harem" (249–51).

6 While the street haunter earlier seems to flirt with a masculine persona as she leans over the Embankment and remembers the self of six months ago ("His is the happiness of death; ours the insecurity of the future"), that passage confines the delineation of masculine identity to the use of the generic "he," whereas the front door shuts on an extensive itemization of masculine professions, gestures, and accoutrements (such as the umbrella) (*DM*, 33, 28).

7 Virginia Woolf's essay series, "The London Scene," appeared in *Good Housekeeping* in the following order: "The Docks of London," December 1931; "Oxford Street Tide," January 1932; "Great Men's Houses," March 1932; "Abbeys and Cathedrals," May 1932; "'This is the House of Commons,'" October 1932; "Portrait of a Londoner," December 1932 (B. J. Kirkpatrick, *A Bibliography of Virginia Woolf*). "Portrait of a Londoner" was originally entitled "A London Character." With the exception of that essay, the essays were reissued as *The London Scene*. John F. Hulcoop has suggested that Woolf's "Six Articles on London Life" (the alternate title of the "London Scene" group) "were originally intended to be written in the form of 'Six Letters,'" of which "Letter One," now held in the Berg Collection of the New York Public Library, was the first. John F. Hulcoop, "Note Appended to 'Letter One,'" [Virginia Woolf, (Articles), Berg Collection of the New York Public Library], March 8th, 1971.

8 Malcolm Bradbury, "The Cities of Modernism," 100.

9 Virginia Woolf, "The Port of London," in "Six Articles on London

Life: St. Paul's, Great Men's Houses, The Port of London, Abbeys and Cathedrals, Streets and Shops, The House of Commons," holograph, unsigned, first dated 13 March 1931, Berg Collection, New York Public Library.

10 Ibid.

11 Jane Marcus, "*The Years* as Greek Drama, Domestic Novel, and *Götterdämmerung*," 301.

12 Notice how Woolf speaks here for and with the *Good Housekeeping* readership, whereas in the previous version she spoke for and with the toiling "housekeepers." The switch is ironic, in a magazine of that name.

13 G. Robert Stange, "The Victorian City and the Frightened Poets," 629.

14 Eliot and Lawrence dramatized urban alienation in "The Love Song of J. Alfred Prufrock" and the "Creme de Menthe" chapter (6) of *Women in Love*, whereas Georg Simmel used sociological analysis to explain its origins in the urban money economy in his brilliant essay "The Metropolis and Mental Life." Woolf's vision of the city as a "breeding ground, a forcing house of sensation" (*LS*, 17) recalls Simmel's view of it as an environment perpetually assaulting the citydweller with unfamiliar experiences. Yet Simmel proposed that the urban individual protects his consciousness from the demands of this sensory overload by screening out experiences and responding intellectually rather than emotionally to the "threatening currents and discrepancies of his external environment which would uproot him" (48). In contrast, Woolf imagines the city-dweller thriving on sensation in an almost visceral way.

15 Thomas Carlyle, *On Heroes, Hero-Worship, and the Heroic in History*, 5–6. I am grateful to Helen Cooper for pointing out this important contrast between Carlyle's vision and Woolf's in "Great Men's Houses."

16 Ibid., 207.

17 Ibid., 6.

18 Ibid., 206.

19 The Carlyles' house reflects a similar spatialization of social and sexual relations: just as mistress and maid are linked in the mind of the Victorian man by their shared embodiment of the frightening force of female sexuality, so in this essay mistress and maid are linked in the spaces of both home and city through their shared physical labor. Leonore Davidoff, "Class and Gender in Victorian England," 97.

20 Jerry Wasserman, "'A Curious Kind of Relationship,'" 6.

21 Woolf, "The London Scene II: Oxford Street Tide," 5, 18.

22 Woolf, "The London Scene IV: Abbeys and Cathedrals," 18.

23 Ibid., 19.

24 Woolf, "'This is the House of Commons,'" 18.

25 Woolf, "A London Character," in "The London Scene," Berg Collection, New York Public Library.

1 E. M. Forster wrote, "*Night and Day* . . . is the simplest novel she has written, and to my mind the least successful. Very long, very careful, it condescends to many of the devices she so gaily derides in her essay on 'Mr. Bennett and Mrs. Brown.' . . . In view of what preceded it and of what is to follow, *Night and Day* seems to me a deliberate exercise in classicism" ("The Novels of Virginia Woolf," 173).

2 "It was when the lights went up in the evening that society came into force. During the daylight one could wear overalls; work. There was the Academy for Nessa; my Liddell and Scott and the Greek choruses for me. But in the evening society had it all its own way" (*MB*, 129–30).

3 Irving Howe, "The City in Literature," 62.

4 Raymond Williams, *The Country and the City*, 62; Howe, "The City in Literature."

5 Forster, "Novels," 173.

6 Harold Child, "Unsigned Review, *Times Literary Supplement*"; *ND*, 68.

7 Katherine Mansfield, "Review." Quentin Bell describes Mansfield's "private opinion" of *Night and Day*: "it was 'a lie in the soul.' 'The war has never been: that is what its message is . . . I feel in the *profoundest* sense that nothing can ever be the same—that, as artists, we are traitors if we feel otherwise: we have to take it into account and find new expressions, new moulds for our new thoughts and feelings'" (*Virginia Woolf: A Biography*, II: 69).

8 John Henry Raleigh, "The Novel and the City," 302.

9 See, e.g., the above-cited reviews by Forster and Mansfield.

10 Williams, *The Country and the City*, 46.

11 Dorothy Brewster, *Virginia Woolf's London*, 34. By my count, Ralph has fifteen walking scenes, in comparison to Katharine's thirteen, Mary's seven, Rodney's five, and Cassandra's four. A correlation emerges between the openness to change that the city fosters and the experience of mobility, particularly in the city. Mary Datchet, however, is an exception to this rule: her role as a secondary character may account for the discrepancy between her affirmation of city life with the innovation it makes possible, and the relatively small number of walking scenes in which she figures.

12 See *Moments of Being* for discussion of the differences between life at 22 Hyde Park Gate, where Virginia Stephen lived until her father's death in 1904, and at 46 Gordon Square, where the Stephen children then moved. The contrast between Kensington and Bloomsbury, she wrote in October 1918, as she was writing *Night and Day*, "was the gulf between respectable mum[m]ified humbug & life crude & impertinent perhaps, but living" (*D*, I: 206).

13 Howe, "The City in Literature," 64.
14 Allen McLaurin, *Virginia Woolf*, 10.
15 Walter Benjamin, *Illuminations*, 163, 165.
16 Jane Marcus, "Enchanted Organs, Magic Bells: *Night and Day* as Comic Opera," 109.
17 For further discussion of how fictional forms constrain real lives, and how fictions constrain fictions, see Margaret Homans, *Women Writers and Poetic Identity*, esp. introduction, and Jean Strouse, *Alice James*.
18 In this anxiety, of course, Virginia Woolf was far from alone, as contemporary feminist scholarship reveals. See particularly Homans, *Women Writers and Poetic Identity*, and Sandra Gilbert and Susan Gubar, *The Madwoman in the Attic*.

CHAPTER 5

1 Although Mary Datchet remains at work in London, she is only a secondary character in *Night and Day*. The protagonist, Katharine Hilbery, plans a retreat from London paralleling her creator's.
2 Leon Edel, *Bloomsbury: A House of Lions*, 53.
3 Stella McNichol, "Introduction," *Mrs. Dalloway's Party*, 9. For some "Second Thoughts" on this edition, see John Hulcoop's article thus titled.
4 Hélène Cixous, "Sorties," 91.
5 Ibid., 90.
6 For the most useful recent discussions of the female psychic structure as it is created in the nuclear family of patriarchal society, see Nancy Chodorow, *The Reproduction of Mothering*; Elizabeth Abel, "(E)merging Identities"; Judith Kegan Gardiner, "The (US)es of (I)dentity"; and Marianne Hirsch, "Mothers and Daughters."
7 Abel, "(E)merging Identities," 417.
8 Of course, as a writer Woolf was also actively involved in public, professional life.
9 For more discussion of the split between figure and ground, and its significance for individuals and society, see Ch. 2.
10 David Daiches and John Flower trace the movements of the characters in *Mrs. Dalloway* through London, but do not consider the significance of those movements for the novel as a whole (*Literary Landscapes of the British Isles*, 84).
11 Clarissa feels "like a Queen whose guards have fallen asleep and left her unprotected (she had been quite taken aback by this visit—it had upset her) so that anyone can stroll in and have a look at her where she lies with the brambles curving over her . . ." (*MD*, 65). Beverly Ann Schlack also makes this point in *Continuing Presences*, 60.

12 Simone de Beauvoir, *The Second Sex*, 207–8.
13 Paul Fussell, *Abroad*, 210–11.
14 de Beauvoir, *Second Sex*, 208.
15 Roy Schafer, *Language and Insight*, 150.
16 Ibid.
17 Ibid., 144.
18 Ibid., 141.
19 Brenda R. Silver, "*Three Guineas* Before and After," 271.
20 Ibid.
21 *MD*, 21; Gloria Levitas, "Anthropology and Sociology of Streets," 230.
22 Septimus's vision of lunatics resembles Woolf's own, on 9 January 1915, corroborating a reading of Septimus as a double or scapegoat for Clarissa Dalloway, and for women in general: "On the towpath we met & had to pass a long line of imbeciles. The first was a very tall young man, just queer enough to look twice at, but no more; the second shuffled, & looked aside; & then one realised that every one in that long line was a miserable ineffective shuffling idiotic creature, with no forehead, or no chin, & an imbecile grin, or a wild suspicious stare. It was perfectly horrible. They should certainly be killed" (*D*, I: 13).
23 For an illuminating discussion of Clarissa's existential freedom, see Lucio P. Ruotolo, *Six Existential Heroes*, 13–35.
24 Kenneth Burke, *The Philosophy of Literary Form*, 45.
25 Ibid.
26 Ibid., 39.
27 Edel, *Bloomsbury*, 92.
28 Ibid.
29 Definition of *valour* from *The Compact Edition of the Oxford English Dictionary*, II: 3586.
30 Thomas V. Czarnowski, "The Street as a Communications Artifact," 207.
31 Ibid.

CHAPTER 6

1 For a discussion of the marginalization of animals, see John Berger's fascinating essay, "Why Look at Animals?" in *About Looking*, 1–26. See also Virginia Woolf, "Speech of January 21, 1931," in *The Pargiters*, ed. Mitchell A. Leaska, xxix–xxx.
2 See Jane Marcus's treatment of London as "Capital of the Patriarchy" in "Thinking Back through Our Mothers."
3 See my "'A Track of Our Own'" for a similar vision of a fallen patriarchal civilization, which Woolf wrote at approximately the same time.

4 Virginia Woolf, "Aurora Leigh," *Second Common Reader*, 186.
5 Gertrude Himmelfarb, "The Culture of Poverty," 727.
6 Ibid., 721.
7 Anthony Keating, "Fact and Fiction in the East End," 593.
8 *The Fatal Caress*, ed. Richard Baker, 192. The *Times* coverage appeared when Woolf was an exceedingly literate six year old, daughter of a father given to reading aloud.
9 Quoted in Keating, "Fact and Fiction in the East End," 594. As Keating points out, "The image of the East End which first emerged during the last two decades of the nineteenth century, and which survives little changed today," was the product of, among others, Jack the Ripper (586).
10 On 26 January, 1931, shortly before finishing *The Waves*, Woolf noted in her diary her memory of the day's headlines: "Gandhi set free. Pavlova to be buried on Golders Green. Ripper murder on Blackheath." The three headlines, intermingling justified disobedience, art, and the Ripper theme of violence against women, anticipate *Flush*, which Woolf was working on only seven months later (*D*, IV: 8). See Judith R. Walkowitz, "Jack the Ripper and the Myth of Male Violence," for an insightful discussion of the class and gender issues shaping the "Jack the Ripper" legend.
11 There are numerous similarities between Flush's return to London after his shearing and Orlando's return to London after her sex change. Like Orlando (and like Woolf), Flush after his shearing sees life anew: society holds no further terror or fascination, and London appears newly oppressive when seen through the eyes of one identified now not with insiders, but with women and other outsiders.
12 Jane Marcus, "*The Years* as Greek Drama, Domestic Novel, and *Götterdämmerung*."
13 Like *Flush*, *Orlando* can be seen as the confluence of two developmental dramas, both of which take place largely in the city. While *Flush* charted the parallel developments of a dog and a woman poet, *Orlando* chronicles two narratives in one body: the making of a poet and the "making" of a woman. Drawing on *Moll Flanders* while subverting the influence of the "Defoe narrative," Woolf follows Orlando's growth from insider to outsider, from youthful male lover to mature mother. Moreover, in its conclusion the novel affirms the rich diversity of character and experience made possible by a woman's marginal role, as Orlando unites womanhood, motherhood, and "poethood." The celebrated episode of Orlando's sex change, in Constantinople, uses an exotic urban setting to commingle the novel's two narrative streams: from that time forward, Orlando's two identities are merged, womanhood being driven by the desire to write poetry, and "poethood" being both constrained and broadened by Orlando's experience as a woman.

The passage during which Orlando's son is born, offstage, celebrates the social, sexual, and literary ecstasy possible in the modern city. Forced by biographical conventions to turn away from describing Orlando's *accouchement*—a topic which in its social and sexual freedom is unsuitable for the biographer's pen, Woolf ironically implies—the biographer manages to go one better, by describing the entire city as an arena permitting "all fulfillment of natural desires." Here the portrait of the city revises the classical modernist view of London as a place of chaotic commercialism, linguistic plurality, and excessive stimulation; if to writers like Eliot and Joyce London is Purgatory at best, and Hell at worst, to Woolf it is a gloriously mundane and fertile Heaven.

> "Wait! Wait! The kingfisher comes; the kingfisher comes not.
>
> Behold, meanwhile, the factory chimneys, and their smoke; behold the city clerks flashing by in their outrigger . . . Behold them all. Though Heaven has mercifully decreed that the secrets of all hearts are hidden so that we are lured on for ever to suspect something, perhaps, that does not exist; still . . . we see blaze up and salute the splendid fulfillment of natural desires for a hat, for a boat, for a rat in a ditch . . .
>
> Hail! natural desire! Hail! happiness! divine happiness! and pleasure of all sorts, flowers and wine, though one fades and the other intoxicates; and half-crown tickets out of London on Sundays, and singing in a dark chapel hymns about death, and anything, anything that interrupts and confounds the tapping of typewriters and filing of letters and forging of links and chains, binding the Empire together. Hail even the crude, red bows on shop girls' lips . . . kingfisher flashing from bank to bank, and all fulfillment of natural desire, whether it is what the male novelist says it is; or prayer; or denial; hail! in whatever form it comes, and may there be more forms, and stranger. [*O*, 192–93]

In this choric interlude, Woolf celebrates London in images that recall not merely her own *Kew Gardens* (1919), but also Eliot's *The Waste Land*, which Hogarth Press published in 1923: flowers and factory workers, rats on the riverbank, typists, clerks, and shop girls, day excursions to London's parks, hymn singing in dark city churches, the often crude shapes of natural desire. Encircling the whole passage is the image of "the kingfisher flashing from bank to bank," an opaque natural inversion of the Fisher King myth central to Eliot's poem. Although in its imagery this passage clearly draws on *The Waste Land*, it departs from Eliot's vision. *The Waste Land* is concerned with impotence, both personal and national; Woolf, in contrast, affirms both emotional and sexual potency, the fulfillment of "all natural desire . . . in whatever form it comes." While *The Waste Land* mourns the loss of a meaningful form for personal, political, and spiritual experience (embodied for Eliot in the floundering kingdom of the Fisher King, which provides one mythic source for the poem), Woolf applauds whatever undermines patriarchal order and affirms a multiplicity of forms for the varieties of human experience. She not only cheers anything which "interrupts and confounds . . . [the] forging of links and chains binding the Empire together," but, by choosing this choric passage to mark the birth of Orlando's child, she celebrates the modern flowering of maternal power. See my "Tradition and Revision in Woolf's *Orlando*."

CHAPTER 7

1 For a discussion of Woolf's revisions of *The Years*, see Grace Radin, "'Two enormous chunks.'" See also Susan Squier, "'A Track of Our Own.'"
2 Virginia Woolf, *The Pargiters*, ed. Mitchell A. Leaska.
3 Mitchell A. Leaska, "Virginia Woolf, the Pargeter," 173.
4 *The Years* spends ten of the first seventeen pages about the tea table; while it begins at Colonel Pargiter's club, the sense of frustrated energies experienced by the Pargiter women in the tea-time scene is crucial to the "1880" chapter, as to the novel as a whole.
5 Olive Banks, *Faces of Feminism*, 73. Note Butler's assumption, characteristic of many social reformers of the period, that sexual desire is unique to men.
6 Ibid., 131.
7 Sallie Sears, "Notes on Sexuality." The entire issue of the *Bulletin* in which Sears's article appears contains among the best early treatments of *The Years*. In addition to Sears's essay, I am particularly indebted to Margaret Comstock, "The Loudspeaker and the Human Voice," and Jane Marcus, "*The Years* as Greek Drama, Domestic Novel, and *Götterdämmerung*."
8 See also Squier, "'A Track of Our Own.'"
9 It was defeated.
10 Squier, "'A Track of Our Own,'" 204.
11 Percy Bysshe Shelley, "Ozymandias," quoted from *English Romantic Writers*, ed. David Perkins, 971.
12 Ibid.
13 Squier, "'A Track of Our Own,'" 203.
14 Woolf borrowed this image from Oliver Strachey, who borrowed it in turn from Sir James Jeans. Characteristically, Woolf subverted Strachey's sexual and Jeans's scientific meanings, using the image to symbolize the enduring feminist civilization of the future (*D*, IV: 66–67).
15 For another example of Woolf's analysis of how domestic labor cre-

ates fellowship between women, see my discussion of "Great Men's Houses," in Ch. 2, above.

16 Squier, "'A Track of Our Own,'" 223.

17 Ibid., 224.

18 Ibid.

19 Grace Radin and Mitchell Leaska both make this point in their essays in *Bulletin of the New York Public Library* 80: 2 (Winter 1977).

20 For a further analysis of these deleted passages, see Radin, "'Two enormous chunks.'" Further references to these deleted passages will follow in the text.

21 See also Ch. 2, above. The phrase was borrowed by Woolf from Lady Astor.

22 Erich Neumann, *The Great Mother*, 38.

23 For a similar treatment of the suburban environment as epitome of a conventional, limited state of mind, see my discussion of Ralph Denham's home in Highgate, in Ch. 4, above.

24 Thomas Hardy, "Hap," quoted in *The Norton Anthology of English Literature*, II, 1766.

25 Radin, "'Two enormous chunks,'" 235.

26 Comstock, "The Loudspeaker and the Human Voice," 264.

27 Paul Tillich, "The Strange and the Familiar in the Metropolis," 347.

28 Ibid., 347–48.

29 Ibid., 347.

30 Mitchell A. Leaska, "Introduction" to his edition of *The Pargiters*, vii–xxii.

31 See Radin, "'Two enormous chunks,'" for a full treatment of this question.

32 Grace Radin has suggested that Woolf's deletions of the "1917" and "1921" sections lightened the tone of *The Years*, making possible a more optimistic conclusion than would otherwise have been possible (ibid., 227).

33 Leaska, "Introduction" to *The Pargiters*, vii.

34 See Comstock, "The Loudspeaker and the Human Voice," 255.

35 I am grateful to Jane Marcus for this information. The sultan theme recalls Kitty Lasswade's retreat from the new freedom of her widowhood, "chaperoned" by her big dog, Sultan, in the excised "1921" chapter.

36 David Mitchell, *The Fighting Pankhursts*, 32.

CHAPTER 8

1 Brenda R. Silver, "*Three Guineas* Before and After." For a discussion of *The Years* as a novel charting the decline of the British Empire, see Jane Marcus, "*The Years* as Greek Drama, Domestic Novel, and *Götterdämmerung*."

2 Virginia Woolf, *A Writer's Diary*, 161. See also Silver, "*Three Guineas* Before and After."

3 See my "Mirroring and Mothering" for a further discussion of Woolf's analysis of "subconscious Hitlerism" as the origin of war.

4 Here I read "Thoughts on Peace in an Air Raid" rather differently from Jane Marcus. For Marcus, the essay is "a defensive position taken under extreme pressure," whereas I see it as an aggressive redefinition of the concepts of militancy and patriotism to include the feminist fight against male oppression of women and outsiders. See Jane Marcus, "Storming the Toolshed."

5 See Silver, "*Three Guineas* Before and After."

6 Ibid. The phrasing is Silver's, from an earlier, unpublished draft of "*Three Guineas* Before and After."

7 Ibid., 271.

8 For an illuminating exploration of the loudspeaker's meaning in Woolf's works, see Margaret Comstock, "The Loudspeaker and the Human Voice."

9 Silver, "*Three Guineas* Before and After," 270.

10 William Blake, "Milton," quoted in *English Romantic Writers*, ed. David Perkins, 115.

11 Raymond Williams, *The Country and the City*, 235.

12 "Virginia Woolf's *The Journal of Mistress Joan Martyn*," ed. Susan M. Squier and Louise A. DeSalvo. See also DeSalvo's "Shakespeare's Other Sister."

13 See Sallie Sears, "Theater of War: Virginia Woolf's *Between the Acts*."

BIBLIOGRAPHY

Abel, Elizabeth. "(E)merging Identities: The Dynamics of Female Friendship in Contemporary Fiction by Women." *Signs* 6 (Spring 1981): 413–35.

Anderson, Stanford, ed. *On Streets*. Cambridge: MIT Press, 1978.

Baker, Richard, ed. *The Fatal Caress*. New York: Duell, Sloan and Pearce, 1947.

Banks, Olive. *Faces of Feminism*. New York: St. Martin's Press, 1981.

Beker, Miroslav. "London as a Principle of Structure in *Mrs. Dalloway*." *Modern Fiction Studies* 18 (Autumn 1972): 375–85.

Bell, Quentin. *Virginia Woolf: A Biography*. New York: Harcourt Brace Jovanovich, 1972.

Benjamin, Walter. *Illuminations*. Ed. Hannah Arendt; trans. Harry Zohn. New York: Schocken, 1969.

Berger, John. *About Looking*. New York: Pantheon, 1980.

Berman, Marshall. *All That Is Solid Melts into Air*. New York: Simon & Schuster, 1982.

Blake, William. "Milton." P. 115 in *English Romantic Writers*, ed. David Perkins. New York: Harcourt, Brace & World, 1967.

Bradbury, Malcolm. "The Cities of Modernism." Pp. 96–104 in *Modernism: 1890–1930*, ed. Malcolm Bradbury and James McFarlane. Harmondsworth, England: Penguin, 1976.

Brewster, Dorothy. *Virginia Woolf's London*. New York: New York University Press, 1960.

Burke, Kenneth. *The Philosophy of Literary Form*. Berkeley: University of California Press, 1973.

Byrd, Max. *London Transformed: Images of the City in the Eighteenth Century*. New Haven: Yale University Press, 1978.

Carlyle, Thomas. *On Heroes, Hero-Worship, and the Heroic in History*. Philadelphia: Henry Altemus, 1894.

Chevigny, Bell Gale. "Daughters Writing: Toward a Theory of Women's Biography." *Feminist Studies* 9 (Spring 1983): 79–102.

———. *The Woman and the Myth: Margaret Fuller's Life and Writings*. Old Westbury, N.Y.: Feminist Press, 1976.

Child, Harold. "Unsigned Review, *Times Literary Supplement*." P. 75 in *Virginia Woolf: The Critical Heritage*, ed. Robin Majumdar and Allen McLaurin. London: Routledge & Kegan Paul, 1975.

Chodorow, Nancy. *The Reproduction of Mothering*. Berkeley: University of California Press, 1978.

Cixous, Hélène. "The Laugh of the Medusa." Pp. 249–51 in *New French*

Feminisms, ed. Elaine Marks and Isabelle de Courtivron. Amherst: University of Massachusetts Press, 1980.

———. "Sorties." Pp. 90–98 in *New French Feminisms* (see above).

Comstock, Margaret. "'The Current Answers Don't Do': The Comic Form of *Night and Day*." *Women's Studies* 4 (1977): 153–71.

———. "The Loudspeaker and the Human Voice: Politics and the Form of *The Years*." *Bulletin of the New York Public Library* 80 (Winter 1977): 252–75.

Cooper, Helen. "Elizabeth Barrett Browning." Unpublished MS.

Czarnowski, Thomas V. "The Street as a Communications Artifact." In *On Streets*, ed. Stanford Anderson. Cambridge: MIT Press, 1978.

Daiches, David, and Flower, John. *Literary Landscapes of the British Isles: A Narrative Atlas*. New York and London: Paddington Press, 1979.

Davidoff, Leonore. "Class and Gender in Victorian England: The Diaries of Arthur J. Munby and Hannah Cullwick." *Feminist Studies* 5 (Spring 1979): 87–141.

de Beauvoir, Simone. *The Second Sex*. Trans. H. M. Parshley. New York: Bantam Books, 1979.

DeSalvo, Louise A. "Shakespeare's Other Sister." Pp. 61–81 in *New Feminist Essays on Virginia Woolf*, ed. Jane Marcus. London: Macmillan Press, 1981.

———. "1897: Virginia Woolf at Fifteen." Pp. 78–108 in *Virginia Woolf: A Feminist Slant*, ed. Jane Marcus. Lincoln: University of Nebraska Press, 1983.

———, and Squier, Susan M., eds. "Virginia Woolf's *The Journal of Mistress Joan Martyn*." *Twentieth Century Literature* 25 (Fall/Winter 1979): 237–69.

Di Battista, Maria. *Virginia Woolf's Major Novels: The Fables of Anon*. New Haven: Yale University Press, 1980.

Dinnerstein, Dorothy. *The Mermaid and the Minotaur: Sexual Arrangements and the Human Malaise*. New York: Harper & Row, 1976.

Edel, Leon. *Bloomsbury: A House of Lions*. Philadelphia and New York: J. B. Lippincott, 1979.

Fanger, Donald. *Dostoevsky and Romantic Realism*. Cambridge: Harvard University Press, 1972.

Forster, E. M. "The Novels of Virginia Woolf." First published in *New Criterion*, April 1926; reprinted on pp. 171–78 in *Virginia Woolf: The Critical Heritage*, ed. Robin Majumdar and Allen McLaurin. London: Routledge & Kegan Paul, 1975.

Fussell, Paul. *Abroad*. New York: Oxford University Press, 1980.

Gardiner, Judith Kegan. "The (US)es of (I)dentity: A Response to Abel on (E)merging Identities." *Signs* 6 (Spring 1981): 436–41.

Gilbert, Sandra, and Gubar, Susan. *The Madwoman in the Attic: The Woman Writer and the Nineteenth-Century Literary Imagination*. New

Haven: Yale University Press, 1979.

Goffman, Erving. *Frame Analysis*. New York: Harper Colophon Books, 1974.

Grace, Sherrill E. "Quest for the Peaceable Kingdom: Urban/Rural Codes in Roy, Laurence, and Atwood." Pp. 193–209 in *Women Writers and the City: Essays in Feminist Literary Criticism*, ed. Susan M. Squier. Knoxville: University of Tennessee Press, 1984.

Hardy, Thomas. "Hap." P. 1717 in *The Norton Anthology of English Literature*, II, 3rd ed., ed. M. H. Abrams. New York: W. W. Norton, 1974.

Harris, Neil. *Humbug*. Boston: Little, Brown, 1973.

Hawthorn, Jeremy. *Virginia Woolf's "Mrs. Dalloway": A Study in Alienation*. London: Sussex University Press, 1975.

Hill, Katherine C. "Virginia Woolf and Leslie Stephen: Literary History and Literary Revolution." *PMLA* 96 (May 1981): 351–62.

Himmelfarb, Gertrude. "The Culture of Poverty." Pp. 707–36 in *The Victorian City: Images and Realities*, II, ed. H. J. Dyos and Michael Wolff. London: Routledge & Kegan Paul, 1973.

Hirsch, Marianne. "Mothers and Daughters." *Signs* 7 (Autumn 1981): 200–222.

Homans, Margaret. *Women Writers and Poetic Identity: Dorothy Wordsworth, Emily Bronte, and Emily Dickinson*. Princeton: Princeton University Press, 1980.

Howe, Irving. "The City in Literature." *Commentary* 51 (May 1971): 61–68.

Hulcoop, John F. "Note Appended to 'Letter One.'" Virginia Woolf [Articles] Berg Collection of the New York Public Library. 8 March 1971.

———. "Second Thoughts." *Virginia Woolf Miscellany* 3 (Spring 1975): 3–4, 7.

Hunter, Diane. "Hysteria, Psychoanalysis, and Feminism: The Case of Anna O." *Feminist Studies* 9 (Fall 1983): 465–88.

Jaye, Michael C., and Watts, Ann Chalmers, eds. *Literature and the Urban Experience: Essays on the City and Literature*. New Brunswick, N.J.: Rutgers University Press, 1981.

Keating, Anthony. "Fact and Fiction in the East End." Pp. 585–602 in *The Victorian City: Images and Realities*, II, ed. H. J. Dyos and Michael Wolff. London: Routledge & Kegan Paul, 1973.

Kirkpatrick, B. J. *A Bibliography of Virginia Woolf*. Oxford: Clarendon Press, 1980.

Leaska, Mitchell A. "Introduction." *The Pargiters: The Novel-Essay Portion of* The Years, ed. Mitchell A. Leaska. New York: New York Public Library, 1977.

———. *The Novels of Virginia Woolf*. New York: The John Jay Press, 1977.

______. "Virginia Woolf, the Pargeter: A Reading of *The Years*." *Bulletin of the New York Public Library* 80 (Winter 1977): 172–210.
Levitas, Gloria. "Anthropology and Sociology of Streets." Pp. 225–40 in *On Streets*, ed. Stanford Anderson. Cambridge: MIT Press, 1978.
Mansfield, Katherine. "Review." First published in *Athenaeum*, 21 November 1919; reprinted on pp. 79–82 in *Virginia Woolf: The Critical Heritage*, ed. Robin Majumdar and Allen McLaurin. London: Routledge & Kegan Paul, 1975.
Marcus, Jane. "Enchanted Organs, Magic Bells: *Night and Day* as Comic Opera." Pp. 96–122 in *Virginia Woolf: Revaluation and Continuity*, ed. Ralph Freedman. Berkeley: University of California Press, 1980.
______. "Putting Her in Her Place: New Approaches to Virginia Woolf." *Virginia Woolf Miscellany* 4 (Fall 1975): 3–4.
______. "Storming the Toolshed." *Signs* 7 (Spring 1982): 622–40.
______. "'Taking the Bull by the Udders': Sexual Difference in Virginia Woolf, A Conspiracy Theory." Unpublished MS.
______. "Thinking Back through Our Mothers." Pp. 1–30 in her *New Feminist Essays on Virginia Woolf* (see below).
______. "*The Years* as Greek Drama, Domestic Novel, and *Götterdämmerung*." *Bulletin of the New York Public Library* 80 (Winter 1977): 276–301.
______, ed. *New Feminist Essays on Virginia Woolf*. London: Macmillan, 1981.
______. *Virginia Woolf: A Feminist Slant*. Lincoln: University of Nebraska Press, 1983.
Marks, Elaine, and de Courtivron, Isabelle, eds. *New French Feminisms*. Amherst: University of Massachusetts Press, 1980.
McLaurin, Allen. *Virginia Woolf: The Echoes Enslaved*. Cambridge: Cambridge University Press, 1973.
McNichol, Stella, ed. "Introduction." *Mrs. Dalloway's Party*, ed. Stella McNichol. New York: Harcourt Brace Jovanovich, 1973.
Mitchell, David. *The Fighting Pankhursts*. New York: Macmillan, 1967.
Mitchell, Juliet. *Psychoanalysis and Feminism*. New York: Random House, 1975.
Moore, Madeline, ed. "Special Issue: Virginia Woolf." *Women's Studies* 4 (1977).
Neumann, Erich. *The Great Mother*. Princeton: Princeton University Press, 1963.
Ortner, Sherry B. "Is Female to Male as Nature Is to Culture?" Pp. 67–88 in *Women, Culture & Society*, ed. Michelle Z. Rosaldo and Louise Lamphere. Stanford: Stanford University Press, 1974.
Pike, Burton. *The Image of the City in Modern Literature*. Princeton:

Princeton University Press, 1982.
Radin, Grace. "'Two enormous chunks': Episodes Excluded during the Final Revisions of *The Years*." *Bulletin of the New York Public Library* 80 (Winter 1977): 221–51.
———. *Virginia Woolf's "The Years": The Evolution of a Novel*. Knoxville: University of Tennessee Press, 1981.
Raleigh, John Henry. "The Novel and the City: England and America in the Nineteenth Century." *Victorian Studies* 11 (March 1968): 291–328.
Rosaldo, Michelle Z. "Women, Culture, and Society: A Theoretical Overview." Pp. 17–42 in *Women, Culture & Society*, ed. Michelle Z. Rosaldo and Louise Lamphere. Stanford: Stanford University Press, 1974.
Rubin, Gayle. "The Traffic in Women: Notes on the Political Economy of Sex." Pp. 157–210 in *Toward an Anthropology of Women*, ed. Rayna Reiter. New York: Monthly Review Press, 1975.
Ruddick, Sara. "Learning to Live with the Angel in the House." *Women's Studies* 4 (1977): 181–200.
———. "Private Brother, Public World." Pp. 185–215 in *New Feminist Essays on Virginia Woolf*, ed. Jane Marcus. London: Macmillan, 1981.
Ruotolo, Lucio P. "*Mrs. Dalloway*: The Journey Out of Subjectivity." *Women's Studies* 4 (1977): 173–78.
———. *Six Existential Heroes: The Politics of Faith*. Cambridge: Harvard University Press, 1973.
Schafer, Roy. *Aspects of Internalization*. New York: International Universities Press, 1968.
———. *Language and Insight*. New Haven: Yale University Press, 1978.
Schlack, Beverly Ann. *Continuing Presences: Virginia Woolf's Use of Literary Allusion*. University Park: Pennsylvania State University Press, 1979.
Schorske, Carl E. "The Idea of the City in European Thought: Voltaire to Spengler." Pp. 95–114 in *The Historian and the City*, ed. Oscar Handlin and John Burchard. Cambridge: MIT Press, 1963.
Sears, Sallie. "Notes on Sexuality: *The Years* and *Three Guineas*." *Bulletin of the New York Public Library* 80 (Winter 1977): 211–20.
———. "Theater of War: Virginia Woolf's *Between the Acts*." Pp. 212–35 in *Virginia Woolf: A Feminist Slant*, ed. Jane Marcus. Lincoln: University of Nebraska Press, 1983.
Sennett, Richard, ed. *Classic Essays on the Culture of Cities*. Englewood Cliffs, N.J.: Prentice-Hall, 1969.
———. *The Fall of Public Man*. New York: Alfred A. Knopf, 1977.
———. *The Uses of Disorder: Personal Identity and City Life*. New York: Alfred A. Knopf, 1970.
Shelley, Percy Bysshe. "Ozymandias." P. 971 in *English Romantic Writers*,

ed. David Perkins. New York: Harcourt, Brace & World, 1967.

Showalter, Elaine. *A Literature of Their Own*. Princeton: Princeton University Press, 1977.

Silver, Brenda R. "*Three Guineas* Before and After: Further Answers to Correspondence." Pp. 254–76 in *Virginia Woolf: A Feminist Slant*, ed. Jane Marcus. Lincoln: University of Nebraska Press, 1983.

______. *Virginia Woolf's Reading Notebooks*. Princeton: Princeton University Press, 1983.

Simmel, Georg. "The Metropolis and Mental Life." Pp. 47–60 in *Classic Essays on the Culture of Cities*, ed. Richard Sennett. Englewood Cliffs, N.J.: Prentice-Hall, 1969.

Skura, Meredith. *The Literary Uses of the Psychoanalytic Process*. New Haven: Yale University Press, 1981.

Smith-Rosenberg, Carroll. "The Female World of Love and Ritual: Relations between Women in Nineteenth-Century America." *Signs* 1 (Autumn 1975): 1–30.

Spears, Monroe K. *Dionysus and the City: Modernism in Twentieth-Century Poetry*. Oxford: Oxford University Press, 1972.

Spitz, René. *The First Year of Life*. New York: International Universities Press, 1965.

Squier, Susan M. "Mirroring and Mothering: Reflections on the Mirror Encounter in Virginia Woolf's Works." *Twentieth Century Literature* 27 (Fall 1981): 272–88.

______. "'A Track of Our Own': Typescript Drafts of Virginia Woolf's *The Years*." *Modernist Studies: Literature & Culture 1920–1940* 4: 218–31. Reprinted in *Virginia Woolf: A Feminist Slant*, ed. Jane Marcus. Lincoln: University of Nebraska Press, 1983.

______. "Tradition and Revision in Woolf's *Orlando*: Defoe and the Jessamy Brides." *Women's Studies*, 1984.

______, ed. *Women Writers and the City: Essays in Feminist Literary Criticism*. Knoxville: University of Tennessee Press, 1984.

______, and DeSalvo, Louise A., eds. "Virginia Woolf's *The Journal of Mistress Joan Martyn*." *Twentieth Century Literature* 25 (Fall/Winter 1979): 237–69.

Stange, G. Robert. "The Victorian City and the Frightened Poets." *Victorian Studies* 11 (Summer 1968): 627–40.

Stimpson, Catharine R., ed. "Women and the American City: Special Issue." *Signs* 5 (Spring 1980).

Strouse, Jean. *Alice James: A Biography*. Boston: Houghton Mifflin, 1980.

Szladitz, Lola L. "The Life, Character and Opinions of Flush the Spaniel." *Bulletin of the New York Public Library* 74 (April 1970): 211–18.

Tillich, Paul. "The Strange and the Familiar in the Metropolis." Pp.

346–48 in *The Metropolis in Mental Life*, ed. Robert Moore Fisher. New York: Russell & Russell, 1955.

Vidler, Anthony. "The Scenes of the Street: Transformations in Ideal and Reality, 1750–1871." Pp. 29–112 in *On Streets*, ed. Stanford Anderson. Cambridge: MIT Press, 1978.

Walkowitz, Judith R. "Jack the Ripper and the Myth of Male Violence." *Feminist Studies* 8 (Fall 1982): 543–74.

Wasserman, Jerry. "'A Curious Kind of Relationship': Virginia Woolf and Logan Pearsall Smith." *Virginia Woolf Miscellany* 10 (Spring-Summer 1978): 5–6.

Welsh, Alexander. *The City of Dickens*. Oxford: Clarendon Press, 1971.

Williams, Raymond. *The Country and the City*. New York: Oxford University Press, 1973.

Winnicott, D. W. *Playing and Reality*. Harmondsworth, England: Penguin, 1971.

Wolff, Cynthia Griffin. *A Feast of Words: The Triumph of Edith Wharton*. New York: Oxford University Press, 1977.

Woolf, Virginia. "Abbeys and Cathedrals." *Good Housekeeping* 21: 3 (May 1932): 18–19, 102.

———. "'Anon' and 'The Reader': Virginia Woolf's Last Essays." Ed. Brenda Silver. *Twentieth Century Literature* 25 (Fall/Winter 1979): 356–68.

———. *Between the Acts*. New York: Harcourt Brace Jovanovich, 1969.

———. *The Captain's Death Bed and Other Essays*. New York: Harcourt Brace Jovanovich, 1950.

———. *The Common Reader*. New York: Harcourt, Brace & World, 1953.

———. *The Death of the Moth and Other Essays*. New York: Harcourt Brace Jovanovich, 1970.

———. *The Diary of Virginia Woolf*. Ed. Anne Olivier Bell. New York: Harcourt Brace Jovanovich. I, 1915–19 (1977); II, 1920–24 (1978); III, 1925–30 (1980); IV, 1931–35 (1982).

———. "The Docks of London." *Good Housekeeping* 20: 4 (December 1931): 16–17, 114, 116–17.

———. *Flush: A Biography*. New York: Harcourt Brace Jovanovich, 1961.

———. "Great Men's Houses." *Good Housekeeping* 21: 1 (March 1932): 10–11, 102–3.

———. *Granite & Rainbow*. New York: Harcourt Brace Jovanovich, 1958.

———. *A Haunted House*. Harcourt, Brace & World, 1949.

———. "Introductory Letter." Pp. xv–xxxix in *Life as We Have Known It*, by Co-operative Working Women. Ed. Margaret Llewelyn Davies. New York: W. W. Norton, 1975.

———. "Virginia Woolf's *The Journal of Mistress Joan Martyn.*" Ed. Susan M. Squier and Louise A. DeSalvo. *Twentieth Century Literature* 25 (Fall/Winter 1979): 237–69.

———. *The Letters of Virginia Woolf.* Ed. Nigel Nicolson and Joanne Trautmann. New York: Harcourt Brace Jovanovich. I, 1888–1912 (1975); II, 1912–22 (1976); III, 1923–28 (1977); IV, 1929–31 (1978); V, 1933–35 (1979); VI, 1936–41 (1980).

———. *The London Scene*. New York: Frank Hallman, 1975; London: Hogarth Press, 1982.

———. *The Moment*. New York: Harcourt Brace Jovanovich, 1947.

———. *Moments of Being: Unpublished Autobiographical Writings*. Ed. Jeanne Schulkind. New York: Harcourt Brace Jovanovich, 1976.

———. *Mrs. Dalloway*. New York: Harcourt, Brace & World, 1953.

———. *Night and Day*. New York: Harcourt Brace Jovanovich, 1948.

———. *Orlando: A Biography*. New York: Signet, 1960.

———. "Oxford Street Tide." *Good Housekeeping* 20: 5 (January 1932): 18–19, 120.

———. *The Pargiters: The Novel-Essay Portion of* The Years. Ed. Mitchell A. Leaska. New York: New York Public Library, 1977.

———. "Portrait of a Londoner." *Good Housekeeping* 22: 4 (December 1932): 28–29, 132.

———. *A Room of One's Own*. New York: Harcourt, Brace & World, 1957.

———. "Street Music." *National Review* 45 (1905): 144–48.

———. *The Second Common Reader*. New York: Harcourt, Brace & World, 1960.

———. "'This is the House of Commons.'" *Good Housekeeping* 22: 2 (October 1932): 18–19, 110–12.

———. *Three Guineas*. New York: Harcourt, Brace & World, 1966.

———. *To the Lighthouse*. Harcourt, Brace & World, 1955.

———. *A Writer's Diary*. Ed. Leonard Woolf. New York: Harcourt Brace Jovanovich, 1954.

———. *The Years*. New York: Harcourt, Brace & World, 1965.

INDEX